D1375986

"In *Rhymin' and Stealin'*, Justin Williams achieves s[...] remarkable, adeptly conjoining sharp musicological an[...] inquiry, and cultural theory to enhance our understanding of hip-hop's sonic appropriation and musical construction. In a highly original manner that is consistently lucid and whip smart, he weaves together a compelling narrative about the relationships between hip-hop aesthetics and the diverse concepts of technology, mobility, memory, nostalgia and death. People will surely 'borrow' ideas from this book for quite some time."

—Murray Forman, Northeastern University

"*Rhymin' and Stealin'* starts from a basic idea—that hip-hop aesthetics involve borrowing from the past—and, in the spirit of hip-hop's consummative ingenuity, explores the varied possibilities for re-coding, re-situating, and re-envisioning it. Moving beyond the notion of digital sampling, Justin Williams provides a theoretically sophisticated, musicologically adept, and richly interdisciplinary look at hip hop's intertextual traditions and how they impact rap music's reception. In the process, Williams talks all that jazz, reminisces over rap's most canonical figures, and lets readers ride along a fantastic voyage through hip-hop's instinctive modes of meaning making."

—Anthony Kwame Harrison, Virginia Tech, author of *Hip Hop Underground: The Integrity and Ethics of Racial Identification*

"With the ear of a musician, the eye of a scholar, and the heart of a fan, Justin Williams guides us through the complex and creative ways in which hip-hop borrows and transforms existing sounds into astonishingly original art. *Rhymin' and Stealin'* digs deep—into music, aesthetics, and culture—and in the process rewards readers with crucial insights into one of the most vital musical traditions of our time."

—Mark Katz, University of North Carolina at Chapel Hill

BARNSLEY COLLEGE

00135451

30002153

Rhymin' and Stealin'

U.C.B.
LIBRARY

TRACKING POP

SERIES EDITORS: LORI BURNS, JOHN COVACH, AND ALBIN ZAK

In one form or another, the influence of popular music has permeated cultural activities and perception on a global scale. Interdisciplinary in nature, Tracking Pop is intended as a wide-ranging exploration of pop music and its cultural situation. In addition to providing resources for students and scholars working in the field of popular culture, the books in this series will appeal to general readers and music lovers, for whom pop has provided the soundtrack of their lives.

Rhymin' and Stealin'

MUSICAL BORROWING IN HIP-HOP

Justin A. Williams

The University of Michigan Press
Ann Arbor

First paperback edition 2014

Copyright © by the University of Michigan 2013

All rights reserved

This book may not be reproduced, in whole or in part, including illustrations, in any form (beyond that copying permitted by Sections 107 and 108 of the U.S. Copyright Law and except by reviewers for the public press), without written permission from the publisher.

Published in the United States of America by

The University of Michigan Press

Manufactured in the United States of America

⊗ Printed on acid-free paper

2017   2016   2015   2014   5   4   3   2

A CIP catalog record for this book is available from the British Library.

ISBN 978-0-472-11892-2 (cloth : alk. paper)

ISBN 978-0-472-02939-6 (e-book)

ISBN 978-0-472-03619-6 (pbk. : alk. paper)

To my lovely wife, Katherine,
and in memory of my grandmother Edith Burton.

ACKNOWLEDGMENTS

This book is the result of advice, encouragement, and support from many who deserve my thanks and appreciation. The seeds of this project were sown many years ago when I was a Stanford University undergraduate and my early music professor, Kerry McCarthy, commented in a written assignment on my comparisons of borrowing in the music of Josquin des Prez and Will Smith: "Articles need to be written about this!" Though the end result looks very different from what we both envisioned initially, it nevertheless is the product of her early encouragement and of more general early-stage musicological mentoring and support from Phil Ford, Tom Grey, Stephen Hinton, and Luke Roberts.

I received generous support during my research as a PhD student at the University of Nottingham, including the Overseas Research Scheme, the Graduate School's Travel Prize, and Universitas 21 Scholarships, as well as a research grant from the Royal Musical Association. I also thank the staff and facilities of the British Library and the Harvard (formerly Stanford) Hip-Hop Archive, particularly Marcyliena Morgan and Dawn-Elissa Fisher (aka the D.E.F. Professor), for their help and support. Special thanks go to David Metzer for his advice and careful reading of my work and for his hosting me while I was at the University of British Columbia as a part of the Universitas 21 program. I was blessed with support and encouragement from one of the kindest and most intellectually rich music departments in the world at Nottingham. Thanks to Robert Adlington, Mervyn Cooke, Deniz Ertan, Dan Grimley, Sarah Hibberd, Liz Hickling, Paula Higgins, Sherene Osbourne, and Peter Wright. I have also benefited from advice and discussions among my postgraduate colleagues, including Jan Butler, Mark Clayden, Fiona Ford, Angela Kang, Ben Moss, James Munk, and Tim Shephard.

I would also like to thank the Economic and Social Research Council, UK, for providing me a grant to continue and expand upon my PhD research; this book is one of the products of that grant. Thanks to my mentor John Urry, who gave loads of professional advice at a crucial stage, and thanks to Tim Dant for his kindness and support. Extra special thanks go to the enthusiastic undergraduates at the University of Nottingham, Leeds College of Music, and Anglia Ruskin University, who humored me and let me test my unconventional ideas on them.

Adam Krims deserves a unique mention, as his work informs this book at a deep level. He was an encouraging and calming presence as a PhD supervisor from our earliest email correspondence. I owe him a tremendous amount of thanks for both his groundbreaking theories on rap music and his skills as an advisor. Although Adam is no longer with us, his ideas, methods, and genuine gems of wisdom will remain with me throughout my life. I am also grateful to Mervyn Cooke and Tim Hughes for their thorough reading of my work and for their helpful comments and suggestions.

Thanks to the University of Michigan Press, particularly Chris Hebert for his advice, help, and patience, and project manager Marcia LaBrenz as well as editorial assistants Susan Cronin and Christopher Dryer. Additional publication costs were supported by the AMS 75 PAYS Endowment of the American Musicological Society, funded in part by the National Endowment for the Humanities and the Andrew W. Mellon Foundation.

Some of the material in this book has been published in earlier versions. Thanks to the University of California Press, Equinox Press, and Waxmann for permission to adapt "The Construction of Jazz Rap as High Art in Hip-Hop Music," *Journal of Musicology* 27, no. 4 (2010): 435–59 (chapter 2); "'You never been on a ride like this befo': Los Angeles, Automotive Listening, and Dr. Dre's 'G-Funk,'" *Popular Music History* 4, no. 2 (2010): 160–76 (chapter 3); and "Historicizing the Breakbeat: Hip-Hop's Origins and Authenticity," in *Jahrbuch des Deutschen Volksliedarchivs "Lied und populäre Kultur / Song and Popular Culture"* (Münster: Waxmann, 2011) (chapter 1). Special thanks to Taylor and Francis for permission to reproduce the table in the introduction of this book and to the Crutchfield Corporation for permission to reproduce the car audio diagram in chapter 3.

Additional thanks to Jane Brandon and Carlo Cenciarelli for their friendship, advice, and proofreading and to the "Bucho crew" of Sacramento and San Francisco. To the last group: without them, I would not have developed an interest in the recording studio compositional process and would not have had such incredible tour experiences with such great musicians. Thanks to Roger Cox, Josh Lippi, Leon Moore, Gerald Pease, Ryan Robertson, Ben Schwier, and Derek Taylor, and especially Anthony Coleman II for making it all happen.

My family has been extremely supportive of this project. Thanks to my sister, Whitney, my mother, Vicki, and my father, Richard. My late grandmother Edith Burton provided an overwhelmingly large amount of love and support throughout our time together. I thank them all for teaching me to love music and for encouraging me to share that love with others.

My wife and soulmate, Katherine, receives the biggest "thank you" of all. Her extremely high level of productivity allows her to wear numerous hats in our life together: loving and supportive wife, intellectually challenging academic colleague, bandmate (jazz *and* ska), proofreader, music software technician, and best friend. This would not have been possible without her love, encouragement, and intellect.

Grateful acknowledgment is made to the following for permission to reprint previously published materials:

Check The Rhime

> Words and Music by Leon Ware, Minnie Riperton, Richard Rudolf, Kamal Ibn Fareed, Malik Taylore, Muhammad Ali, Owen McIntyre, Roger Ball, Alan Gorrie, James Stuart, Stephen Ferrone and Malcolm Duncan
> (c) 1991 JOBETE MUSIC CO. INC., DICKIE BIRD MUSIC, UNIVERSAL MUSICEZ TUNES LLC, JAZZ MERCHANT MUSIC and JOE'S SONGS

All Rights for JOBETE MUSIC CO. INC. and DICKIE BIRD MUSIC Administered by MUSIC SALES CORPORATION

All Rights Reserved International Copyright Secured Used by Permission

Acontains elements of "This Love I Have" by Leon Ware, Minnie Riperton and Richard Rudolph, (c) 1975 (Renewed 2003) Jobete Music Co. Inc. and Dickie Bird Music

Reprinted by Permission of Hal Leonard Corporation

A Dream

Words and Music by Shawn Carter, Sean Combs, Christopher Wallace, Jean Claude Olivier and James Mtume

(c) 2002 EMI APRIL MUSIC INC., CARTER BOYS PUB-LISHING, JUSTIN COMBS PUBLISHING COMPANY INC., BIG POPPA MUSIC, JUMPING BEANS SONGS LLC and MTUME MUSIC

All Rights for CARTER BOYS PUBLISHING, JUSTIN COMBS PUBLISHING COMPANY INC. and BIG POPPA MUSIC Controlled and Administered by EMI APRIL MUSIC INC.

All Rights Reserved International Copyright Secured Used by Permission

Acontains elements of "Juicy Fruit"

Reprinted by Permission of Hal Leonard Corporation

Excursions

Words and Music by Kamaal Ibn John Fareed, Ali Shaheed Jones-Muhammad and Malik Izaak Taylor

Copyright (c) 1991 by Universal MusictZ Tunes LLC and Jazz Merchant Music

All Rights Administered by Universal MusicmZ Tunes LLC

International Copyright Secured All Rights Reserved
Reprinted by Permission of Hal Leonard Corporation

Ghetto Gospel

Words and Music by Elton John, Bernie Taupin, Tupac Shakur,
Marshall Mathers, Luis Resto and Deon Evans
Copyright (c) 2004 UNIVERSALIDICK JAMES MUSIC LTD.,
UNIVERSAL MUSIC CORP., EIGHT MILE STYLE
MUSIC, RESTO WORLD MUSIC and BACK ON POINT
MUSIC
All Rights for UNIVERSAL/DICK JAMES MUSIC LTD. in
the United States and Canada Controlled and Administered by
UNIVERSALAPOLYGRAM INTERNATIONAL PUB-
LISHING, INC.
All Rights for EIGHT MILE STYLE MUSIC and RESTO
WORLD MUSIC Administered by KOBALT MUSIC PUB-
LISHING AMERICA, INC.
All Rights Reserved Used by Permission
Acontains elements of "Indian Sunset"
Reprinted by Permission of Hal Leonard Corporation

Hip Hop Is Dead

Words and Music by Nasir Jones, William Adams, Jeremiah Lordan
and Douglas Ingle
Copyright (c) 2006 by Universal MusictZ Songs, BMG Sapphire
Songs, i am composing llc, Francis Day And Hunter Ltd., Cotil-
lion Music, Inc., Ten-East Music and Iron Butterfly Music
All Rights for BMG Sapphire Songs and i am composing llc Ad-
ministered by BMG Rights Management (US) LLC
All Rights for Francis Day And Hunter Ltd. in the U.S. and Canada
Administered by Regent Music Corporation

All Rights for Ten-East Music and Iron Butterfly Music Administered by Cotillion Music, Inc.
International Copyright Secured All Rights Reserved
contains elements of "Apache" and "In-A-Gadda-Da-Vida"
Reprinted by Permission of Hal Leonard Corporation

In Da Club

Words and Music by Curtis Jackson, Andre Young and Michael
Elizondo
Copyright Y 2003 UNIVERSAL MUSIC CORP., 50 CENT MU-
SIC, BUG MUSIC-MUSIC OF WINDSWEPT, BLOTTER
MUSIC, ELVIS MAMBO MUSIC, WB MUSIC CORP. and
AIN'T NOTHIN' BUT FUNKIN' MUSIC
All Rights for 50 CENT MUSIC Controlled and Administered by
UNIVERSAL MUSIC CORP.
All Rights for BUG MUSIC-MUSIC OF WINDSWEPT,
BLOTTER MUSIC and ELVIS MAMBO MUSIC
Controlled and Administered by BMG RIGHTS MANAGE-
MENT (US) LLC
All Rights for AIN'T NOTHIN' BUT FUNKIN' MUSIC Con-
trolled and Administered by WB MUSIC CORP.
All Rights Reserved Used by Permission
Reprinted by Permission of Hal Leonard Corporation

Indian Sunset

Words and Music by Elton John and Bernie Taupin
Copyright (c) 1970 UNIVERSAL/DICK JAMES MUSIC LTD.
Copyright Renewed
All Rights in the United States and Canada Controlled and Admin-
istered by UNIVERSALnSONGS OF POLYGRAM IN-
TERNATIONAL, INC.

All Rights Reserved Used by Permission
Reprinted by Permission of Hal Leonard Corporation

It Has Been Said

Words and Music by Marshall Mathers, Obie Trice, Leroy Watson
and Christopher Wallace
Copyright (c) 2005 SHROOM SHADY MUSIC, ALMO MU-
SIC CORP., OBIE TRICE PUBLISHING, ANIYA NICOLE
PUBLISHING, EMI APRIL MUSIC INC., B.I.G. POPPA
MUSIC and JUSTIN COMBS PUBLISHING
All Rights for SHROOM SHADY MUSIC Controlled and Ad-
ministered by SONGS OF UNIVERSAL, INC. All Rights for
OBIE TRICE PUBLISHING Controlled and Administered by
ALMO MUSIC CORP.
All Rights Reserved Used by Permission
Reprinted by Permission of Hal Leonard Corporation

It's Good To Be Here

Words and Music by Ishmael R. Butler
(c) 1993 GLIRO MUSIC, INC. and WIDE GROOVES MUSIC
All Rights Controlled and Administered by EMI BLACKWOOD
MUSIC INC.
All Rights Reserved International Copyright Secured Used by
Permission
Reprinted by Permission of Hal Leonard Corporation

Nuthin' But A G Thang

Words and Music by Frederick Knight, Leon Haywood and Cordo-
zar Calvin Broadus

Copyright (c) 1993, 1994 IRVING MUSIC, INC., TWO-KNIGHT PUBLISHING CO., SONGS OF UNIVERSAL, INC., MARI KNIGHT MUSIC, SNOOP DOGGY DOGG PUB DESIGNEE, SUGE PUBLISHING and WB MUSIC CORP.
All Rights for TWO-KNIGHT PUBLISHING CO. Controlled and Administered by IRVING MUSIC, INC.
Worldwide Rights for SNOOP DOGGY DOGG PUB DESIGNEE and SUGE PUBLISHING Administered by BMG RIGHTS MANAGEMENT (US) LLC
All Rights Reserved Used by Permission
Reprinted by Permission of Hal Leonard Corporation

Patiently Waiting

Words and Music by Curtis Jackson, Mike Elizondo, Luis Resto and Marshall Mathers
Copyright (c) 2003 50 CENT MUSIC, BUG MUSIC-MUSIC OF WINDSWEPT, ELVIS MAMBO MUSIC, BLOTTER MUSIC, RESTO WORLD MUSIC and EIGHT MILE STYLE MUSIC
All Rights for 50 CENT MUSIC Controlled and Administered by UNIVERSAL MUSIC CORP.
All Rights for BUG MUSIC-MUSIC OF WINDSWEPT, ELVIS MAMBO MUSIC and BLOTTER MUSIC
Administered by BMG RIGHTS MANAGEMENT (US) LLC
All Rights for RESTO WORLD MUSIC and EIGHT MILE STYLE MUSIC Administered by KOBALT MUSIC PUBLISHING AMERICA, INC.
All Rights Reserved Used by Permission
Reprinted by Permission of Hal Leonard Corporation

Rebirth Of Slick (Cool Like Dat)

Words and Music by Ishmael Butler and Mary Ann Vieira
(c) 1993 GLIRO MUSIC, INC. and WIDE GROOVES MUSIC
All Rights Controlled and Administered by EMI BLACKWOOD
    MUSIC INC.
All Rights Reserved International Copyright Secured Used by
    Permission
Acontains elements of "Stretchin"
Reprinted by Permission of Hal Leonard Corporation

Thugz Mansion (N.Y.)

Words and Music by Tupac Shakur, Johnny Jackson, Nasir Jones,
    Claudio Cueni, Michael Herring and Larry Loftin
Copyright (c) 2002 UNIVERSAL MUSIC CORP., UNIVER-
    SAL MUSIC - MGB SONGS, BLACK HISPANIC MUSIC,
    UNIVERSAL MUSICCZ SONGS, UNIVERSAL MUSIC-
    ZZ TUNES LLC, COLOR BLIND FISH and FROM THE
    SOUL MUSIC
All Rights for BLACK HISPANIC MUSIC Controlled and Ad-
    ministered by UNIVERSAL MUSICAMGB SONGS
All Rights Reserved Used by Permission
Reprinted by Permission of Hal Leonard Corporation

Where Are They Now

Words and Music by Nasir Jones, Salaam Remi, James Brown,
    Bobby Byrd and Ronald Lenhoff
Copyright (c) 2006 by Universal MusictZ Songs, EMI April Music
    Inc., Salaam Remi Music, Unichappell Music Inc. and Crited
    Music, Inc.

All Rights for Salaam Remi Music Controlled and Administered by EMI April Music Inc.

All Rights for Crited Music Inc. Controlled and Administered by Unichappell Music, Inc.

International Copyright Secured All Rights Reserved

Icontains elements of "Get Up, Get Into It, Get Involved"

Reprinted by Permission of Hal Leonard Corporation

Who Am I (What's My Name)

Words and Music by Calvin Broadus, George Clinton Jr., William "Bootsy" Collins, Mose Davis, Garry Shider, David Spradley and Bernard Worrell

Copyright (c) 1993 Snoop Doggy Dogg (ASCAP), Suge Publishing (ASCAP), Bridgeport Music, Inc. (BMI) and Southfield Music, Inc. (ASCAP)

Worldwide Rights for Snoop Doggy Dogg and Suge Publishing Administered by BMG Rights Management (US) LLC

International Copyright Secured All Rights Reserved

Reprinted by Permission of Hal Leonard Corporation

CONTENTS

Rhymin' and Stealin'

INTRODUCTION

Because mutiny on the bounty's what we're all about.

—THE BEASTIE BOYS, "RHYMIN' AND STEALIN'" (1986)

Rhymin' and Stealin' begins with a crucial premise: the fundamental element of hip-hop culture and aesthetics is the overt use of preexisting material to new ends. Whether it is taking an old dance move for a breakdancing battle, using spray paint to create street art, quoting from a famous speech, or sampling a rapper or 1970s funk song, hip-hop aesthetics involve borrowing from the past. When these elements are appropriated and reappropriated, they become transformed into something new, something different, something *hip-hop*.

Although all music genres use and adapt preexisting material in different ways, hip-hop music celebrates and flaunts its "open source" culture through highly varied means. It is this interest in the web of references, borrowed material, and digitally sampled sounds that forms the basis of this book—sampling and other types of borrowing becomes a framework with which to analyze hip-hop music and wider cultural trends.

From its onset, hip-hop music was founded on the manipulation of preexisting material; DJs were borrowing instrumental excerpts from records (known as "breaks" or "breakbeats") to craft their sets, either looping passages with two copies of the same record or stringing passages together from different records. (See chap. 1 for a longer description of hip-hop music's origins.) Joseph Schloss writes that "the looping aesthetic . . . combined a traditional African American approach to composition with new technology to create a radically new way of making music."[1] As digital sampling technology improved and became more affordable in the mid- to late 1980s, many hip-hop DJ practices (such

1

as "crate digging," looping, and collage techniques) shifted to the "hip-hop producer." As digital sampling emerged in hip-hop culture, it has been said, it aligned itself with the early days of the hip-hop aesthetic: "Indeed, the story of sampling is a tale of technology catching up with the DJ, of equipment being created that could do faster, more accurately and more easily what a DJ had long been able to."[2] Bill Brewster and Frank Broughton argue convincingly that sampling was just a faster, more complex and permanent way of recreating what the DJs had been doing all along.[3]

Because of the tightening of copyright legislation for sampling in the late 1980s and early 1990s, collage-style albums like those from Public Enemy and De La Soul would be too expensive to make commercially in the mid-1990s and after.[4] Hip-hop music production post-mid-1990s is too varied to define comprehensively, but it often includes a mix of technology such as samplers, sequencers (machines that put samples together), synthesizers, drum machines, and more traditionally "live" instruments. Above all, the most unifying sonic thread within hip-hop is the particular drum timbres that have their origins in 1970s funk.[5]

The openness of the funk break allows hip-hop producers to sample and borrow from myriad types of music and other sounds, thus permitting a high degree of tempo manipulation in general. This is how a breakbeat like the introduction from the Honeydrippers' "Impeach the President" (1973) can be looped with Beethoven's "Für Elise" for Nas's "I Can" and can also be used on the synthesizer-heavy "Chronic (Intro)," produced by Dr. Dre. Both examples fit neatly in the hip-hop music genre yet utilize strikingly disparate material.[6] These rhythmic structures act as the anchor, often looped as part of a "basic beat" as the structural foundation of a track.[7] The foundational role of the drum and its specific timbres, as in many African-based musics, is what gives hip-hop its identity as a genre. Even when the drums are not present (such as in an a cappella rap), I would argue that particular drum sounds are implied as counterpoint to the rapper's delivery. As its primary defining feature, then, the funk break seems to yield limitless possibilities for the varieties of musical borrowing in hip-hop and other breakbeat-based musics.

Musical Borrowing, Digital Sampling, and Signifyin(g)

In academic studies of hip-hop's musical appropriations, "sampling" has been the dominant term, usually without any in-depth or critical description.[8] For example, Joanna Demers's article on the lineage between gangsta rap and 1970s blaxploitation film begins: "Musical borrowings, or samples, have long been a means of creating lineage between hip-hop and older genres of African-American music such as funk, soul, and rhythm and blues."[9] I find it more productive, however, to create a distinction between musical borrowing and digital sampling as a special case of musical borrowing. In contrast, I have chosen to use the terms *autosonic quotation* and *allosonic quotation,* from Serge Lacasse, to differentiate between sampled and nonsampled quotations, respectively. Autosonic quotation is quotation of a recording by digitally sampling it (digital or analogue), as opposed to allosonic quotation, which quotes the previous material by way of rerecording or performing it live (like a quote in jazz performance), rather than sampling from the original recording.[10]

A number of metaphors have been used to discuss sampling in hip-hop. For example, Russell Potter describes sampling as raids, politically subverting traditional author functions, as well as traditional roles of production and consumption.[11] His reading of hip-hop is largely through a postmodern lens, one that sees the play of postmodernism, in this case, to be highly political, as a form of resistance and a strategy for solidifying communities and traditions.[12]

Potter also describes sampling as a form of Signifyin(g), a concept theorized by Henry Louis Gates Jr. in African American literary studies and adapted to black musics by Samuel A. Floyd Jr.[13] To quote Potter:

> Simply put, Signifyin(g) is repetition *with a difference;* the same and yet not the same. When, in a jazz riff, a horn player substitutes one arpeggio for a harmony note, or "cuts up" a well-known solo by altering its tempo, phrasing, or accents, s/he is Signifyin(g) on all previous versions. When a blues singer, like Blind Willie McTell, "borrows" a cut known as the "Wabash Rag" and re-cuts it as the "Georgia Rag," he is Signifyin(g) on a rival's recording.[14]

Like ragtime, swing music, bebop, hard bop, cool, reggae, dub, dance remixes, and mash-ups, hip-hop is a musical form that was Signfyin(g) on what came before. Furthermore, musical texts Signify upon one another, troping and revising particular musical ideas. These musical "conversations" can therefore occur between the present and the past or synchronically within a particular genre.

To Signify is to foreground the signifier, to give it importance for its own sake. The language of the Signifying Monkey from African folklore is playful yet intelligent and can be found in hipster talk and radio DJs of the 1950s, comedians such as Redd Foxx, 1970s blaxploitation characters such as Dolemite, and countless rap lyrics. In addition to Signifying as masterful revision and repetition of tropes, it also includes double-voiced or multivoiced utterances that complicate any simple semiotic interpretation.[15]

In his 2004 ethnographic study *Making Beats*, Joseph Schloss is largely concerned with the practices and "ethics" of a relatively small, albeit tight-knit and influential, hip-hop producer community. I choose to cast my net wider than he does, focusing largely on reception rather than production, as well as accounting for the entire hip-hop recording rather than just the production of the beats. Schloss's interviews and insights have been undoubtedly important in forwarding the study of sample-based hip-hop and crucial to the study of hip-hop compositional process, particularly emphasizing the role that aesthetics has in the motivation to sample from a particular record.[16]

It is worth considering what sets digital sampling apart from other forms of borrowing, as it arguably has radicalized music making and listening. Chris Cutler provides a definition:

> Digital sampling is a purely electronic digital recording system which takes samples or "vertical slices" of sound and converts them into binary information, into data, which tells a sound producing system how to *reconstruct*, rather than *reproduce* it. Instantly . . . it is stored rather as discrete data, which act as *instructions* for the eventual reconstruction of a sound (as a visual object when electronically scanned is translated only into a binary code).[17]

Digital sampling, particularly its ability to reproduce sounds or groups of sounds so accurately, has changed the musical landscape in a number of ways.[18] Additionally, one also needs to consider how new technologies extend rather than replace existing musical practices. Mark Katz, for example, embraces multiple traditions that predate sampling by considering Public Enemy's "Fight the Power" as a digital form of Signifyin(g), linking it to African traditions, while at the same time acknowledging sampling as a form of musical borrowing that has a long history in Western classical music. He believes that what sets digital sampling apart from other quotation is what he calls "performative quotation"—"quotation that recreates all the details of timbre and timing that evoke and identify a unique sound event."[19] And though the patterns of 0s and 1s stay the same in digital sampling, these samples can become transformative through their specific contexts.

Intertextuality in hip-hop culture always lies at the crossroads between technology and history, between African and African American artistic traditions and newer technologies like digital sampling that allow practitioners to extend older traditions in new and varied ways.[20] Each composer and listener hears particular, varied elements from this chronological imaginary spectrum, and from this, larger patterns and questions can emerge. For example, the investigation of how earlier material is borrowed in primarily 1990s and 2000s US mainstream hip-hop music has unearthed questions on larger issues, most broadly questions of history (chap. 1), genre (chap. 2), space (chap. 3), death/memorial (chap. 4), and lineage (chap. 5). Each chapter begins with these broader themes and ideas from within hip-hop culture, narrowing toward closer readings of hip-hop texts to show how text and context work together to elucidate these broader ideas.

Musical Borrowing in Hip-Hop

My choice of the term *hip-hop* instead of *rap music* is deliberate, even though all the subsequent case studies fall under the latter classification as well. (I do not investigate other hip-hop musical forms such as turntabilism, Bristol "trip-hop," or the "instrumental hip-hop" of artists like DJ Shadow, Madlib, and Flying Lotus.[21]) My decision to use the term stems from the fact that the instances of borrowing that I highlight in this study are part of a larger hip-hop aesthetic that encompasses all the so-called four elements of hip-hop culture (rapping, DJing, graffiti, and breakdancing).[22] For example, Schloss writes of borrowing as lineage in terms of incorporating "foundational" moves in contemporary b-boy (breakdancing) routines. Borrowing and quotation are arguably just as important to b-boying as they are to rap music. He also adds that "graffiti writers, for example, often use specific letter styles as tributes to their teachers, while stylistic lineages are also valued—and can be heard—in hip-hop production."[23]

My decision to use the term *hip-hop*, then, is threefold: I wish to emphasize, first, that my music examples reflect wider processes throughout multiple artistic forms considered part of a wider "hip-hop culture"; second, that there exists a wider hip-hop community, an imagined community, that interprets these intertextualities; and third, that my work acts as an open text in an effort to initiate a dialogue with others interested in borrowing in hip-hop cultures. It would be most fruitful to collaborate on a comparative analysis of borrowing in graffiti, hip-hop music (rap music and turntabilism), and breakdancing in future scholarly endeavors. I discuss only one of these elements in great detail at present, but implicit in this study is the fact that these practices and attitudes are manifest in multiple realms of hip-hop culture.

Furthermore, I use the term *musical* of *musical borrowing* to encompass all aspects of hip-hop texts, sound recordings, and music videos, including aspects of quotation and references in lyrics and music video imagery, in addition to musical complements to rap delivery ("the beat").[24] As a musicologist, I aim to emphasize *sounds* rather than present a lyric-based approach, and it is important to state that I am looking at music in the broadest sense of these sounds. Though this book engages deeply with social cultures and contexts, my investigations begin and end with musical texts, seeking a deeper understanding of meaning within these recordings and what their reception says about larger cultural practices.

I also use the terms *beat* and *flow* to separate the lyrical content and delivery of the rapper(s) from its musical complement, acknowledging that they are nevertheless inextricably linked.[25] I do want to foreground all sounds in the musical text of the recording, mediated by their sociohistorically situated interpretations, while concurrently recognizing that music can also act a mediator.[26]

Borrowing is the term that creates the widest net for my purposes, but I could have easily used the word *appropriation* or even stronger value-laden terms such as *stealing* or *theft*. (The title "Musical Theft in Hip-Hop Music," however, suggests too large a value judgment for my taste.) The fact is that artists have "stolen" since time immemorial: Shakespeare from Ovid and Plutarch, Renaissance mass composers from Gregorian chant, Bartók from folk melodies, Bob Dylan from everyone, and blues singers from each other. Jonathan Lethem writes, "As examples accumulate . . . it becomes apparent that appropriation, mimicry, quotation, allusion, and sublimated collaboration consist of a kind of *sine qua non* of the creative act, cutting across all forms and genres in the realm of cultural production."[27] Of course, by no means is the term *borrowing* value free, quite the opposite. To borrow something implies that it should be returned intact or that it *can* be. And perhaps in some ways it *is* returned, albeit transformed in both old and new contexts. For my purposes, however, *borrowing* sidesteps the ethical arguments in favor of more detailed analysis and places these hip-hop practices within a well-established lineage of musical borrowing in both African-based and European-based musics.[28]

Textually Signaled and Unsignaled Borrowing

As stated previously, the initial premise of the book is that hip-hop presupposes an unconcealed intertextuality. Much of this has to do with the hip-hop community's expectations (its "generic contract"),[29] but this is not meant to imply that all hip-hop musical texts draw attention to their borrowing equally. In his book on pastiche, Richard Dyer points out that pastiche as an imitative artistic form is "textually signaled" as such; in other words, the text itself draws attention to the fact that it contains imitative material. Catherine Grant and Christine Geraghty, in the context of film adaptation theory, believe that textually signaling is crucial to an adaptation, that the film somehow recalls the source novel: "the most important act that films and their surrounding discourses need to perform in order to communicate unequivocally their status as adaptations is to [make their audiences] *recall* the adapted work, or the cultural memory of it. There is no such thing . . . as a 'secret' adaptation."[30] In the case of pastiche and film adaptation, and in forms like parody and homage, recognizing that these works are referring to something that precedes them is crucial to their identity as that form, necessary to their *working* as such.

The table below, from Richard Dyer's study of pastiche, shows how pastiche as imitation "fits" into qualitative categories as compared to other forms of imitation: whether it conceals its imitation as plagiarism and forgeries do; whether the text itself draws attention to its imitation (to be "textually signaled") or not; and whether the imitative form, by its nature, already suggests some sort of preconceived evaluative response (as in parody).

In the context of hip-hop music, those knowledgeable of a broad range of hip-hop styles will see that the genre does not actually fall neatly into just the "not textually signaled" or "textually signaled" categoriza-

CONCEALED		UNCONCEALED	
NOT TEXTUALLY SIGNALLED		TEXTUALLY SIGNALLED	
EVALUATIVELY OPEN			EVALUATIVELY PREDETERMINED
plagiarism	copies	pastiche	emulation homage
fake forgery hoax	versions		travesty burlesque mock epic
	genre		parody

TABLE 1. From Richard Dyer, *Pastiche* (London: Routledge, 2007), 24

tion.[31] Though I argue that unconcealed borrowing forms a crucial part of hip-hop aesthetics, hip-hop songs can textually signal their borrowing overtly or not do so, and both approaches can be manifested in a number of ways. Consider two songs discussed in subsequent chapters, "Rebirth of Slick (Cool like Dat)" by Digable Planets (chap. 2) and "Who Am I? (What's My Name)" by Snoop Doggy Dogg (chap. 3). The hiss of vinyl can be heard faintly in the introduction of "Rebirth of Slick," textually signaling that some of the song has its roots elsewhere, that elements have been borrowed. In contrast, "Who Am I?" contains many elements derived from earlier songs but was rerecorded in a studio (apart from its two-bar introduction) and does not contain any vinyl popping or hiss characteristic of sample-based hip-hop songs. In other words, the intertextuality of "Who Am I?" is not textually signaled. Its sources of material are not obvious in themselves, and to a young listener unknowledgeable of 1970s soul and funk, it can sound strikingly "original" (as it did to me when I first heard it at age eleven).

The musical distinctions between "Who Am I?" and "Rebirth of Slick" show that hip-hop recordings can be categorized based on whether or not the borrowing employed draws attention to its past. Many times, digitally sampling a well-known lyric or beat is akin to showing part of a song's inner workings or inner parts or at least signaling that it has its origins elsewhere. And in other songs, such as the Dr. Dre example, borrowings are streamlined into sounding new, though their inner parts are taken from songs decades earlier. To consider music in such a way shifts the argument from how original a work actually is to how original it *appears to be*. At the risk of overgeneralizing major music genres, rock 'n' roll and rock music's intertextualities have been generally more concealed and textually unsignaled in terms of their intra- and extramusical discourses than the intertextualities of hip-hop, though any such statement is always more complicated at a closer level of detail.[32]

Examples of textually signaled borrowing in hip-hop music include but are not limited to the following:

1. *In lyrics and flow*: drawing attention to the source of a quotation, for example, when 50 Cent says in "Patiently Waiting" (3:43): "Snoop said this in '94: 'We don't love them hoes'" (from Snoop's "Gin and Juice"

[0:55]). 50 Cent also imitates Snoop's delivery of the line as a true al-losonic quotation of the text, as well as attributing the source of his quo-tation in the lyrics. Another example is using short snippets of dialogue from television or radio that seem incongruous to the other parts of the song (such as the autosonic quotation "Meanwhile, deep underground somewhere outside the city" on Jurassic 5's "High Fidelity" [1:50]).

2. *In beat:* vinyl hiss and popping, scratching, looped beats, chopped-up beats (as producers and rappers may use a sample as an opening phrase and proceed to chop the phrase for its basic beat, such as Kanye West does on his own "Champion" and on Talib Kweli's "In the Mood"),[33] breakbeats that fall firmly within the breakbeat canon, heavy collages of sound (the Bomb Squad, DJ Shadow), and sped-up samples (such as the use of Chaka Khan's "Through the Fire" on Kanye West's "Through the Wire"). In addition, sampling could be textually signaled if the borrowed fragment "doesn't quite fit" with the rest of the material, for example, if the sample is slightly out of tune with other elements (the "de-tuned lay-ers" that Adam Krims discusses) or if the duration of the sample does not fit any "regular" pattern (i.e., a 4- or 8-bar pattern).

These distinctions are important to make, in light of the fact that on an abstract level, "everything is borrowed," a phrase that I myself borrow from an album title of the UK hip-hop artist The Streets.[34] But what is compelling for the purposes of this book is how particular communities incorporate borrowing, celebrate it or conceal it, and discuss it. It is from here that I outline hip-hop as an imagined community, for my purposes the most appropriate way to preface this study and to answer questions regarding borrowing reception in hip-hop music.

Hip-Hop as Imagined Community

It is safe to say that hip-hop culture has become its own "art world" (to invoke sociologist Howard Becker's influential study).[35] This is a concept fundamental to Schloss's approach to studying hip-hop, both his groundbreaking book on sample-based hip-hop production and his book on b-boying. He acknowledges that hip-hop culture is self-reflexive and self-critiquing:

> But to understand hip-hop's powerful self-critique, we need to understand hip-hop *on its own terms*. Not only because it has interesting symbolic, political, and social implications (although they are important), not only because it confirms our theories about the work of art in the age of electronic reproduction (although that's valuable, too), but simply because the way hip-hop sees the world is itself a legitimate and consistent and fascinating intellectual system.[36]

I claim that this hip-hop world is an "imagined community," to borrow a term from Benedict Anderson's writings on nationalism.[37] To quote Anderson, "It is imagined because the members of even the smallest nation will never know most of their fellow-members, meet them, or even hear of them, yet in the minds of each lives the image of their communion."[38] A given community will be maintained through print and electronic media, solidifying traditions, histories, identities, and cultural objects that contribute to its continuity (such as a national anthem and/or era-defining events and individuals). As in any nation, its demographic contains a number of highly heterogeneous negotiating identities. To be a fan and practitioner of hip-hop music (in any of its forms and sub-genres) is to belong to a musical culture, and it is toward this culture that borrowing practices are aimed, including the listeners who interpret it most thoughtfully.

In 1999, perhaps not coincidentally the year after hip-hop officially outsold country music as the United States' best-selling music genre, a number of journalists acknowledged the existence of a "Hip-Hop Nation." In "I Live in the Hiphop Nation," journalist Touré recounts that there is no single president of the nation, but a number of MCs who act as senators: "Unlike rhythm and blues, hiphop has a strong memoiristic impulse, meaning our senator-MCs speak of themselves, their neighborhoods, the people around them, playing autobiographer, reporter, and oral historian."[39]

The self-referential nature of this imagined community is crucial to understanding the intramusical and extramusical discourses in the genre. As hip-hop matured as a genre, observes journalist Oliver Wang, it became an internalized discourse. The number of peer references, linguistic idiosyncrasies, and quotes became a feature not just of rap lyrics and music but also of the relevant journalism: "Once the music and culture had a long-enough internal history, writers began to write more insularly. References no longer had to bounce off people, idea, and events outside of hip-hop; a writer could simply nod to someone or something within hip-hop, and readers understood."[40] The same can be said for intertextual references within hip-hop recordings—the listeners understood many of the references. References not only draw attention to hip-hop's internalized discourse but often draw attention to various traditions outside of hip-hop as well. And what is considered intrageneric rather than outside the genre is largely evaluated by who is listening and by an ever-shifting play of signifiers that may or may not become embedded in a generic nexus.

Additionally, in terms of any given musical imagined community, there exist certain ideological attitudes toward borrowing and "originality."[41] For example, certain early music cultures (e.g., those who compose cantus firmus, paraphrase and parody masses) resemble the hip-hop world in their unconcealed intertextualities, in that borrowing was a large part of the compositional practice, and overtly so, in contrast to nineteenth-century Romantic ideologies where composers often denied their precursors in an attempt to appear purely original.[42] As Raymond Knapp writes, "nineteenth-century composers endeavored to create original masterworks consisting primarily of musical clichés on all levels, while somehow disguising from their audiences the fact that they had, in an important sense, heard it all before."[43] While this quote could be applied to much of popular music today, hip-hop music largely celebrates its intertextualities and references, and knowledgeable listeners will no doubt understand certain references even when the borrowing is not textually signaled.

In addition to how a musical culture treats the concept of originality, another important question to ask of a musical culture is whether or not it places more value on the individual or on the collective. It is safe to say that the Romantic musical world placed its emphasis on the individual, and this ideology has seeped into rock music most noticeably. Hip-hop music is not without its individual "stars," as the culture often intersects with Romantic/individualistic notions of authenticity quite forcefully, but these stars also use references and intertextualities to bolster their own stardom, and later artists reference these stars to heighten their own authenticities (see chaps. 4 and 5). In other words, while individuality certainly exists in hip-hop culture, it is frequently supported by a collective or collaborative ethos in line with thee ethoses of jazz, funk, gospel, and other African-based musics that place a high emphasis on the collective as part of the "changing same" of black music.[44]

Imagined Communities as Interpretative Communities

In studies of borrowing, there is always the question of whether to favor compositional process or cultural reception or, to invoke Jean-Jacques Nattiez, to place emphasis on the *poiesic* or the *esthesic* dimension, respectively.[45] Christopher Reynolds, in his study of allusion in nineteenth-century German instrumental music, asks whether an allusion needs to be recognized in order to be successful. He says that it does not and writes that "allusions are therefore more important for how music is made than for how it is heard."[46] Or should the focus be placed on reception? To quote David Metzer's study of quotation in twentieth-century music: "Recognition then forms a crux for quotation, especially in its role as a cultural agent. Simply put, if a borrowing is not detected then it and its cultural resonances go unheard."[47] And if the latter is to be preferred, whose reception is it exactly? For Metzer, it is the study of "cultural agency" in quotation,[48] though he does not always devote sufficient space to locating and describing the cultures that would recognize those quotations. More important in this case, how can a study of musical borrowing in hip-hop not simply become the private reflections of an idiosyncratic white middle-class academic such as myself, risking a danger of implicitly making the spurious claim that these references on which I chose to focus as a musicologist can generally be heard by "all"?

The answer lies within the imagined community of hip-hop. Most crucially, this imagined community is also as an "interpretive community," to make reference to Stanley Fish and reader-response theory:

> Indeed, it is interpretive communities, rather than either the text or the reader, that produce meanings and are responsible for the emergence of formal features. Interpretive communities are made up of those who share interpretive strategies for not reading but for writing texts, for constituting their properties. In other words these strategies exist prior to the act of reading and therefore determine the shape of what is read rather than, as is usually assumed, the other way around.[49]

In any given reference in a rap song, some listeners will understand the reference, and some will not, to varying degrees. This is not to suggest that there are one or more fixed meanings, or a dialectic between past and present, or necessarily between a hip-hop song and its source sample, but multiple imagined "sources," based on the previous knowledge of specific songs, artists, or genres. It is the reading and misreading of these sources, as reflected by constantly shifting and negotiating interpretations within hip-hop's imagined communities, that form the foundation of this project. These hip-hop interpretative communities (to which, as a fan and scholar of hip-hop music, I also belong) bring their experiences to the understanding of hip-hop texts, shaping and inflecting these texts through the interaction involved in the listening and interpreting experience.

Despite variations that are inevitable with a group's interpretation of any given utterance, I would argue that there exists an audience expectation that hip-hop is a vast intertextual network that helps to form and inform the generic contract between audiences and hip-hop groups and artists. And in many cases, hip-hop practitioners overtly celebrate their peers, ancestors, and musical pasts, though the reasons for this may diverge and though the way in which references and sources are textually signaled (or unsignaled) varies on an imaginary spectrum that roughly corresponds to a timeline of traditions and technical innovations. Whereas certain rock ideologies that borrow from Romantic notions of musical genius attempt to demonstrate an illusionary originality, hip-hop takes pride in appropriating and celebrating other sounds and ideas. It is reflective of a long lineage of African American and pre-Romantic-Western music making that has embraced the collective in different ways.[50]

Musical codes can work on a number of levels in borrowing and not simply along the lines of textually signaled or not, or autosonic versus allosonic borrowings. Musical codes can exist on the level of genre recognition (in the case of jazz in chap. 2) or that of a recognizable artist voice (in the case of 2Pac and Notorious B.I.G. in chaps. 4 and 5). In other words, listeners do not have to have knowledge of the *exact* song being borrowed for it to communicate meaning. And again, this will vary among listeners: some will know the exact song, some will recognize a genre, and some will realize that it could reference a number of elements, as hip-hop is often a multivocal discourse. Two examples will suffice.

Ingrid Monson, discussing Signifyin(g) in jazz, uses the example of John Coltrane's "My Favorite Things" as an example of ironic Signification, troping on a Broadway song and transforming it into a song with new meanings.[51] The hip-hop group OutKast also covers "My Favorite Things" on *Speakerboxxx/The Love Below* (2003), with a prominent "drum and bass" feel, and include a soprano saxophone characteristic of Coltrane. In analyzing the OutKast version, are we to consider this a two-way relationship between the OutKast and the Coltrane versions because of the soprano saxophone, or can we also include the original *Sound of Music* version in the analysis? Borrowing in hip-hop is highly multivocal, and there may be more than one source or in fact a lineage that complicates any sort of dialectical reading between "old" and "new" texts.[52]

A second example involves how best to theorize the relationship of James Brown to hip-hop culture. Elizabeth Wheeler, in her study of the dialogic nature of sampling, states that "quoting James Brown is always an act of homage."[53] But it may be worth asking: at what moment does "homage to James Brown" become a more general (or generic) homage to hip-hop? Or is it now always double-voiced? That is, is it demonstrating a quasi-DuBoisian double-consciousness, at once representing both hip-hop and funk? Wheeler's comment came in 1991, only eleven years after the first hip-hop on record. But twenty years after Wheeler's article, at the time of this writing, perhaps rather than homage to James Brown and funk music, such quoting has become homage to hip-hop as its own self-conscious genre. The possibility is open that the racial, political, and other associations attached to James Brown stay intact and that a James Brown reference now represents both hip-hop culture *and* James Brown as one its forefathers. These meanings depend on who is interpreting the samples (as James Brown's voice and breakbeats are normally sampled rather than borrowed), but treating James Brown as hip-hop signifier can potentially show that academic discourse on hip-hop can engage thoughtfully with references from within its own genre, in addition to the vast amount of previous academic discussion on sampling's link to pre-hip-hop forms.[54]

Ingrid Monson, in the context of jazz, has provided a useful explanation of the varied ways that borrowing can be utilized and interpreted within a musical culture:

> The reference may be as specific as a melodic quotation from a particular piece or as diffuse as a timbre or style of groove. It might be from within or without mainstream jazz repertory. The important point is that a chain of associations may be set off that engage the listener and unite her or him with a community of other individuals who share a similar musical point of view. Quotations are only the most obvious examples of the thick web of intertextual and intermusical associations to which knowledgeable performers and listeners react. Theoretically almost any musical detail or composite thereof could convey a reference, so long as a community of interpreters can recognize the continuity. The key here is "community of interpreters" (which includes both performers and audience), for a sonic detail becomes sonically meaningful and actionable only in an at least partially shared context of use.[55]

Monson locates a jazz community that will understand the web of intertextual references, similar to the kind of interpretations and communications from the hip-hop communities in the following chapters.

The imagined community of the hip-hop world prepares the framework for the first case study in chapter 1. As hip-hop is now over thirty years on record, rappers and producers now borrow from hip-hop's *own* past, creating a web of references that demonstrate "insider knowledge" of this genre, solidifying further the hip-hop community around the world. In this chapter I locate borrowing as a demonstration of "historical authenticity," using signifiers said to belong to the hip-hop world's past as a marker of authenticity within the genre. This is a special case of what I call "intrageneric borrowing," literally borrowing from elements said to represent hip-hop culture. As hip-hop on record is now over thirty years old, there exists a vast network of signifiers already embedded in this generic nexus. This form of intertextuality only strengthens this already self-conscious genre and shows one particular strategy for artists and groups to establish authenticity in a genre that is often obsessively concerned with such matters.

Chapter 2 shifts the focus from intrageneric borrowing to intergeneric borrowing, sampling or borrowing from another genre. This case study explores the sampling of jazz music in hip-hop as suggesting a high-art identity of sophistication and intellectualism in the subgenre commonly categorized as "jazz rap." I make the case that these "jazz codes" were recognized by a mainstream US audience because of the ubiquity of a specific style of jazz in the 1980s. Furthermore, jazz's associations with art music and with the black middle class were key aspects of the dominant ideology for jazz in the 1980s, and I show that these connotations were reflected in the recognition and reception of jazz codes in late-1980s/early-1990s rap music. This study of cross-generic interaction is a particularly fruitful method of borrowing analysis, a hermeneutics rarely approached in popular music studies.

Chapter 3 begins to explore musical borrowing for particular playback spaces, more specifically, for the automobile. I focus on Los Angeles based gangsta rap producer Dr. Dre and his albums *The Chronic* (1992) and *Doggystyle* (1993). Dr. Dre consciously decided to use fewer samples in his production at this time, instead choosing to rerecord preexisting material. This study also underlines music's intersections with geography, both the influence of urban geography on music production and the geography of particular listening spaces. As borrowing is central to hip-hop's ethos, Dr. Dre's production reflects how musical materials become reused for a new space, updated and customized for the automotive listening experience.

Chapter 4 shifts the borrowing focus to digital sampling, but instead of examining digital sampling in the context of hip-hop beats, as other studies have done, I wish to look at digitally sampling the voice of the rapper. In particular, I will discuss the voice as relic, deployed to reference the hip-hop martyrs Notorious B.I.G. and Tupac Shakur. Rappers Jay-Z (Shawn Carter) and Nas (Nasir Jones) both embed these late artists in examples of what I call "postmortem sampling," that is, the use of a recording (sound or image) of a deceased artist with great cultural heft (e.g., Elvis Presley, Kurt Cobain, Freddie Mercury, John Lennon, Michael Jackson). In postmortem borrowing, the authenticity lies in the recorded sound or image, in spite of its recontextualization. Close investigations of examples involving the Notorious B.I.G. (by Jay-Z) and Tupac Shakur (by Nas) will compare the sonorities of the old and new contexts, a juxtaposition that demonstrates the fact that the sonority of the beats themselves, often neglected in studies of rap, is integral to the presentation of any rap song. Thus, when the voice of a deceased rapper is used in a new context, both the voice (with its biographical associations) and sonorities from the beat provide meaning. Rappers who use the symbolic immortality of hip-hop martyrs Tupac Shakur and the Notorious B.I.G. to their own ends create specific identities for the deceased artists and themselves, both creating memorial processes and encouraging canon formation.

Chapter 5 is a companion to chapter 4, as they deal with similar themes, notably allusions to and borrowing from the canonized rappers Tupac Shakur and the Notorious B.I.G. As chapter 4 looks at some of their contemporaries, chapter 5 looks at the "next generation" of artists, the construction of Eminem and 50 Cent into a particular gangsta rap lineage. I look closely at Eminem's production style, his "sonic signature," as providing an authorial presence beyond his rapping. For example, 50 Cent's "Patiently Waiting," produced by Eminem, shows a web of references that places 50 Cent as an heir to a lineage that includes Eminem, Dr. Dre, and "ancestor" Tupac Shakur. By no means are the case studies intended to be exhaustive, but they provide examples that demonstrate that a thorough study of musical borrowing in hip-hop requires attention to the texts (hip-hop recordings), their reception, and wider cultural contexts.

As Richard Shusterman has written, "Artistic appropriation is the historical source of hip-hop music and still remains the core of its technique and a central feature of its aesthetic form and message."[56] This practice fits within a long lineage of other musical genres and cultures, but appropriation in the digital era means that there are even more possibilities that hip-hop practitioners can utilize to create their music. Bounding the hip-hop world as imagined community makes the discussion more productive, and the variety of case studies presented is an attempt to approach borrowing from different angles, in order to draw the greatest knowledge from the most perspectives. Though these recordings are open to many interpretations, the following chapters intend to show that intertextuality is a crucial part of hip-hop music's composition and reception.

CHAPTER 1

HISTORICIZING THE BREAKBEAT
Hip-Hop's Origins and Authenticity

Hip hop today thrives on a sense of its own past.

—BILL BREWSTER AND FRANK BROUGHTON, *LAST NIGHT A DJ SAVED MY LIFE*

Some say this is the first generation of black Americans to experience nostalgia.
And it all showed up in the music.

—NELSON GEORGE, *HIP-HOP AMERICA*

With hip hop, born in the Bronx, these guys created something out of nothing.
That's amazing. That's alchemy. That's magic.

—JOHAN KUGELBERG, *BORN IN THE BRONX*

The complex relationship between an artistic culture and its history can be investigated from two large-scale methodological angles. First, there is the "ancestral method"—the relationship between a culture and its historical influences and precedents, linking past to present to form a network of lineage or traditions. The second method ("intracultural hermeneutics") looks at the relationship between a self-conscious culture and its own internal history: its origins, development, or evolution and its defining features.[1] Though elements of a culture shift over time, the importance of a culture's defining features (e.g., lifestyles, worldview, philosophies, images, objects, and products) is what keeps cultural objects bounded in an imagined community. While such objects and concepts are never fully bounded in actuality, these features are the crucial signifiers that form cultural identity and, to many, its essence. Despite the contestation that some of an art world's essentialism may invite, the truth content (*Wahrheitsgehalt*) of an artistic culture is of great importance for those who participate. In popular music cultures, this "truth content" is part of a larger issue, widely theorized in popular music scholarship, known as authenticity.[2] This chapter, by way of the second method, explores the links between hip-hop's self-conscious cultural history and notions of authenticity through the variety of ways newer artists borrow and sample from their predecessors in the hip-hop world.

African American culture, and its reception, has had a unique and problematic relationship with history, exposed to interpretations ranging from praise of artistic lineages (Stuckey, Gates, Floyd, Demers, Cobb) to claims of having no history at all (Hegel's contention of African culture's "historylessness"/*Gesehichtslosigkeit* as antithetical to Europe's).[3] In terms of culture produced from the African diaspora, there may exist what Lois Zamora calls an "anxiety of origins" within North American and Latin American (more specifically "New World") literary cultures.[4] Zamora writes: "I consistently find that an anxiety about origins impels American writers to search for precursors (in the name of community) rather than escape from them (in the name of individuation); to connect to traditions and histories (in the name of a usable past) rather than dissociate from them (in the name of originality)."[5] Zamora sees the use of traditions, clichés, interest in origins, and repetition as a result of this historical anxiety.

More specifically, links in scholarship between hip-hop and earlier forms of African or African American expression have been abundant. These include connections with griots, Jamaican toasting, jazz, blues, and 1970s blaxploitation film. While the connections with pre-hip-hop ancestry are useful and enlightening, this chapter analyzes hip-hop history and borrowing from *within* the "hip-hop world" or "Hip-Hop Nation." Rather than consider long-term or cross-generational links with earlier forms of African American arts, hip-hop can now be treated and discussed as its own cultural field for hermeneutical investigation. Hip-hop discourse acknowledges, and debates within, its own field with its own intracultural traditions, and this genre consciousness among fans, artists, and media is crucial both to identity and to understanding. Exploring these more internalized dynamics will help elucidate notions of cultural definition, canon formation, and authenticity. This investigation of borrowing from *within* the hip-hop world, focusing on the origins and romanticization of a "prerecording" hip-hop performance culture, demonstrates a pervasive source of hip-hop authenticity. A number of artists and groups borrow from the "old school" as representative of a historically authentic hip-hop identity. I call this concern with hip-hop history *historical authenticity*.[6]

Rather than theorize answers as to why genre self-consciousness is so abundant in hip-hop, this chapter shows *how* the specific relationship between hip-hop and its own history is embedded within hip-hop music.[7] Concern with hip-hop's internal history is more prominent with some artists than others; artists such as KRS-One, Common, and Nas comment on hip-hop as a larger culture and, as I will argue, borrow from the early period of hip-hop to signify authenticity.[8] Artists who assert and invoke the past as the essence of *true* hip-hop demonstrate that knowledge in a number of ways. Historical authenticity in hip-hop becomes an extramusical and intramusical debate that contributes to construction of these genres and communities.

Historical Accounts of the Origins of Hip-Hop

While it is not the aim of this chapter to show how it really was ("Wie es eigentlich gewesen"),[9] it is important to present some accounts of the origins of hip-hop music as a frame of reference. Many of these accounts have evolved from interviews over the years, and various anecdotes have become canonized through frequent citations in books, magazines, and documentary films. Since hip-hop's origins were largely unrecorded (which contributes to its mystique), we will never have an entirely accurate account of how it was, but these accounts are nonetheless important in forging a usable past for historical authenticity.

For certain hip-hop purists, the truest form of hip-hop culture existed from 1973 to 1979, before hip-hop was "commercialized" in the form of recordings. It was during this time period that what became known as the "four elements" of hip-hop arose in the South Bronx (graffiti, breakin', DJing, and MCing). These artistic movements were linked, all sharing the same urban space, with artists often engaging with more than one of these elements. The following will give an account of those early days, culled from various secondary sources.

Though graffiti and what became known as breakdancing emerged as early as the late 1960s, no specific date is associated with their birth. The origin of hip-hop music, however, can be traced back to a single time and place: 1520 Sedgwick Avenue in Morris Heights (in the Bronx) on August 11, 1973, when Jamaican-born DJ Kool Herc threw his first party. What separated Herc from other DJs at the time was that he did something different with the records. First, he used two turntables (as contemporaneously used in disco to create a smooth flow from one song to another), and he began to monitor the crowd for responses.[10] Second, he decided to use the instrumental break of records, since that was the part of the record that dancers seemed to like the most. The often quoted account is from David Toop's 1984 book *The Rap Attack*: "Initially, Herc was trying out his reggae records but since he failed to cut ice he switched to Latin-tinged funk, just playing the fragments that were popular with the dancers and ignoring the rest of the track. The most popular part was usually the percussion break."[11] Herc developed a technique called the "merry-go-round" where he would play a continuous flow of breakbeats, one after the other. He was then able to use the same breakbeat on two copies of the same records, alternating the two to create a continuous instrumental flow. A number of breakbeats are mentioned in these accounts, most notably the middle section of James Brown's "Give It Up or Turnit A Loose" and the Incredible Bongo Band's version of "Apache." Bill Brewster and Frank Broughton provide a quote from an interview with DJ Kool Herc:

> Herc recalls the records he used that night. "There was the 'clap your hands, stomp your feet' part of James Brown's 'Give it up or Turnit a Loose,' 'Funky Music Is The Thing' by the Dynamic Corvettes, 'If You Want To Get Into Something' by the Isley Brothers and 'Bra' by Cymande." All this was topped off with the percussion frenzy of the Incredible Bongo Band's "Apache," a record destined to become Herc's signature tune, a Bronx anthem, and one of the most sampled records in hip hop.[12]

There is no debate within the hip-hop community as to the individual who most directly "invented" hip-hop music: DJ Kool Herc is universally recognized and respected. Accounts almost always note his unusually large sound speakers (a tradition brought with him from the Caribbean), as well as his own size (6'5" tall). As the story goes, after a few parties, Herc began to establish a reputation for himself in the Bronx.

DJ and former South Bronx gang member Afrika Bambaataa organized his first party in November 1976 at the Bronx River Community Center, inspired by Herc's break-centered style, as opposed to a song-centered DJ style.[13] He founded an organization called the Zulu Nation to promote an end to gang warfare in the Bronx. He played a wide variety of records: in addition to funk music, he played instrumental portions of the Monkees, the Beatles, Aerosmith, and Kraftwerk.[14] For Bambaataa, using the instrumental fragment eradicated an element of racial identity and genre categorization; artist and genre mattered less than sound and danceability. Bambaataa, in an oft-cited statement to David Toop in 1984, recalled:

> I'd throw on *Sgt Pepper's Lonely Hearts Club Band*—just that drum part. One, two, three, BAM—and they'd be screaming and partying. I'd throw on the Monkees, "Mary, Mary, where are you going?"—and they'd start going crazy. I'd say, "You just danced to the Monkees." They'd say, "You liar. I didn't dance to no Monkees." I'd like to catch people who categorise records.[15]

His individualism was rooted in leadership of a musical democracy. In other words, if the crowd had not responded favorably to the records, it would not have worked. The events became extremely popular, and partygoers went all over New York City to look for the eclectic records that Bambaataa played. The astounding variety of his records frequently became a metaphor for peace and coexistence in later reception.[16]

As Joseph Schloss and others have stated, hip-hop represented a new way of thinking about records and, ultimately, a new way of making music.[17] Rather than a linear harmonic progression in the Western art music sense, the looping repetition of dance music creates a pleasure arising from a process, rather than satiating a goal-oriented desire (what Luis

Manuel Garcia calls "process pleasure").[18] Broadly speaking, the break-beat was part of an artistic tradition of recontextualizing "found objects" (e.g., Duchamp's *Fountain*) and of Signifyin(g) on past styles, adapting and appropriating records to fit new contexts for collective enjoyment and active engagement. It was a form of musical fetishization, but un-like Adorno's criticisms of fragmented listening, I do not use the term in a pejorative sense. Dancers were now able to enjoy the pleasures of their musical fetishes to the fullest. Most important, this music culture began as a dance culture—it was about the energy of parties. The break-beat involves a freedom, a freedom of the DJ as listener to foster cre-ativity with the collage of cultural information he or she had available. The focus on the dancer and the community invokes what Herbert Gans calls the "user-orientation" of popular music as opposed to the "creator-orientation" of high art music and its canons.[19] This early hip-hop focus on the party conjures up notions of the pleasure-field, as described and theorized by Richard Middleton, a "loss of the subject" in experiencing *jouissance*.[20]

The importance of collectivity and audience to historical authenticity cannot be overstated. While the individual innovators are acknowledged and celebrated, the notion of the collective (crews, audience, battles, community, diversity) became intertwined with hip-hop. As was the case with many cultural births, the diverse mix of people found in an urban environment played a crucial role—what Robin Kelley calls "polycultur-alism."[21] Dancers and DJs mutually influenced each other, and it is safe to say that hip-hop music would not have formed and expanded in the Bronx without either's contributions.

Other DJs began to emerge and improve on the conceptual approach initiated by DJ Kool Herc, such as Grandmaster Flash, credited with advances in mixing, and Grand Wizzard Theodore, who is credited with inventing record scratching as a turntable technique. MCs arrived soon after, speaking over the instrumental tracks and forming groups and as-sociations with certain DJs.[22]

As time passed, parties grew, and reputations increased. In 1977, a blackout brought the opportunity for the looting of turntables and other equipment, increasing the number of DJs in the Bronx. By October 1979, hip-hop music reached a much greater audience with the release of the first hit rap single, "Rapper's Delight" by the Sugar Hill Gang. It received copious amounts of radio play and sold numerous units. This was the moment when hip-hop music reached a national audience and eventually the whole world.

The South Bronx and *Wild Style* (1982)

Hip-hop's origins in the South Bronx became the romantic mythology of an artistic culture born out of dismal socioeconomic conditions. City planner Robert Moses built the Cross Bronx Expressway in 1959, which went through working-class ethnic communities. Many middle-class families left the Bronx, and poorer groups were relocated into blue-collar housing units. The South Bronx became a symbol of ruin, poverty, and the apparent hopelessness of postindustrial abandonment.[23] Afrika Bambaataa has said, "It was so bad in the South Bronx, they said it was the worst place in the United States. And there was the culture of hip hop, this music. We always had the musical aspect in the Bronx. And we had the drugs, the dope, the coke—that was plaguing the community."[24] The energy of parties in the Bronx was created in isolation (away from any media coverage), as if the trope of the alienated, suffering artist could now be applied to an entire community.

Frequently cited as the most accurate representation of the early hip-hop period, the film *Wild Style* (1982) has had a colossal effect on hip-hop culture. The film depicts the urban landscape of the Bronx, along with the coexistence of these new artistic ideas in various party scenes. Melle Mel (of the Furious Five) said in an interview, "*Wild Style*, that was the one movie that captured more of the true essence of hip hop."[25] Though filmed in 1981, *Wild Style* is considered the quintessential hip-hop film because it sought to capture the energy of prerecording, pre-1979 hip-hop.

Written, produced, and directed by Charlie Ahern, *Wild Style* was the brainchild of Frederick Braithwaite (Fab 5 Freddy),[26] who contributed music and acted in the film. The plot centers on a young graffiti artist named Ray (painting under the name "Zoro" and played by real-life graffiti artist Lee Quinones) who isolates himself from the graffiti crews, though he becomes romantically involved with a graffiti crew leader named Rose (Sandra "Lady Pink" Fabra). The film includes a number of performers from the early hip-hop world, including MC Chief Rocker Busy Bee, Grandmaster Flash, the Treacherous 3, breakdancers the Rock Steady Crew, and a rap battle on a basketball court (the "basketball throwdown") between the Fantastic 5 and the Cold Crush Brothers. The climax of the film is the "jam" at the East River Park Amphitheatre. Set against a graffiti mural backdrop of two hands shooting lightning bolts toward a large blue star (painted by Quinones), this party/jam features the previously mentioned performers, as well as Lil' Rodney Cee and K. K. Rockwell, formerly of the Funky Four +1, now under the name Double Trouble, performing a rap entitled "Double Trouble." After their rap, Grandmaster Flash cuts and scratches Chic's "Good Times," as if to reterritorialize it for pre-1979 hip-hop.[27] Flash's virtuosic DJ riffs on the song continue, with images of the outdoor party persisting through to the end credits sequence.

Many involved with the film attest to its importance as depicting authentic forms of early hip-hop. Ahern tellingly writes that "*Wild Style* was the first movie to capture hip-hop culture at its roots."[28] Fab 5 Freddy said that the intention of the film was to portray the scene not as it was in 1982, but as it had been a few years before (pre-Rapper's Delight"). Fab 5 Freddy writes, "When we were making *Wild Style*, we wanted to set the movie in the 70s. Because 'Rappers Delight' had already come out, MCs were making records, so we wanted to go back a few years earlier, and set it at a point when hip hop was completely underground, when the form was raw and pure."[29] Using real graffiti artists and musicians adds to the perceived realness of the film, as Quinones comments to Ahern in 2007: "You was in the moment. It was a magical, special moment. You captured an innocent moment, like, we weren't acting."[30]

The climactic gig at the Amphitheatre in the film demonstrates that, although the genre largely uses prerecorded materials for its musical sources, this version of hip-hop authenticity strays little from the authenticity of the "live gig." Sarah Thornton writes:

> While authenticity is attributed to many different sounds, between the mid-fifties and mid-eighties, its main site was the live gig. In this period,

"liveness" dominated notions of authenticity. The essence or truth of music was located in its performance by musicians in front of an audience. Interestingly, the ascent of "liveness" as a distinct musical value coincided with the decline of performance as both the dominant medium of music and the prototype for recording.[31]

The live hip-hop gig involves creative alteration of preexisting recordings, whereas the live rock gig is concerned with more traditional forms of originality and instrumental performance; they are both nevertheless symbolic of a live gig in their respective genres. In hip-hop, the content is significantly different and involves an arguably more complex web of mixed media (graffiti, breakin', DJing, MCing, and the audience all elemental to the performance in its idealized realizations), but the form remains the same. In 2007, *Wild Style* was inducted into VH1's Hip-Hop Honors, acknowledging the influence the film has had on hip-hop culture. *Wild Style* becomes crucial to this study not for investigating its historical accuracy, but for the ideologies it promotes and how subsequent artists uphold them.

Wild Style is now canonized along with other artifacts from early hip-hop culture. A twenty-fifth-anniversary DVD edition of the film has now been released, exemplary of what David Shumway would call "commodified nostalgia."[32] There exists an irony, of course, in commodifying nostalgia for an era praised for its "uncommercialness," but such is the case for a number of twentieth-century countercultures. As the stories go, DJs like Herc and Baambaataa transcended fixed categories, decanonizing the range of artists they played. Thirty years on, these DJs, and the breakbeats they played, have in themselves been canonized. Herein lies the paradox of the hip-hop canon: hip-hop, to quote Neil Kulkarni, "was resistant to precisely those ideas of fixed cultural worth which other, more hierarchal art forms quickly created for themselves";[33] but hip-hop then became canonized and hierarchical (with classic breakbeats, radio shows devoted to "Old School" hip-hop, icons of the movement, bus tours, multiple halls of fame, and a presumed "Golden Age" in the late 1980s/early 1990s). Kodwo Eshun's comment that the break was used "to groove rob not ancestor worship"[34] may contain truth for many DJs, but there is certainly another strand of contemporary hip-hop culture that uses "classic breaks" as homage or ancestor worship. Furthermore, citing or borrowing from early DJs, fashion, breakbeats, books, and other elements that signify the origins of hip-hop culture contains a high degree of subcultural capital and thus is used to the benefit of artists who borrow and sample from such signifiers.

Intrageneric Borrowing and Historical Authenticity in Hip-Hop Recordings

As stated earlier in the chapter, many historical accounts romanticize the prerecorded period of hip-hop, from 1973 to 1979. In fact, Jeff Chang calls "Rapper's Delight" "the first death of hip-hop."[35] His history, *Can't Stop Won't Stop: A History of the Hip-Hop Generation,* is a narrative of decline, romanticizing the South Bronx artistically, while simultaneously portraying its dismal economic and social conditions. For him and others, this was when hip-hop was urban, spontaneous, live, full of creativity, and innovative. It was a DIY culture where competition was collaboration; it was often perceived as a peaceful solution to gang warfare and was unmediated by "business" (in the form of corporate infrastructures).[36] And, unlike the misogyny expressed in the lyrical content of later rap styles, women had important artistic roles in the formative stages of the culture.[37]

Historical authenticity in hip-hop is seen by many as a live phenomenon about having fun and rocking the party. Although there is no denying that selling recordings of hip-hop music brought about drastic changes to its form and substance, canonizing the origins of hip-hop through a nostalgic lens contributes to notions of prerecorded hip-hop as romantic, unmediated space.[38] Knowledge of the history and origins of hip-hop empowers both artist and fan with historical authenticity. For those who evoke the past, whether sampling a classic breakbeat or saying the name of an old legend, these gestures signify hip-hop authenticity. Historical authenticity is a special case of Thornton's "subcultural authenticity," which "is grounded in the performer in so far as s/he represents the community."[39] KRS-One and Nas, while authenticating themselves by

Typology of Intra-generic Borrowing and Historical Authenticity

	DEFINITION/EXAMPLES	FOUND IN:
A. Image	Breakdancing, graffiti, turntables, live battles, fashion, urban space	Music videos, cover art, CD booklets, live performances, etc.
B. Sampling and borrowing	Using "classic breakbeats" (e.g., "Apache," "The Big Beat") Scratching and other vinyl sounds	Musical signifyin(g) in hip-hop beats
C. Peer references	Referencing rappers, historically important DJs, breakdancing crews	Lyrical content
D. Verbal quotation	Allosonic and autosonic quotations from hip-hop films and recordings	Lyrical content
E. Stylistic allusion	Imitating earlier styles of rap music, flow, of a particular artist without direct quotation. Using older techno-logical equipment (such as the Roland TR-808 drum machine).	Either (or both) beat or flow
F. Nostalgia	Often based on art vs. commerce "Back in the day" as pure, peaceful, fun, more creative, uncorrupted	Lyrical content, though nostalgia can be a sentiment demonstrated by all above types of borrowing

TABLE 1.1. Historical Authenticity in Hip-hop

flaunting their subcultural capital, represent and teach members of the "Hip-Hop Nation," a notion that resonates with the idea that these art-ists acknowledge, work within, and help construct hip-hop culture.

A. Image

Artists and groups use imagery to evoke the historical authenticity of hip-hop as a cultural movement wider in scope than simply "rap music." This includes showing images of breakdancing in music videos (Run-DMC's "It's Like That," Chemical Brother's "Galvanize," and Wyclef Jean's "We Trying to Stay Alive," which featured the Rock Steady Crew), graf-fiti (Naughty by Nature's "Hip Hop Hooray," KRS-One's "5 Boroughs"), DJs and turntables (Eric B. and Rakim's "Paid in Full," DJ Premier's "Classic"), as well as posters made in the style of 1970s hip-hop parties (the CD booklet of De La Soul's album *The Grind Date*, shown below,

It's Like That

Featuring: Carl Thomas

Published
by Krioketspit
Publishing (BMI),
80's Kid Music
(BMI), Maseo Music
(BMI)
Rugged Jointz (ASCAP).
Thom Tunes Publishing
administered by EMI
April Music (ASCAP).

**Written by De La Soul,
Dave West and Carl
Thomas**

Produced
by Supa
Dave West for
Hot Sauce Inc.
Vocals by Kelvin
Mercer and David
Jolicoeur. Recorded by
Brian Garten at Right
Track Studios,NYC.
Assistant Engineer
Justin Shturtz. Mixed by
Gimel "Young Guru"
Keaton for Loreal Inc. at
Baseline Studios,NYC.
Assistant Engineer
Dave Brown. Additional
Vocals by Carl Thomas.

Carl Thomas appears Courtesy of Bad Boy Records.

Figure 1.1: Inside CD booklet of De La Soul's *The Grind Date* (Sanctuary/ BMG, 2004)

and the opening of Jay-Z's "Roc Boys" video).[40] A number of music videos emphasize the liveness of the hip-hop event, reminiscent of hip-hop's "live gig"/"rockin the party" aesthetics: Nas's "Made You Look" video ends with an a cappella rap in front of a live crowd (similar to Eminem's in the live battle sequences in *8 Mile*). To use a much earlier example, Afrika Bambaataa's "Planet Rock" (1982) music video includes early breakdancing footage along with Bambaataa's stage performance. The KRS-One (produced by Marley Marl) "Hip-Hop Lives" (2007) music video surveys

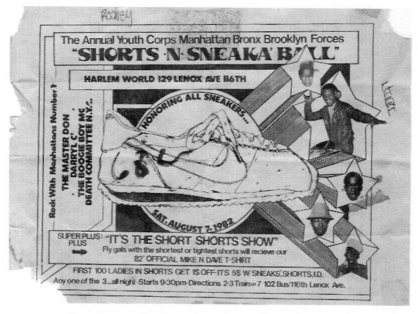

Figure 1.2: Flyer for 1982 hip-hop show in Kugelberg. Courtesy of Toledohi-phop.org

the entire history of hip-hop in images so that breakdancing, graffiti, and turntablism feature prominently.

Most crucial to the imagery of hip-hop historical authenticity are representations of urban space. The urban landscape of the Bronx provided the landscape for graffiti art on subway cars and buildings and provided space for breakdancers and DJs (who wired their systems into lamp posts in the city). Examples of this particular appropriation of urban space can be found in *Wild Style*, in which one scene focuses on what Ahern calls the "rolling art gallery" of the subway trains that emerge into the sunlight of the Bronx.[41] This film and many subsequent hip-hop videos focus heavily on a specific manifestation of what Adam Krims refers to as an "urban ethos."[42] The urban ethos of historical authenticity is one that depicts multiple elements or signifiers of hip-hop culture with a focus on the party or jam, epitomized in the collective polyculturalism of the *Wild Style* "amp jam."

One example of this "of the street" notion of hip-hop as subcultural capital was the Beastie Boys's 2004 performance on *Late Night with David Letterman* of "Ch-Check It Out." While most bands conventionally perform on the side stage of the Ed Sullivan Theatre, the Beastie Boys opened by rapping while emerging from the New York subway, rapping down the street, through the backstage area, and eventually onto the stage to unite with their DJ, Mix Master Mike, already on stage. Inhabiting the spaces of "the street," the geographical specificity of New York City, and the presence of a live DJ are all elements closely linked to early hip-hop historical authenticity. Such attention to geography is crucial to many forms of hip-hop authenticity, about which both Murray Forman and Adam Krims have written extensively.[43] Though rap is subject to a spectrum of visual representations,[44] representations of the mid-1970s Bronx as site of hip-hop's origins continue to be a powerful force as it pervades a large sector of hip-hop imagery.

B. Historically Self-Aware Sampling and Borrowing

Some believe that rap music production in general has stayed close to its early roots, and quite self-consciously so. From the perspective of DJ historians Brewster and Broughton, hip-hop has aimed to create the sounds of the street, trying to recreate a particular ethos in a way that other DJ cultures do not strive to represent:

> Even now, with a twenty-five-year body of work behind it and an ever more sophisticated approach to production, hip hop is still about recreating in the studio the kind of music that a DJ would make in a basketball park in the shadow of a Bronx tower block.[45]

While this drastically simplifies the multifaceted approaches of hip-hop producers, it goes to show the pervasiveness of the "staying true to your roots" ideology within the genre. And this ideology is very much embedded in the sounds of the examples that follow.

There certainly exists a breakbeat canon, one that communicates a deep signification of hip-hop to knowledgeable interpretive communities.[46] In addition, Schloss's thorough study of b-boying points out the existence of a "b-boy canon," one that has changed little since its origins in the 1970s. For this community of dancers, using the classic breakbeats solidifies their traditions, acknowledges the foundations of their artistic practices, strengthens their community, and validates their livelihood.[47]

One of the most canonized breakbeats is derived from the Incredible Bongo Band's cover of "Apache," as first used by DJ Kool Herc and featured on a number of subsequent recordings.[48] Examples include the Roots' "Thought@Work" and Nas's "Made You Look" (produced by Saalam Remi), the latter of which is significantly slowed down compared to the tempo of the original. The distinctive sound of the bongos is crucial to its recognizability, particularly when producers change the original tempo and add other layers to the beat. The break was cited for its importance as early as 1984: "The record on which everybody concurs—the quintessential hip-hop track—is 'Apache' by The Incredible Bongo Band."[49] Kool Herc, in a *New York Times* article, called "Apache" the national anthem of hip-hop.[50] Other well-known beats circulate widely, such as Billy Squier's "The Big Beat," used by Jay-Z for "99 Problems" and by British rapper Dizzee Rascall for "Fix Up, Look Sharp." Rapper Nas wrote of beats like those from "Apache" and the Incredible Bongo Band's version of "In-A-Gadda-Da-Vida": "Those breaks are so hip-hop. I'm going to continue to use them again and again."[51]

Run-D.M.C, perceived by many to usher in a new phase of hip-hop music, were also using beats from an earlier, more localized instance of performance. For example, "Walk This Way," their famous collaboration with Aerosmith in 1986, supposedly emerged through Rick Rubin recognizing what was known simply as a breakbeat at parties. DMC recalls:

> One day me and Jay was in the studio and we was sampling Aerosmith and Rick said, "Yo, do you know who that is?" and we was like, "No, but we like this beat." We used to always rap over that beat in the 'hood. We didn't know the group name or anything. So Rick gave us the 411, the whole history of the band. We had our own rhymes over the beat, but Rick said, "No do *their* lyrics."
>
> When Steven Tyler came into the studio, Jay was cutting up [Aero-

smith's original version of] "Walk This Way" and he said, "Here's what we used to do with your record." And Steve said, "Yo, when are you gonna hear *me?*" And Jay looked up and said, "We never get to hear you. After this guitar riff, it's back to the beginning." And Steve thought that was so amusing. Those guys were real cool.[52]

This rock-rap collaboration, which was so heavily touted at the time, seems to have been valued as a hip-hop beat even before the collaboration occurred. The success of the single canonized it as one of the earliest rock-rap collaborations, and reception in the mainstream media often treated it as an unprecedented occurrence.[53]

Borrowing sounds associated with hip-hop's origins is by no means limited to breakbeats. Cheryl Keyes locates sounds associated with the urban landscape, considering their function as an intensification of the lyrical topics (such as automobile horns and sirens in Grandmaster Flash and the Furious Five's "The Message").[54] While gangsta rap has taken urban landscapes and soundscapes in different directions, artists who try to recreate a party atmosphere on record (usually by adding the sound of audience response) also engage with historical authenticity, what Elizabeth Wheeler labels as part of the "rock-the-house" subgenre of rap music.[55]

The sound of vinyl scratching, one particular technique of the DJ, has also become a production tool to signify authenticity. The sounds of vinyl can invoke nostalgia, as well as the "digging in the crates" aspect of hip-hop producer purism. The vinyl popping and hiss can be heard in such records as the Pharcyde's "Passin' Me By," which includes a sample of Quincy Jones's "Summer in the City." As is the case with many once-radical-sounding musical signifiers, scratching has spilled over into other genres, and it has become so ubiquitous in popular music that it has lost much of its once-radical meaning. With the advancement of recording technologies, vinyl scratches can be produced by a button on the mixing board or laptop computer. It can be a production technique that simply does not have the same contextual relevance as it once did, yet the code itself still signifies hip-hop (and associations with hipness). One example stems from the 1999 Britney Spears debut album *Hit Me Baby One*

More Time, a release firmly placed in the mainstream pop/"bubblegum pop" tradition—the single "Crazy" features vinyl scratches, and another, a cover version of "The Beat Goes On," contains the hissing and popping sound of vinyl.[56]

The use of a DJ at live performances, as well as turntablistic hip-hop codes (e.g., scratching, vinyl pop and hiss) on recordings, forms a primary defining feature of historical authenticity. Groups like the Beastie Boys, Jurassic 5, Gang Starr, and Eric B and Rakim feature DJs as central to their aesthetic (and these DJs have equal status to the others in the group).[57] The hip-hop group the Roots, criticized in the past for their decision to use live instruments over recorded samples, is one of the groups most overtly knowledgeable of hip-hop's history. They demonstrate a historical authenticity in a number of ways, but one includes their "hip-hop 101" segments in live shows, interludes of classic hip-hop songs often in medley form.[58] Drummer ?uestlove (Amhir Thompson) of the Roots aims for hip-hop authenticity, but by different means: the timbre of his drum beats aims to sound sampled, as he attempts on his drum kit to recreate many of the "classic" breakbeats of the late 1960s and 1970s.[59]

C. Peer References

The use of peer references in hip-hop is abundant and multipurpose: to display associations with a collective (e.g., Native Tongues, G-Unit), to give respect (or disrespect) to contemporaries, to mention the producer of the track (a tradition going back to when early MCs rapped the praises of the DJ), and to give homage to hip-hop icons of the past. The mention of hip-hop icons has a dual purpose: to provide knowledge about the genre's past, particularly to rappers who have been neglected in current times, and to demonstrate some sort of connection with the artists named. For example, Nas's "Where Are They Now?" (2006) provides a long list of artists that Nas suggests have been forgotten:

> Red Head Kingpin, Tim Dogg, have you seen 'em?
> Kwame, King T of King Son
> Superlover C, Cassanova Run

Antwoinette, Rob Base never showin' up
You seen Black Sheep, Group Home, Busy Bee?
Ask Ill and Al Scratch "Where my Homies?"
Leave it to y'all, these niggas left for dead
Last week my man swore he saw Special Ed
Rap is like a ghost town, real mystic
Like these folks never existed
They the reason that rap became addictive
Play their CD or wax and get lifted. (0:10–0:37)

The Roots'"WAOK Roll Call" from their *Phrenology* (2002) album provides a list of names of influential hip-hop artists, reminiscent of the
roll-call scene in Spike Lee's *Do the Right Thing* (1989), when radio DJ
Mister Señor Love Daddy delivers an extensive list of African American musicians. This ancestral impulse creates a canon based on African
American artistic expression (in the case of the Spike Lee film) or, in the
case of the Roots and Nas, a canon based on hip-hop history. In addition
to references to other rappers, artists can also mention other elements
(breakdancing and graffiti) to acknowledge the wider sense of hip-hop
culture (such as KRS-One's mention of the Rock Steady Crew in "South
Bronx").

D. Verbal Quotation

Regarding sampling from hip-hop itself, Felicia Miyakawa has written:

> When sampling from vinyl, DJs tend to avoid taking from hip-hop's own
> history unless there is a specific reason to do so. As several songs in this
> study illustrate, however, sampling rap vocals in order to pay homage to
> rap's historical heavyweights is clearly acceptable.[60]

There are myriad ways to quote earlier rappers or to allude to a particular
style. Many rappers will paraphrase a quote or appropriate it for themselves. For example, KRS-One's "MCs Act like They Don't Know" (1995)
opens with an allosonic quotation of material from the Kurtis Blow sin-

gle "The Breaks" (1980), the first rap single to sell five hundred thousand units. Blow's version opens as follows:

> Clap your hands everybody, if you've got what it takes
> Cause I'm Kurtis Blow and I want you to know that these are the breaks.

And KRS-One's opens (with the same rhythm and vocal emphasis), to a slower tempo:

> Clap your hands everybody, if you've got what it takes
> Cause I'm KRS and I'm on the mic and Premier's on the breaks.[61]

Another example of an allosonic quotation of Blow is Nas's 1996 "If I Ruled the World," which uses the melody of Kurtis Blow's "If I Ruled the World,"[62] sung in the later version by Lauren Hill.[63] The lines become blurred here, as these quotations do refer to recorded hip-hop rather than a "prerecording" era, but I would argue that this still represents a nostalgia for the history of the genre in line with earlier examples.

Extremely influential to electronic dance music, "Planet Rock" (1982) by Afrika Bambaataa and John Robie (produced by Arthur Baker) has also been canonized in hip-hop and is a frequent source of hip-hop quotation and stylistic allusion. In particular, one four-bar passage toward the end of the single has been paraphrased by a number of artists:[64]

Example 1.1: Transcription of "Planet Rock" (4:45). Examples 1.2 and 1.3 show some of its influences.

For example, Talib Kweli and Mos Def paraphrase it for "We Got the Beat" and Mos Def's collaboration with the Roots ("Double Trouble"), respectively:

Example 1.2: Talib Kweli, "We Got the Beat" (1:58)

Example 1.3: Mos Def, "Double Trouble" (5:08)

"Double Trouble" is a reference to the film *Wild Style*, and the group Double Trouble (K. K. Rockwell and Lil' Rodney C), who performed at the Amphitheatre. Mos Def quotes from the film:

> Here's a little story that must be told,
> about two cool brothers that were put on hold. (4:25–4:29)

Mos Def's "Double Trouble" (imitation of the same rhythm and inflections as the original):

> Say, here's a little story that must be told
> About two young brothers who got so much soul. (4:36–4:4)

The collaboration with Black Thought and Mos Def represents both allosonic quotation (from Mos Def) and overall stylistic allusion, recreating an earlier tag-team style of rap exemplified by Double Trouble (and Run-D.M.C and, in a later era, Jurassic 5).

The Beastie Boys' album *To the 5 Boroughs* (2004) contains a track entitled "Triple Trouble" that also quotes the Double Trouble rap from *Wild Style*:

"Double Trouble" (*Wild Style*) (0:00): If you (if you), wanna know (wanna know), the real deal about the two (let us tell ya), let us tell ya we're double trouble girls and we're doing it just for you.

"Triple Trouble" (Beastie Boys) to the same rhythm (1:18): If you (if

Figure 1.3: Cover of the Beastie Boys, *To the 5 Boroughs* (2004) (Capitol, 2004)

you), wanna know (wanna know), the real deal about the three, well let me tell ya, we're triple trouble y'all, we're gonna bring you up to speed.

DJ Mix Master Mike scratches and fragments the opening from "Rapper's Delight" as core to its basic beat on the verse and chorus and scratches more virtuosically in the "middle eight" section of the song. *To the Five Boroughs* can be interpreted as homage to the early days of hip-hop, with a number of quotations and stylistic allusions to this time. In addition, the cover of the album is a cityscape of New York City, including the two towers of the World Trade Center, perhaps in nostalgia for pre-9/11 society. These allusions were not lost on reviewers; as Alan Light writes, their album was "never straying from pass-the-mix-style old-school beats and rhymes."[65]

Autosonic quotations of other hip-hop media also exist, particularly from *Wild Style*. Former professional basketball player and amateur rapper Shaquille O'Neal used the "y'all can't ball" quotation (from Waterbed Kevie Kev in "basketball throwdown") for "I Hate to Brag" from his debut album, *Shaq Diesel* (1993). Nas's debut album, *Illmatic* (1994), opens with the conversation between Zoro and his brother, followed by *Wild Style*'s "Subway Theme."[66] This can be also manifested in non-US-based hip-hop, such as the March 1991 German release of LSD's *Watch Out for the Third Rail* (itself a quote from *Wild Style*) and autosonic quotations of the film for its single "Brand New Style."[67]

E. Stylistic Allusion

Artists also allude to earlier rap styles, rather than quoting directly, such as in Pharcyde's "Return of the B-Boy,"[68] which attempts allusion to earlier hip-hop styles. In this example, the group attempts to emulate an earlier delivery of rap that Krims categorizes as the "sung style,"[69] including call-and-response phrases, record scratching, and raps responding to a party atmosphere. In such stylistic allusion, artists and groups can suggest the "old school" without direct references to the past. These allusions occur in both beat and flow, in the case of the former, often utilized by technology associated with the era such as the Roland T-808 drum machine.

Hip-hop group Jurassic 5 is exemplary of the "tag-team" style mentioned earlier. The group consists of four MCs (Mark 7, Chali2na, Akil, and Soup), DJ Nu Mark, and DJ Cut Chemist; groups of MCs and DJs as a collective suggest an earlier era of groups such as the Cold Crush Brothers, Funky Four +1, and the Furious Five. As one album review writer comments, Jurassic 5 "has spent the past ten years recreating the aesthetic of early rap crews like the Treacherous Three and Crash Crew, intricately weaving their voices in and out of each other, finishing each other's lines, and harmonizing their choruses."[70] Tom Breihan calls this "retro formalism," similar to what the Stray Cats did in the 1980s with an earlier swing music style.[71] Trumpeter Russell Gunn stylistically alludes to the electro-pop style of "Planet Rock" in his "Skate King" from the album *Krunk Jazz* (2008). Gunn's music mixes bebop-style heads and other jazz elements with beats from hip-hop and other dance cultures, and although Gunn cannot be placed firmly in a single genre (jazz or hip-hop), he nevertheless demonstrates a hip-hop historical authenticity by alluding to this early hip-hop style.

F. Nostalgia

The element of nostalgia is a particularly pervasive one, not only in books on hip-hop but also in the lyrical topics of rap songs. As Jurassic 5 say in the chorus of "Concrete Schoolyard": "Let's take it back to the concrete streets, original beats with real live MCs." "Concrete Schoolyard" also quotes the opening (kazoo line) of Grandmaster Flash and the Furious Five's "Freedom" (which is from a popular breakbeat—Freedom's "Get Up and Dance," anthologized on the *Ultimate Breaks and Beats Collection*).

Common's "I Used to Love H.E.R." uses a woman as personification of hip-hop culture, lost love as a frequent object of nostalgia.[72] Common confesses his love for an earlier style of hip-hop, one that was associated with the urban ("She used to only swing it with the inner-city circle") but has now moved out to suburbs and larger audiences. The "love affair" detailed attests to the self-consciousness of hip-hop culture and its construction (and critique) of hip-hop identity. Such sentiments are commonplace in hip-hop (and other genres), particularly hip-hop that tries to separate itself from contemporary mainstream styles. And as Brewster and Broughton note, "hip-hop contains a few endlessly repeated fables, some respectful nods to its legendary creators and a great deal of misty-eyed clichés about 'back in the day.'"[73] As Q-Tip, MC of A Tribe Called Quest, said of their second album, *The Low End Theory*: "Hip-hop is moving farther and farther away from its true starting point. And what we're trying to do with this album is bring it a little bit closer to home."[74] While the exact nature of this "home" is subject to multiple interpretations, this quote is telling; the truth content of hip-hop seems to lie in the past, rather than in the present. The past becomes an authority figure; the "true starting point" becomes a utopian space and an archetype that becomes the referent for later artists to invoke.

The many ways that a historical authenticity can be demonstrated in the recordings are subject to overlap and often combined in the same single. One example of this is Nas's "Hip-Hop Is Dead" (produced by will.i.am), from his 2006 eponymous album. His music video features Nas rapping in a warehouse full of fans, emphasizing the early party and collective elements, including showing images of turntables that accompany his rap. "Hip-Hop Is Dead" also uses two classic breakbeats, which layer on top of the basic beat at different points in the song, the "Apache" break and Billy Squier's "The Big Beat." The "breakdown" section (3:01) has Nas rapping a cappella with a chanting crowd, showing his ability to stage hip-hop as a live phenomenon. Vinyl scratches also allude to the time when hip-hop began (as the trope states) with "two turntables and one mic." The sampling of Iron Butterfly's "In-A-Gadda-da-Vida" is worth noting since this song was used in the early disco scene and was covered on the Incredible Bongo Band's 1973 album *Bongo Rock* (along with "Apache").[75] Nas looks back to an earlier era in his lyrics, emphasizing a commercial/noncommercial divide that pervades hip-hop nostalgia rhetoric:

Everybody sound the same, commercialize the game

Reminiscin' when it wasn't all business. . . .
Went from turntables to mp3s
From "Beat Street" to commercials on Mickey D's. (3:10–3:14; 3:27–
3:31)

"Hip-Hop Is Dead" also reflects the genre's preoccupation with an all-too-real intersection with death and loss. Signaling the death of a genre is not particularly new, and it can be a useful critique of that field, identifying and defining important elements of that culture and what the artist/critic values within that culture. And while many current rappers are technically far more complex than the early MCs and DJs, historical authenticity has little to do with virtuosity as much as it does with fetishization of and nostalgia for the past.

Conclusion: The Quest for Origins

I would argue that this form of hip-hop authenticity is intrinsically concerned with the pursuit of the origin (the "true starting point" to which Q-Tip alludes). Foucault, in his essay "Nietzsche, Genealogy and History," quotes Nietzsche from *The Wanderer and his Shadow*:

> The lofty origin is no more than "a metaphysical extension which arises from the belief that things are most precious and essential at the moment of birth." We tend to think that this is the moment of their greatest perfection, when they emerged dazzling from the hands of a creator or in the shadowless light of a first morning. The origin always precedes the Fall. It comes before the body, before the world and time; it is associated with the gods, and its story is always sung as a theogony.[76]

In the case of the historiography of hip-hop, the early DJs (Herc, Bambaataa, and Grandmaster Flash) become these "gods."

The origins, in hip-hop, thus become the site of truth and purity in the eyes of historically conscious rap artists and writers, an "Eden before the fall," the fall being this "first death of hip-hop" symbolized by commercial success. This historical authenticity reflects an assumption that various popular music genres began in a romanticized space and that any changes to "original" forms become a corruption of the ideal.[77] This viewpoint has important implications for claims regarding the symbolic ownership of and participation within music genres on numerous levels (race, gender, geography, etc.). But as Foucault writes, "What is found at the historical beginning of things is not the inviolable identity of their origin; it is the dissension of other things. It is disparity."[78] In other words, the idea that hip-hop's essence can be found at a fixed origin is a romantic illusion.

Yet there remains a purism in historical authenticity that seeks to use the original impulses of the culture as a scripture to guide future creativity. As one breakdancer from the early period commented, "It's like the Bible, eventually you have to go to the original scripture and the original language it was written in, and I think that everybody on the East and West coast need to re-define our dance and take control of it again."[79] Schloss's study of breakdancers confirms the importance of foundational technique, as Schloss recounts the importance of incorporating original b-boy moves to acknowledge the history of the practice. Ken Swift tells Schloss, "I always try to add some sort of fundamental move in any combination. This way, I keep the traditions of the original style. . . . The finesse behind fundamentals is *serious*."[80] This hip-hop purism at the center of historical authenticity is also aligned with the so-called fifth element of hip-hop: knowledge. Knowledge of hip-hop's origins keeps the field defined in an act of both celebration and self-preservation. What Harrison calls the "formative line of argument" is at work here—the idea that hip-hop authenticity is found in hip-hop's origins. This focus on the origins of the culture has multiple implications for the perceived ownership of hip-hop culture in terms of race (African American and Puerto Rican), geography (New York City, South Bronx more specifically), and gender.[81] And although exactly when the genre's formative period ends is a constantly shifting and negotiated concept that depends on one's interpretive vantage point (the idea of the "old school" is relative), the concept has shaped much of hip-hop culture, its ideologies, and its artistic output ever since.

As it is in most popular music, authenticity is a particularly potent battleground in hip-hop: fans, artists, and critics are quick to distinguish what is "true" or "real" hip-hop from the inauthentic (a brief and informal survey of YouTube viewer responses to hip-hop videos can attest to this). Historical authenticity is simply one strain of hip-hop authenticity, albeit a particularly potent and pervasive one. It arises from a number of impulses: to canonize, to teach, to legitimate; to territorialize as a response to changes in the genre; and to enclose historical authenticity in an arena of nostalgic space. The use of codes, allusions, and quotes additionally becomes a form of Signifyin(g), verbal and musical play that reflects the multivocal discourses in hip-hop culture and African-based musics.

While all music engages in some form of musical borrowing, the intertwining concepts of history, borrowing, and authenticity in the hip-hop world all contribute to intrageneric borrowing as demonstrating a historical authenticity. As Zamora writes, "I agree with Merleau-Ponty that all cultural texts are intertexts, but writers and readers respond to their textual traditions in different ways and for different purposes, often according to *the importance given by a culture to its own history* and the history of its interactions with other cultures" (my emphasis).[82] As borrowing is fundamental to hip-hop aesthetics, and since hip-hop often has an equally overt relationship with its history, borrowing from this history forms a key feature within the music.

Hip-hop textually signals its own history, making listeners aware of its past in a number of ways. A musical shibboleth such as a classic breakbeat or quotation can educate, demonstrate "insider knowledge," and help define cultural boundaries. Hip-hop's origins as a performance-based culture rising from the poverty of the Bronx became a source of its "essence" for many and became a primary source of authenticity. With the genre now at over thirty years old, historical authenticity will become more significant and widespread as hip-hop undergoes further processes of canonization.

CHAPTER 2

THE CONSTRUCTION OF JAZZ RAP AS
HIGH ART IN HIP-HOP MUSIC

For doubters, perhaps rap + jazz will = acceptance.

—CHRISTOPHER JOHN FARLEY, "HIP-HOP GOES BEBOP"

"The so-called jazz hip hop movement is about bringing jazz back to the streets. It got taken away, made into some elite, sophisticated music. It's bringing jazz back where it belongs."[1] The late rapper Guru made this statement in a 1994 interview with *Vibe* magazine at a time when the "jazz rap" subgenre had been well established in media discourse. This was also toward the end of a flowering of eclectic rap groups and subgenres in the hip-hop mainstream, a period some writers refer to as the "golden age" of the genre (1986–93).[2] During this golden age, multiple subgenres coexisted based on the wide variety of lyrical content, imagery, and eclectic musical styles digitally sampled and borrowed.

This chapter focuses on a particular moment in hip-hop music history, roughly 1989–93, in order to specify the historically situated audience that identified jazz in the music, lyrics, and imagery of those considered to belong in the "jazz rap" subgenre.[3] After outlining and summarizing the status of jazz in the mainstream culture industries in 1980s America, this chapter demonstrates how a large part of the cultural reception of jazz rap took its force from the reception of its jazz codes. Despite Guru's desire to bring jazz "back to the streets," the ideological damage had been done, so to speak—jazz aesthetics and imagery contributed to highbrow distinctions within the hip-hop music world.

While chapter 1 locates a number of borrowing and digital sampling strategies to invoke an earlier era of hip-hop (intrageneric borrowing), this chapter provides an example of musical borrowing of a longer-established genre (intergeneric borrowing). Many studies of popular music tend to focus on one metagenre (e.g., rock, hip-hop, folk, rock-pop), almost as if popular music studies follow the same specializations and divisions as the music industry. In contrast to this, I investigate the interaction between two genres of music, exploring how the cultural reception of one affects that of the other.

More specifically, the process that established jazz rap as a formative rap subgenre saw the construction of an "alternative" to other rap subgenres such as "gangsta" and "pop rap," creating, ideologically speaking, a unique type of high art within the rap music world. I hesitate to use the term *high art* because of its culturally specific associations with Western classical music, but when discussing jazz rap as a high art, this is not referring to notions of "high art" within a general society or culture, but to high art as it functions within the hip-hop world. To discuss rap music or hip-hop as an art form, writers construct certain groups or genres at the top of an authenticity hierarchy, juxtaposed against the lower "mass culture" of gangsta rap and pop rap. Although artists, reviewers, and other commentators may not use the terms *high art* and *mass culture*, the meaning, function, and purpose of this distinction, which has been used for at least a century in American culture, remain consistent with other musics, past and present.[4]

Despite the problematic aspects of any attempt to place artists and groups within subgenres, genre systems are, as Adam Krims suggests, "simply reference points,"[5] a "blunt instrument" that is a "necessary step in grasping representation in rap."[6] In other words, although genres are largely stereotypes or "ideal types," they are constructed and used by the music industry, fans, and the media as structural interpretative frameworks. Examining contemporary music journalism is a particularly useful method by which to gague this type of reception, yet surprisingly, journalism (especially on hip-hop) has arguably received less attention than it should in popular music studies. And reception, rather than composer intentionality or a musicologist's individual interpretation, is a crucial factor for engaging in a productive discussion of digital sampling and other forms of borrowing in hip-hop and other musical cultures.

I use the discursively constructed term *jazz rap* for simplicity, since numerous classifications (e.g., hip-bop, jazz hip-hop, etc.) were given to artists and groups at the time. Jazz codes—sounds, lyrical references, and imagery that were identified as jazz—facilitated the establishment of this subgenre and became a focal point for writers and fans. Although groups belonging to the hip-hop "golden age" sampled from a number of styles, jazz was a cultural product familiar to the popular consciousness of various audiences in 1980s America. Furthermore, ideological associations with jazz helped to shape identities for those who sampled and borrowed from jazz styles, informing a hierarchy within hip-hop largely based on art-versus-commerce rhetoric.

Jazz and the 1980s

Mainstream jazz in the 1980s United States was not a revolution or an evolution, but a revival of older styles. Though jazz has had a number of associations over its century-long history, what seemed to dominate the public jazz discourse in this era was the notion that jazz was serious music. The 1980s witnessed the widespread expansion in the cultural mainstream of what I call a "jazz art ideology," many characteristics of which had developed during the bebop era of the 1940s and 1950s and revived in part because of successful "neo-classical" conservative jazz musicians like Wynton Marsalis.[7] By then, jazz had moved to concert halls, to academic institutions, and in close proximity to the classical section of music stores. Jazz became a symbol for many things: America, democracy, African American culture, and, most important to this study, highbrow art music.[8] Stylistically, the jazz revived in the 1980s became what Stuart Nicholson calls "the hard-bop mainstream,"[9] and its promotion by a number of younger musicians helped usher the music into membership in the cultural aristocracy.

This jazz renaissance occurred in a number of ways, including the touring of jazz artists, reissues of jazz classics, and the aggressive marketing of a younger generation of jazz musicians. Films like *Bird* (1988) and *Round Midnight* (1986) showed tormented genius jazz musicians, and Spike Lee's *Mo' Better Blues* (1990)[10] romanticized the jazz world and put jazz in the cultural consciousness of the hip-hop generation.[11] In terms of print media, dozens of jazz books and autobiographies were published and reissued to create and accommodate demand during this jazz re-surgence.[12] *The Cosby Show*, the most successful American sitcom of the 1980s, presented an upper-middle-class black family, used jazz musicians as guests (including Tito Puente, Dizzy Gillespie, the Count Basie Band, Jimmy Heath, Art Blakey, and Max Roach), and featured jazz-based scoring as music cues between scenes.[13] Though the show has been criti-cized for avoiding explicit issues of race, it reinforced jazz's association with the black middle class, a highbrow sophistication that could be jux-taposed against lower-class African American representation in popular culture, namely the "hood" films of the early 1990s.[14]

TV commercials were also associating jazz with affluence, with jazz used in commercials for Chase Manhattan Bank, American Express, the Nissan Infiniti luxury car, and Diet Coke.[15] In 1988, Yves Saint Laurent designed its fragrance "JAZZ for Men," which ran ads in Rolling Stone magazine and elsewhere.[16] Another advertisement in a 1991 *Rolling Stone* featured British jazz saxophonist Courtney Pine modeling GAP turtle-neck sweaters.[17] Jazz was marketed with high fashion, partially inspired by Wynton Marsalis's taste for fine suits and the preferences of the other young musicians who followed his lead. The clean-cut images portrayed by these jazz musicians suggest the cultural elite, a higher-class ethos compared to the working-class images of many rock and heavy metal performers.

There was a further institutionalization of jazz in education: middle schools and high schools added jazz bands to their lists of ensembles, universities offered classes and degrees in jazz, and the parameters of the music were codified for the purposes of teaching improvisation.[18] As Grover Sales comments in the tellingly titled book *Jazz: America's Clas-sical Music* (first published in 1984), "Monk, Mingus, Dolphy and the Miles Davis Sextet with Coltrane and Evans will fuel musicians of the future, just as Bach and Haydn prepare conservatory graduates."[19]

Wynton Marsalis, more than any other individual, played an impor-tant role in the mass-scale legitimization of jazz in the 1980s. A trumpet player and composer from New Orleans, he was the first recording artist

Figure 2.1: Yves Saint Laurent "Jazz for Men" advertisement

to hold a record contract in jazz and classical music simultaneously (at age nineteen, with Columbia Records) and the first artist to win Grammys in jazz and classical in the same year (1983, repeating the feat in 1984). He cofounded Jazz at Lincoln Center in 1987, firmly placing jazz in the concert hall on a regular basis. Described by Francis Davis as "rebelling against non-conformity,"[20] Marsalis held narrow views of jazz that championed the great composers of acoustic jazz, while dismissing any non-acoustic jazz as a debased derivative of a pure art form. He was even more abruptly dismissive of pop music and hip-hop. Influenced heavily by the jazz ideologies of Stanley Crouch and Albert Murray, Marsalis became, to quote Richard Cook, a "jazz media darling in an age when there simply weren't any others."[21] The subject of interviews in magazines, television, and newspapers, as well as the host of jazz programs on National Public Radio and the Public Broadcasting System, Marsalis became the rare case of a cultural producer (musician/composer) who was also a cultural intermediary, a public intellectual whose influence created boundaries, definitions, and tastes for the public.[22] He was (and still is) a gatekeeper of the "jazz tradition" who reaffirmed the notion that jazz is "America's classical music."

Although no time and place is ever truly ideologically homogeneous, the belief that jazz is a "serious music" became pervasively dominant in media discourse of the 1980s, associating jazz with affluence, sophistication, and a highbrow aesthetic that resists being considered a "popular music."[23] Sonorities identified as jazz were in the mainstream cultural consciousness in the 1980s, and the political legitimacy of jazz would affect the reception of those who borrowed from the imagery and music of the genre.

Jazz Rap

Whereas musicians of the 1980s jazz mainstream were largely performing older styles that were idiomatically intact, hip-hop musicians were thinking about and performing music of the past differently, first through the technology of the turntable, then with samplers and other studio technology to create something new. Both hip-hop and jazz had their origins as dance music, were largely the product of African American urban creativity and innovation, and shared rhythmic similarities: hip-hop and 1950s–60s hard-bop jazz were stylistically defined by a dominance of the beat. It should also be mentioned that bebop jazz was a source of inspiration for many 1950s hipsters and "beat" poets, and poetry was often recited accompanied by jazz (almost as a proto-rap form). Improvisation (more specifically, the ability to improvise in the generic idiom) was linked to authenticity in both jazz and hip-hop.[24] For mainstream jazz, it was what one did with the past that made one authentic, along with technical mastery of one's craft, and battles (or "cutting contests") were not uncommon in the early days of jazz in order for performers to gain respect (and gigs) in the musical community; in certain subgenres of hip-hop, one's ability to freestyle (improvise raps on the spot) and "battle" rap is the sure sign of authenticity in certain "underground" rap and DJ circles.

Rap groups such as De La Soul, A Tribe Called Quest, Gang Starr, and Digable Planets emerged from the late 1980s/early 1990s with categorizations for their music such as jazz rap, jazz-hop, jazz hip-hop, hip-bop, new jazz swing, alternative rap, and others.[25] Most overtly, jazz and hip-hop's shared African American musical lineage became a focus in the reception of jazz rap in interviews and other journalism. From a practical standpoint, these artists' parents and siblings often had record collections that were readily available and could be used to sample.[26] In fact, some rap artists had jazz musician parents, most recognizably rapper Nas, whose father Olu Dara occasionally performs on his son's albums. Rapper Rakim (of Eric B and Rakim) was a saxophone player and had a mother who was a professional jazz and opera singer.[27] Turntablist Grandmaster D.ST's (later DXT) father managed jazz musicians like Clifford Brown and Max Roach.[28] As Butterfly of Digable Planets raps, "my father taught me jazz, all the peoples and the anthem / Ate peanuts with the Dizz and vibe with Lionel Hampton."[29] If jazz and hip-hop are most often treated as separate musical and cultural institutions, then the linking of the two acted as a symbolic exchange, forming an alliance to increase their social capital.[30]

Many groups that sampled jazz were part of a loose collective called the Native Tongues: Jungle Brothers, De La Soul, and A Tribe Called Quest all formed in New York in 1988, rapping politically and socially conscious lyrics while promoting Afrohumanistic identities. They were inspired by Afrika Bambaataa's Zulu Nation, and New York City most directly influenced both their jazz awareness and their knowledge of early hip-hop. Taylor notes that A Tribe Called Quest in particular "steered away from the ubiquitous funk and old-school soul samples of their fellow Tongue members and embraced rock and roll and jazz. . . . They were socially relevant, proudly black and whimsical, quirky and confident, a near perfect amalgamation of the other two groups."[31]

The lyrics and imagery of these groups often displayed an ethos most appropriately identified as bohemian;[32] references would span numerous countercultures, from hippies to Five Percenter culture, beatniks, and blaxploitation film. In the case of Digable Planets, overt references to bebop and hard bop musicians went side by side with their rendering of existential and Marxist philosophies. Album titles such as Digable Planets's *Reachin' (A New Refutation of Time and Space)* and A Tribe Called Quest's *People's Instinctive Travels and the Paths of Rhythm* project the complexity of subject matter through an insider language difficult to decipher (similar to complex bebop song titles such as "Epistrophy" and "Ornithology"). The obscurity of their lyrics combined with jazz sonorities signaled a higher artistic plane, the notion of rap as high art and expander of consciousness.

Jazz Codes

Musical elements that have been identified as jazz codes include a walking acoustic bass, saxophones, trumpet with harmon mute,[33] and a jazz guitar, to name a few.[34] As Steve Redhead and John Street have written, authenticity "is rarely understood as a question of what artists 'really' think or do, but of how they and their music and image are interpreted and symbolized,"[35] and the same could be said of genre identifications. For my purposes, the interpretation of jazz codes is an issue of audience reception rather than intention or accurately locating a jazz sample source. So when Wynton Marsalis complained in the late 1980s that "people don't know what I'm doing, basically, because they don't understand music. All they're doing is reacting to what they think it remotely sounds like,"[36] he acknowledged that authorial intent (or performer intent) may differ greatly from audience interpretation. For example, an acoustic bass may signify a "live" jazz aesthetic, even though it may be achieved through digital sampling. If a rap group samples from a 1970s funk horn line, in its old context, it may be identified as funk, but in the newer context, the instrumentation of sax and trumpet may be interpreted as jazz.

A jazz code falls under what Philip Tagg calls a genre synecdoche— an instrument or musical structure that is shorthand for an entire style or genre—part of something that substitutes for the whole concept or object.[37] In jazz rap, this may be achieved by the timbre of a particular instrument (e.g., saxophone) and the jazz performance approach to an instrument (e.g., "walking" acoustic bass lines). Rather than syntactical processes (melody and harmony and other musical features that can be represented in score notation), parameters such as timbre, instrumentation, and performance approaches are arguably more important to jazz identity. Jazz as a performance approach produces a particular jazz *feel* (notably, "swung" eighth notes and expressive subsyntactical microrhythmic variations),[38] as well as the timbre of the particular instruments from jazz performance. Admittedly, this is better shown through recorded excerpts than through the "categorical perception"[39] represented in a musical score, though I provide some transcriptions for illustrative purposes below. Technically speaking, it is the subsyntactical level of expressive timing (what contributes to Keil's "engendered feeling") that characterizes a swing feel. As Matthew Butterfield argues, the groove in jazz is not from syntactical processes, but from expressive microtiming at the subsyntactical level.[40] It is these parameters that contribute to the identification of jazz codes.

Codes, like music genres, simplify in order to clarify and categorize what is an extremely heterogeneous reality. The audience then interprets meanings with regard to these codes, actively constructing from a text (in this case, a recording) and changing the text in the process. It is not simply a transmission from media to individual, but a conversation between the two. The music industry attempts to fix these unfixed texts with genre categorization, as creating and maintaining genre systems is one of the two strategies the music industry has for controlling unreliable demand (creating stars is the other),[41] but these texts are always sites of constant shifts and change, interpretation largely dependent on the perspective of the listener and/or interpretive communities. In the context of jazz rap, these socially situated interpretations are with respect to the 1980s mainstream jazz art ideology. What follows are examples of "jazz codes" in the lyrics, imagery, and music/"beats" of two canonical jazz rap groups: A Tribe Called Quest and Digable Planets.

A Tribe Called Quest's second album, *The Low End Theory* (1991), features jazz bassist Ron Carter on "Verses from the Abstract," and jazz codes span throughout the album: acoustic bass, saxophone, and vibraphone are most prominent.[42] A recurring theme in Q-Tip and Phife's lyrics (on *The Low End Theory*) is criticism of the music industry and of more "commercial" pop artists, R&B, and "new jack swing."[43] Q-Tip sets himself apart from pop rappers in "Check the Rhime":

> Industry rule number four thousand and eighty,
> Record company people are shady.
> So kids watch your back 'cause I think they smoke crack,
> I don't doubt it. Look at how they act.
> Off to better things like a hip-hop forum.
> Pass me the rock and I'll storm with the crew and. . . .
>
> Proper. What you say Hammer? Proper.[44]
> Rap is not pop, if you call it that then stop. (2:54–3:14)

Example 2.1: A Tribe Called Quest, "Check the Rhime"

Example 2.1 shows the "Check the Rhime" saxophone phrase from the chorus.[45] The jazz code of the saxophone emphasizes such a contrast in lyrical content; in other words, sampling this phrase provided a *musical* alternative to R&B and pop rap and accompanied such distancing in the lyrical content of various songs. Phife invokes a similar distancing from pop on the band's second single, entitled "Jazz (We've Got)," when he claims that their songs are "strictly hardcore tracks, not a new jack swing" (2:02). The chorus of "Jazz" contains a sample of Lucky Thompson playing the first four measures of the jazz standard "On Green Dolphin Street." The song opens with the group chanting "We've got the jazz" repeatedly with a jazz drummer (on brushes) and an acoustic bass pedal point.

Another example of this pop/rap binary on *Low End Theory* is from the first track, "Excursions." After a four-bar bass intro (with no drums), Q-Tip raps the following verse (to solo acoustic bass accompaniment):

Back in the days when I was a teenager
Before I had status and before I had a pager
You could find the Abstract [Q-Tip] listening to hip-hop
My pops used to say it reminded him of bebop
I said, well daddy don't you know that things go in cycles
The way that Bobby Brown is just ampin' like Michael. (0:11–0:25)

In the opening lyrics, we have acknowledgment of the African American lineage from bebop to hip-hop, but there exists juxtaposition, on the one hand, between black "pop music," such as that of Michael Jackson and Bobby Brown, and, on the other hand, hip-hop and bebop. "Excursions" opens with an acoustic bass figure that loops throughout the song (see Example 2.2a):[46]

The acoustic timbre sampled here projects the ideologeme of musical

Example 2.2a: A Tribe Called Quest, "Excursions" (0:00)

Example 2.2b: A Tribe Called Quest, "Excursions" (1:40)

authenticity that finds its roots in the legitimacy of both folk music and jazz. On the chorus, the band also samples from a recording of "Time" from the 1971 album *This Is Madness* by the Last Poets, a borrowing of both lineage and the cultural prestige of poetry.

Just as Wynton Marsalis and other neo-classical conservative jazz musicians in the 1980s distanced themselves from pop music as other, A Tribe Called Quest was distancing rap from pop.[47] In order to classify A Tribe Called Quest as "true" hip-hop, Q-Tip defined himself against pop rappers like MC Hammer. Both beat and flow work together to generate this sense of authentic or "uncommercial" identity. A Tribe Called Quest was using the long-standing art-versus-commerce myth, notions of authenticity that align jazz, so-called alternative rap, and other musics. Similarly, criticizing the popular music industry positions A Tribe Called Quest on the "outside," again distancing them from associations with corruption and decay often attributed to mass music. This gesture of economic denial is a familiar story—more broadly a quality of bourgeois production found in jazz, rap, and many other forms of popular music and art as a testimony of authenticity.[48] Such dichotomies are reminiscent of what Phil Ford calls the "asymmetrical consciousness" of the hipster and the square ("The hipster sees through the square but not *vice versa*"[49])—A Tribe Called Quest's recordings stage an awareness of these mainstream *others*, almost to suggest that artists such as MC Hammer and Bobby Brown are operating under a false consciousness compared to their informed, less mainstream rap counterparts, even if this is not explicitly the case.

Of all the jazz rap groups from this period, Digable Planets arguably most overtly flaunted jazz connections and references, mentioning jazz musicians in many of their lyrics and using numerous jazz samples.[50] Their bohemian image had been largely borrowed from the concept of the 1950s hipster, itself an oblique reference to jazz, using words like "cool," "cat," "hip," and "dig." Jazz was also used as a marketing tool for the group. An ad for their debut album in the *Source* magazine (April 1993) (see fig. 2.2) contained the headline "jazz, jive, poetry, & style." The same issue contained a Digable Planets interview with pictures of the members in a jazz club setting, including both male members being photographed with a trumpet (see figs. 2.3 and 2.4). And their first music video, for "Rebirth of Slick (Cool like Dat)," featured the group performing

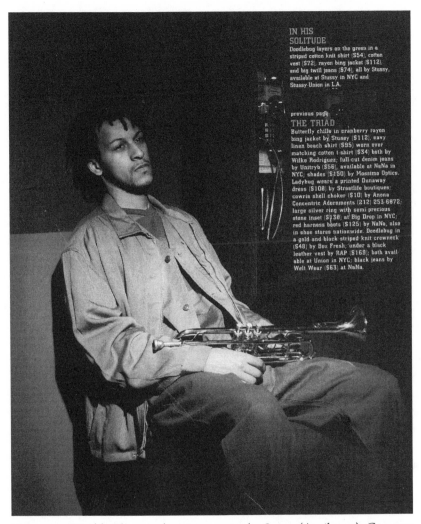

Figure 2.2: Digable Planets advertisement in the *Source* (April 1993). Courtesy of the Harvard Hip-hop Archive.

in a jazz club setting in New York City. Jazz became the vehicle used to market Digable Planets and the framework used for reviews, interviews, and other journalism.[51]

The complex collage of terminology and cultural references in their lyrics borrowed from multiple countercultures, such as the terminology of the 1950s hipsters and beat poets, spoken word poetry, hippies, Five Percenter culture, "old school" hip-hop (Fab 5 Freddy, Crazy Legs of the Rock Steady Crew, Sugarhill Records), and other poets (the Last Poets, Nikki Giovanni, Maya Angelou), as well as myriad jazz references (Charles Mingus, Charlie Parker, Hank Mobley, Dizzy Gillespie, Max Roach), references from 1970s blaxploitation film (e.g., Cleopatra Jones), and other signifiers of African American identity (Afros and other hair references such as "don't cover up your nappy, be happy with your kinkin" from "Examination of What"). As in so many American countercultures, particularly those in the 1950s and 1960s, references to drugs (usually marijuana, as "nickel bags") complemented an antiauthoritarian atmosphere (speaking against Uncle Sam, the "pigs," and "fascist" conservatives). Lyrical references to Sartre and Camus and politically tinged lyrics about abortion (in the song "La Femme Fetal") were frequently mentioned in reviews of the album.

The sonic and visual imagery of the jazz club played a significant role in their music as well as in their media image. At the end of the first track of *Reachin'*, "It's Good to Be Here" (which includes jazz guitar, trumpet, and acoustic bass), an announcer (3:25) begins to introduce the group to the backdrop of a jazz piano vamp, with bass and finger snapping on the backbeat (beats 2 and 4 in 4/4 time):

> Good evening insects, humans too
> The Cocoon Club[52] is pleased to present to you tonight a new band
> [Jazz club motive begins]
> Straight from sector six and the colorful ghettos of outer space
> They are some weird motherfuckers but they do jazz it up
> So let's bring them out here, yeah. (3:25–3:45)

Following this introduction from the announcer, Butterfly introduces the group, then says, "the mind is time / the mind is space / a horn rush, a bass flush / the mind's the taste / so sit back, enjoy the set, yeah," and repeats this line during a fade out. The music video for "Rebirth of Slick" features the members taking the New York subway to a local jazz club where they perform with a Japanese rhythm section for a diverse, yet

Example 2.3: "Jazz Club Motive" from Digable Planets, "It's Good to Be Here" (3:35)

small audience. (The entire video is shot in black and white.) The irony of this is obvious, promoting a "live" aesthetic of a jazz club for a recording that has been constructed through digital sampling. But these jazz instruments suggest "liveness," even when this is not accurately the case.[53] Because of the cultural associations with acoustic jazz (in this case, acoustic bass, piano, and drums playing a jazz vamp), these jazz instruments would be heard as live, one trait of a particular jazz authenticity that suggests unmediated expression and creativity. No doubt the narration of the "announcer" plays a crucial role in creating a jazz club soundscape as well. A similar effect occurs at the end of "Swoon Units," creating a similar jazz club "sound stage" with a jazz rhythm section and the sound of audience talking (as Butterfly says he is "hippin up the nerds"). At the end of the album, each member of the band provides a final stanza, with the earlier jazz club motive in the background. These three separate jazz club interludes on the album use the same musical material, solidifying the interpretation of various jazz tropes as central themes or as fundamental to the group's image and style.[54]

Their debut single, "Rebirth of Slick (Cool like Dat)," is exemplary in the use of jazz codes within hip-hop beats. The opening instrumental introduction is 16 measures (4+4+4+4); the first 4 measures include the solo walking acoustic bass phrase that repeats throughout the song (as bass figure 1).[55]

The second four measures consist of bass figure 1 accompanied by finger snapping on beats 2 and 4. The third set of four measures adds drums, and the fourth four measures add a horn line with saxophone and trumpet. Verses include acoustic bass and drums, with a variation on the bass line on each concluding four measures of the verse (bass figure 2). On the chorus, the words "I'm cool like that" repeat every two beats with the horn line from the intro (with the bass and drums).

The particular sonic texture from the chorus (horns, bass, and drums)

Measures	"Rebirth of Slick" Intro.
mm. 1–4	Solo acoustic bass (bass fig. 1)
mm. 5–9	Bass fig. 1 with finger snaps
mm. 10–14	Bass fig. 1 with finger snaps and drums
mm. 15–19	Bass fig. 1 with snaps, drums, and horn line

TABLE 2.1. "Rebirth of Slick," Opening Measures

Example 2.4a: Digable Planets, "Rebirth of Slick (Cool like Dat)"

Example 2.4b: Digable Planets, "Rebirth of Slick (Cool like Dat)," chorus (0:29)

becomes the central jazz trope in the song. The drum sounds (not included in the transcription) include a modified beat from the Honeydrippers' oft-sampled funk track "Impeach the President" (1973). Despite the fact that the drum sounds derive from funk, "Rebirth of Slick" is still identifiable as jazz, with its use of acoustic bass, trumpet, and saxophone (a point of comparison with a jazz-style drum sound would be the samples on A Tribe Called Quest's "Jazz").[56]

Doodlebug's third verse of "Rebirth of Slick" demonstrates the abstract/specialist language of their lyrics:

We get you free 'cause the clips be fat boss
Them dug the jams that commence to goin' off
She sweats the beats and ask me could she puff it
Me I got crew kid, seven and a crescent
Us cause a buzz when the nickel bag a dealt
Him that's my man with the asteroid belt
They catch a fizz from the Mr. Doodlebig
He rocks a tee from the Crooklyn nine pigs
The rebirth of slick like my gangster stroll
The lyrics just like loot come in stacks and rolls
You used to find the bug in a box with fade
Now he boogies up your stage plaits twist the braids. (2:46–3:15)

Both A Tribe Called Quest and Digable Planets used complex lyrics that may appear incomprehensible to a "square" outsider. As Kyle Adams has argued, the lack of narrative unity or cohesion in the lyrical content of groups like A Tribe Called Quest can be explained through a rapper's desire to match the sounds and rhythm of their "flow" to a precomposed "beat."[57] Even if this is the case, the link with and extension of the 1950s hipster terminology actually creates a loosely unified countercultural or "hip" ethos between beat and flow.[58] Groups like A Tribe Called Quest and Digable Planets were negotiating a complexity of topics and ideas musically and lyrically, and a closer reading of the two groups would show striking differences in a number of ways. But a desire to find unity and order is not simply the concern of many music theorists and analysts; jazz became the identifiable and unifying force in media reception of many of these groups.

Media Reception

Jazz rap groups like A Tribe Called Quest were often defined by their sounds in ways that their counterparts in other rap subgenres could not be. To quote Diana Crane, "Cultural information that is already familiar because of its associations with previous items of culture is more readily assimilated into the core,"[59] the "already familiar" being jazz codes and their attached high art ideologies. The "core," in this case, is the mainstream discourses as framed through various media; print media such as *Rolling Stone*, the *Source*, *Vibe*, and *Rap Pages* contextualized the jazz samples in terms of class, intelligence, and artistic achievement.

One *Rolling Stone* review described the sounds of A Tribe Called Quest's first album as "funkified quiet-storm pseudo-jazz you might expect young Afro-centric upwardly mobiles to indulge in when they crack open that bottle of Amaretto and cuddle up in front of the gas fireplace: plenty of sweet silky saxophones."[60] John Bush wrote, "Without question the most intelligent, artistic rap group during the 1990s, A Tribe Called Quest jump-started and perfected the hip-hop alternative to hardcore and gangsta rap."[61] One writer expressed that the *Low End Theory* "demonstrated that hip-hop was an aesthetic every bit as deep, serious and worth cherishing as any in a century plus of African-American music . . . giving a rap the same aesthetic weight as a Coltrane solo."[62] Journalist Brian Coleman wrote of the group, "Every time they hit the studio they added a serious, studious, jazz edge to their supremely innovative productions."[63] Other adjectives used in the media suggested that they were "more cerebral"[64] than other styles, had a "more intellectual bent,"[65] and were "more reflective."[66] Many of these descriptions are in comparison with an other, real or imagined, to describe the music as "artistic" or as an "aesthetic"—in other words, a bourgeois high art comparable to jazz.

For Digable Planets, media reception of *Reachin'* also focused on jazz as a high cultural facet of their music. Lyrical references to jazz and musical borrowing of jazz codes featured prominently in the reviews. Digable Planets were described as "accessible without succumbing to a pop mentality."[67] Kevin Powell wrote in his review that Digable Planets "is everything hip-hop should be: artistically sound, unabashedly conscious and downright cool. And Digable Planets is the kind of rap act every fan should cram to understand."[68] Both of these reviews mentioned an element of intellectualism in their music, with the former review explicitly citing jazz and existentialist references. Another review wrote that *Reachin'*'s "sampled snatches of music from jazzmen Sonny Rollins and Art Blakey conjure the feel of smoky bebop clubs and two-drink minimums. . . . These jazzy undercurrents give the album a laid-back quality that refutes the riotous stereotype of rap."[69]

The frequent juxtaposition of jazz rap with rapper/producer Dr. Dre is particularly pertinent in the context of Digable Planets since they had albums and singles released at similar instances.[70] Dr. Dre's *The Chronic* (see chap. 3) is often seen as the yardstick historically and generically that marks the point when gangsta rap began to dominate the rap mainstream and crossed over into pop music realms.[71] A Tribe Called Quest had also been directly compared with Dr. Dre, as Kevin Powell wrote that A Tribe Called Quest and De La Soul provided "Nuthin' but 'P' things: poetry, positive vibes, and a sense of purpose."[72] This was a reference to Dr. Dre's "Nuthin' but a 'G' Thang," the first single from *The Chronic*. Thus, when the media reviewed Digable Planets or other jazz rap artists and albums, they contrasted jazz rap with Dr. Dre (and his label Death Row Records) as representative of a gangsta rap mainstream. These comparisons were in terms of sonorities used, lifestyles promoted, and ideologies implied. One article states:

> In the early 1990s, while Suge Knight's Death Row records dominated hip-hop with artists like Dr. Dre and Tupac, Digable Planets chose the same high road that De La Soul and A Tribe Called Quest had already taken—they all but ignored gangsta culture. MCs Doodlebug, Butterfly, and the sweet-voiced Ladybug combined a positive vibe with jazz samples to create ultra-laid-back joints that provoked head bobbing rather than drive-bys. Their debut, *Reachin'*, invaded college boom boxes and

birthed the Top 20 hit and Grammy winner "Rebirth of Slick (Cool Like Dat)."[73]

Placing De La Soul, A Tribe Called Quest, and Digable Planets on a "high road" in opposition to Death Row artists like Dr. Dre and Tupac Shakur juxtaposes the two in terms of subgenre and implies both Digable Planets' perceived audience and their listening space ("college boom boxes"). Though both Dr. Dre and Digable Planets were considered rap music, for many the two represented opposite ends of a rap spectrum. Constructions of identity often involve such positioning, discursively constructed by artists, media, fans, and the industry, all working within these imagined juxtapositions in order to legitimate artists' own practices.[74]

Jazz Codes and Meaning

Jazz is, of course, by no means univocal. It is important to note that the jazz art ideology identified is far from being the only identity existing for jazz in the 1980s and other eras. For example, in 1950s film noir, "crime jazz" often accompanied the corrupted dark side of the city; jazz projected sex, drugs, and other vices of a depraved urban landscape (e.g., in *The Sweet Smell of Success, The Man with the Golden Arm*). As bebop musicians were crafting an elite, virtuosic music appreciated by hipster-intellectuals, jazz-influenced film scores used instruments such as a scooping jazz saxophone to accompany the sexuality of a femme fatale. This is still evident in later parodies of film noir, for example, on the television cartoon *The Simpsons*.[75] And although this essay is primarily concerned with the use of jazz in the hip-hop world, there existed musicians closer to the jazz world collaborating with musicians and ideas from hip-hop scenes in the 1980s and 1990s (that is not to suggest that the two worlds were entirely separate).[76]

At worst, the less-conservative jazz musician who uses elements from hip-hop or the hip-hop producer who digitally samples from jazz records can be criticized as gravitating to whatever was commercially popular and profitable at the time (or as a case of branding, see Greg Osby and

Figure 2.3: Greg Osby ad in the *Source* (April 1993)

J. Spencer in figures 2.3 and 2.4). Record labels, by the same token, could be criticized for fostering hip-hop and jazz collaboration as simply a strategy of rebranding an old genre for the purpose of selling back catalogs. At best, jazz musicians who borrow and collaborate with hip-hop could be said to "improve" the genre, to stay close to their musical lineage, and to try something new in the spirit of jazz as a verb rather than a noun. While jazz codes added a degree of sophistication and cultural elevation to rap, hip-hop codes such as turntable scratches and hiss from sampled vinyl could be heard on a number of jazz recordings as subcultural capital said to signify hipness or coolness.

These examples show that jazz can symbolize a variety of meanings depending on context and interpretive community, such as high culture, the "street," sexuality, hipness, elite tastes, or urban corruption. However, it is jazz constructed as high art that was distributed in the 1980s mainstream culture industries and that was the most pervasive ideology in contemporary cultural interpretations. As Robert Fink has written, there is now a redefinition of art music that includes jazz (and rock); new composers borrow from rock and jazz; and "postminimalism's embrace of alternative rock/jazz culture is arty composers turning not away from artiness, but *toward* it."[77]

In the case of jazz's musical codes, the identification of a general jazz identity or style is sufficient, rather than the need for knowledge of a specific song or artist. With jazz, as an easily identifiable instrumental music that can be linked to an ideology, specific meanings of songs can be less important than what the genre has been imagined to represent. In an attempt to decode meaning, journalists often categorize these jazz rap artists in terms of preestablished frames. A muted trumpet and a walking acoustic bass are recognizable signifiers, sonic elements that have become emblematic of jazz, as interpreted by certain sociohistorically situated interpretive communities. Similar in function to earlier jazz albums and concerts that used string sections as a sign of class (e.g., Paul Whiteman's symphonic jazz of the 1920s, "concert jazz" made famous by Duke Ellington, or *Charlie Parker with Strings* from 1950), acoustic bass and horns have become a sign of class in rap music.[78] Jazz in the 1980s became associated with the middle class, and these meanings are brought to groups

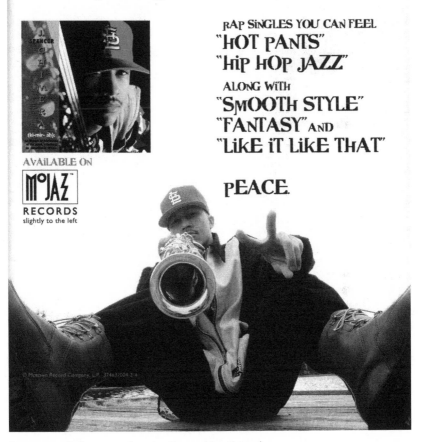

Figure 2.4: J. Spencer ad in the *Source* (April 1993)

that sample jazz. Jazz rap became labeled and defined as a counterculture (though the artists themselves do not use the term), an "alternative" within the rap world, partly defined by jazz signifiers that reinforce preexisting cultural meanings.

Gary Tomlinson's writing on authentic meaning in music is worth quoting here:

> First, all meanings, authentic or not, arise from the personal ways in which individuals, performers and audience, incorporate the work in their own signifying contexts. Clearly the performer can exert only so much influence on the personal context of the listener. . . . Second and more important, the authentic meanings of a work arise from our relating it to an array of things outside itself that we believe gave it meaning in its original context.[79]

Tomlinson is championing the ability of the cultural historian to find meaning in early music performance, but his comments point to the importance of locating a context for the act of relating musical codes "to an array of things outside itself," a crucial component of studying musical borrowing and intertextuality of any era. Perhaps somewhat obvious in a time when academics celebrate the "death of the author," it is still worth emphasizing that both performer and composer/producer (and musicologist, of course) have limited ability to exert meaning onto an audience. And while any piece of music is open to an infinite number of interpretations, the specific context of 1980s jazz as high art has provided a certain frame or "signifying context" for various interpretations of jazz rap.

These jazz codes could easily be identified and contrasted with other rap music sonorities that had largely become the norm. For example, the sound of an acoustic bass ("Can I Kick It?," "Rebirth of Slick [Cool like Dat]," "Excursions") is strikingly different from that of the funk bass or synthesized bass of many rap styles (Dr. Dre's "G-funk" style, for example). Or, the use of a jazz guitar ("Bonita Applebum," "Push It Along," "It's Good to Be Here") is conspicuous in opposition to the use of rock or metal guitars for Rick Rubin's production work with the Beastie Boys and Run D.M.C. The jazz guitar implies a George Benson sound rather than an Eddie van Halen or Jimi Hendrix sound. A muted trumpet, or certain horn lines, may suggest jazz where in many other styles of rap, instrumental horn lines may be synthesized, or more often, drum sounds from funk music will be sampled, with the accompanying horn sounds (e.g., trumpet, trombone, saxophone) omitted.

Taking the bifurcation a step further, if early 1990s gangsta rap suggests the listening space of a car or West Coast block party, then jazz rap may suggest more bourgeois environments, such as the modern-day jazz club or a hi-fi stereo system in one's living room. Jazz rap implied a more introspective or private experience, to be listened to on a Walkman, as opposed to in a dance club (e.g., early 1990s pop rap such as MC Hammer or Vanilla Ice).[80] Musical codes can sometimes imply particular spaces (such as a jazz club), based on a number of factors, including cultural and stylistic associations, and dominant images from our media-saturated society. If jazz is said to create a certain "vibe" or "atmosphere,"[81] then this is further proof that jazz (and other musics) has the ability to imply certain spaces in their recordings. In short, sounds are historically, socially, *and* spatially situated, and musicologists should pay additional attention to this third dimension of musical signification.[82]

As seen in most popular music cultures, the divide between "mainstream" and "alternative" manifests in many forms. As Stuart Hall has written, one of the ideological functions of the media is to classify center and periphery (as well as to promote lifestyles and define reality).[83] But in a subculture, instead of having its legitimacy reinforced, the center becomes the inauthentic, and the periphery becomes the authentic. And having a niche, perceived to be followed by few, also helps to solidify the subcultural identity of the periphery. For example, bebop, with its niche authenticity as opposed to swing music, was one particular subculture. The same niche authenticity can be said to exist in folk music, art films, so-called indie labels, "alternative" musics, and "conscious" or "backpack" rappers. In an "age of mass counterculture" (to borrow Philip Ford's phrase), the constructions of these subgeneric categories are important and ever present, offering membership into an elite society that attempts to appear more closed and marginalized than it manifests in actuality.[84]

These jazz codes have a multitude of meanings among a number of interpretive communities. That both jazz and hip-hop are identified as African American musics may be the most obvious linkage, but the 1980s also solidified the notion that jazz was not only an African American music but also an African American art form. Despite protestation of this labeling from the artists themselves, groups such as A Tribe Called Quest, De La Soul, Digable Planets, and Gang Starr were largely defined by the style of music from which they sampled and borrowed. A walking acoustic bass, a muted trumpet, and saxophones are sonic elements that have become emblematic of jazz, and jazz codes enact commentary with these attached, historically situated ideologies. Hierarchies seem inescapable in music and are also reflective of wider cultural processes; for example, these rap music distinctions belong to a will to elitism or hipness still robust at the end of the cold war in 1980s and early 1990s US culture—and jazz provided the soundtrack. Rap music's borrowing from jazz was a key gesture in the defining of jazz rap as a sophisticated alternative, as part of hip-hop's ongoing struggle for cultural legitimacy.

CHAPTER 3

DR. DRE'S "JEEP BEATS" AND MUSICAL
BORROWING FOR THE AUTOMOTIVE SPACE

I think men's minds are going to change in subtle ways because of automobiles.

—EUGENE MORGAN IN *THE MAGNIFICENT AMBERSONS* (1942)[1]

We're conforming to the way machines play music. It's robots' choice. It used to be ladies' choice— now it's robot's choice.

—DONALD FAGEN, PRODUCER AND STEELY DAN FRONTMAN[2]

The music is just in me now, you know . . . and I know what people like to play in their cars.

—DR. DRE, PRODUCER/RAPPER[3]

In comparing the sonic codes in "Rebirth of Slick (Cool like Dat)" with "Nuthin' but a 'G' Thang" in chapter 2, and later two versions of 2Pac's "Thugz Mansion" in chapter 4, it becomes apparent that not only do musical codes signify certain genres or ideas, but they can imply certain listening spaces as well. In short, sounds can be historically, socially, and *spatially* situated. This chapter follows on from that point and begins to explore musical borrowing for particular playback spaces.

Contemporary culture has seen a shift in the character of urban environments, including a trend toward heightened design intensity in interior spaces; increased use of music as a component of design has strongly affected how playback from music recordings inhabits these locations and, in many cases, influences the music produced for them.[4] This chapter underlines musical borrowing's intersection with geography, both the influence of urban geography on hip-hop music production and the geography of particular listening spaces. Though a number of spaces could be considered (clubs, concert halls, coffee shops, shopping malls), I have chosen the playback space of the automobile because of its tremendous influence on hip-hop music production. My case study focuses on one producer, Dr. Dre, and his creation of a style labeled "G-funk," which according to him, was created and mixed *specifically* for listening in car stereo systems. As borrowing is so central to hip-hop's ethos, Dr. Dre's production reflects how musical materials become reused for a new space, updated and customized for the automotive listening experience.

Dr. Dre's compositional process is but one story in the history of the automobile's shaping of music production. Little has been written on the cross-influences among recorded music, technology, and automobility, and yet the automobile has been an important mixing reference in music production since at least the 1960s. I will consider not only how rap producers consider the automotive space in production but also how they borrow from previous musical material, tailoring it for historically specific playback technology and their idealized listening spaces, just as car customizers individualize automobiles from previous forms and materials.

Hip-Hop Cultures and the Automobile

As it began from playing records through large loudspeakers at block parties in the Bronx (see chapter 1), much of hip-hop music is still largely characterized by its high volume and its attention to the low frequencies in the musical spectrum.[5] Many of these "beats" are intended for listening in car soundsystems, preferably custom ("aftermarket") systems with subwoofers. In mainstream hip-hop culture, cars and car accessories such as rims and grills become cross-marketed in a way that suggests "lifestyle" marketing, together with television shows like *Pimp My Ride* and *Rides* magazine.

The automobile and hip-hop culture form, in a certain sense, a nexus of status symbols (e.g., rims, subwoofers, and car brands) with an accompanying soundtrack. The high status that an upmarket or customized automobile provides to members of the African American community, according to Paul Gilroy, helps to compensate for the disenfranchisement and propertylessness experienced in African American history.[6] Gilroy notes that auto-autonomy is a means of empowerment and resistance for African Americans with a history of coerced labor and that the custom car is an ongoing process that may be "gesturing their anti-discipline to power even as the whirlpool of consumerism sucks them in."[7] African Americans, in 2001, spent forty-five billion dollars on cars and related products, representing 30 percent of the automotive-buying public; yet this demographic only makes up 12 percent of the US population.[8] Race-specific marketing by no means suggests that these accessories are bought solely by the race to which it is targeted, but it projects a certain form of "blackness," real or imagined, that enters the cultural consciousness. Gilroy writes that the automobile is "at the very core of America's complex negotiations with its own absurd racial codings."[9] Others have suggested that the importance of the car harkens back to religious imagery, the chariot metaphor symbolizing the promise of freedom from slavery for the Hebrews and subsequently for antebellum African Americans.[10]

The automobile has been a central object in hip-hop music videos and album covers, ranging from the gangsta rap of Ice-T, Too $hort, and Dr. Dre, to the "Bling Bling" era of Puff Daddy and Ma$e, and, more recently, to the Southern "crunk" music of Lil' Jon and David Banner. The automobile and its powerful sound system is an object central to the boasting traditions in rap music and earlier African-based art forms such as toasting, as Daz Dillinger raps in "My System": "Cruzin' down the block / And my system bangin' out about a million watts / All these suckers wanna stare and jock / And hear my shit subbin' down the block" (0:32–0:38).

Car audio technology and hip-hop styles began to evolve in the 1980s when it became more common for young drivers to have upgraded systems. In automobile-centric Miami, Florida, there emerged a subgenre of rap known as "Miami bass." Miami groups such as 2 Live Crew made a direct connection with bottom-heavy music and bottom-heavy women on their album covers and music videos ("Miami bass" was sometimes referred to as "booty music" or "booty bass").[11] One hit song by the Miami female rap duo L'Trimm rapped of their love of "boom cars" in 1988 as they chanted, "They're always adding speakers when they find the room /

Cuz they know we like the guys with the cars that go boom" (1:33–1:40).[12] Bass music, as popularized largely by 2 Live Crew, expanded in the early 1990s with hits such including "Whoot, There It Is" by Jacksonville's 95 South in 1993, "Whoomp! (There it is)" by Atlanta's Tag Team in 1993, and "Tootsie Roll" by Jacksonville's 69 Boyz in 1994.

The use of the car stereo system is multifaceted. The music can be used for individual driving pleasure or function like a boom box, to accompany and create a space of socialization such as a block party, or it may territorialize (and/or terrorize) the surrounding sonic environment. "Boom cars" have been a source of both intense competition and neighborhood frustration. The International Auto Sound Challenge Association (IASCA) was formed in the late 1980s and regularly holds competitions for the loudest and highest-quality car sound systems, competitions referred to by enthusiasts as "sound-offs," "crank-it-up competitions" or "dB Drag Racing."[13] Others see the boom-car pastime as using sound as a weapon, as activist groups in the United States who consider themselves "victims of audio terrorism" have pressed for legislation to decrease legal decibel levels in cars.[14] The multiplicity of car audio uses demonstrates its interpretive flexibility, and that technology and society influence each other in complex ways. What "boom cars" show more specifically is that the notion of a "good"/pleasurable or "bad"/harmful technology differs not only with users but also with those who are directly or indirectly affected by a given technology.

The primary object that connects the boomy bass of hip-hop to the automotive soundscape is the car subwoofer. Available in the car-stereo "aftermarket" (i.e., custom products, as opposed to "stock" systems that come with the car) since the early 1980s, the subwoofer is a large, enclosed loudspeaker (eight to eighteen inches in diameter) that , like any speaker, turns electric impulses into mechanical energy/soundwaves.[15] The subwoofer specializes in producing the lower-frequency waves in the sound spectrum (roughly 20–120Hz), omni/nondirectional sensations of sound perceived as an amalgamation of pitch recognition and a feeling of pressure (sound measured in decibels is also known as sound pressure level, or SPL).[16] In other words, the lower the frequency, the greater the possibility that one will begin to "feel" the sound. Without the sub-

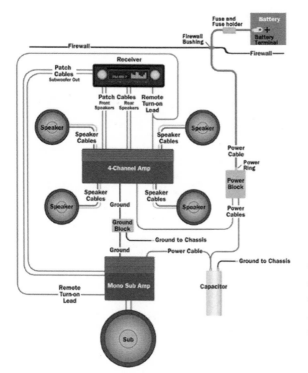

Figure 3.1: Car audio amplifier wiring diagram. Diagram courtesy of Crutchfield Corporation © 2003.

woofer, other noises can cancel the lower frequencies in the music, frequencies that require so much power that one needs a separate amplifier for them.[17] Most road noise is in the 100–200 Hz range and will cancel out this band of a recording's audio spectrum; therefore, one function of the subwoofer is to bring out the lower frequencies in the music.[18] A custom system creates an a auditory division of labor in speaker types, with higher frequencies supported by tweeters, middle frequencies by midrange speakers, and lower frequencies by the woofers and subwoofers.[19] In choosing these and other types of speakers, one has to think of qualities such as "resonant frequency," the frequency at which the speaker naturally wants to vibrate, and "transfer function": "a measure of how the volume of an enclosure, such as a room or a car, effects the way a speaker sounds."[20] The attention given to specific technology such as loudspeaker types and their playback qualities, and to the character of specific playback spaces, is important to car audiophiles and a fruitful lens through which to consider and analyze music production and recordings.

Like those inhabiting custom car cultures before them, car audio enthusiasts form a community with shared interests, while expressing a sense of individuality. The design intensity and niche marketing of the car audio aftermarket can be said to participate in the so-called post-Fordist society; the fact that *The Car Audio and Electronics Buyer Guide* listed 3,195 different speakers available in just one year (1998) attests to this.[21] But many forget that the emblematic symbol of Fordism, the Model T, had over 5,000 accessories available in its lifetime, suggesting that the desire to customize the car is as old as automotive mass production itself.[22] Rather than invoke discourses of Fordism, perhaps it is more useful in popular music production to invoke the influence of Sloanism, named after General Motors president Alfred Sloan, the creator of the annual model, who produced different car models in a stylistic hierarchy and led the first separate design division for a car company in the 1920s (led by Harley Earl for over thirty years).[23] Hip-hop music, for example, with its heavy use of borrowing and sampling, adds surface features to old frameworks in some ways analogous to Sloanist production methods and functions within a constantly shifting subgeneric hierarchy of cultural products.

The Automobile and Music Production

The automobile forms an exemplary object of twentieth-century mass production, transforming time, space, and "the everyday," as well as urban and emotional geographies. It is safe to say that this "quintessential manufactured object of Fordism"[24] had influence on a number of production methods, including recorded music production. And as Michael Bull reminds us, "While the 20th century is sometimes interpreted as both the century of the automobile and of the moving image, it is also the century of mechanically reproduced sounds."[25]

It was Galvin Manufacturing Company that built the first commercially successful car radio in the early 1930s, known as the Motorola 5T71, an amalgamation of the words "motor" car and "Victrola." (The company would later change its name to that of its most successful product.)[26] By 1952, automobile radios were in just over half of America's cars but had a significant boom after this due to the 1953 invention of the transistor, which made car radios more reliable and affordable. By 1980, the start of a decade that saw the rapid growth of both the car audio aftermarket and rap music, that percentage had increased to 95 percent.[27]

The automobile sound system has been an important listening reference in many styles of music production since at least the 1960s, with the advent of Top 40 radio and the car's role in youth cultures. Steven Pond writes, "Bowing to the importance of radio airplay, pop producers up to the late sixties routinely calibrated their final mixes to cheap car speakers, which could accommodate only a limited frequency range."[28] Perhaps appropriately, given its location in the car manufacturing mecca of Detroit, Motown Records was attentive to this new listening market, as by 1963, fifty million automobiles had car radios.[29] Suzanne Smith writes:

> At Hitsville Studios the proliferation of the car radio was not overlooked but capitalized on. Both the musical form and the audio fidelity of Motown hits such as "My Girl" and "Shop Around" were well suited and often produced with a car radio audience in mind. Some of the first critical commentary on the Detroit sound noted that "Motown's light, unfussy, evenly stressed beat, its continuous loop melodies, [are] the ideal accompaniment for driving."[30]

Motown made its singles extra short to help ensure radio play and tested them for compatibility with car radio speakers. Motown was also aware that the majority of car radio listeners belonged to the baby-boomer teenage market it was trying to attract. As producers tailored their mixes to the car stereo, the needs of automotive listening surely impacted the timbre and volume of the music produced. As Warren Belasco has written, "The greatest success in rock 'n' roll usually goes to those whose music suits the hyperkinetic formats of the Top-40 stations that transmit primarily to car radios and transistor receivers."[31]

Radio stations since the 1960s have heavily "compressed" (i.e., used dynamic range compression) the sounds coming through the airwaves, as compression decreases the overall range of the dynamics to make music sound louder without increasing peak amplitude. Television commercials also often have compressed sound, which is why commercials often sound louder than programs. One reason producers utilized this "loudness" effect from compression was to compete with rival radio stations, to sound more exciting and keep the listener's attention; but another reason was to produce a consistent dynamic level that could be heard over the road and engine noise of an automobile. Music producers also use dynamic compression in mixing to compete with other "loud" albums but also when they expect albums to be played in loud environments such as bars, shopping malls, restaurants, and automobiles.[32]

Automotive listening (particularly for those with "stock systems") demands a high level of dynamic consistency; listening to Berlioz's *Symphonie Fantastique* or Schubert's *Unfinished Symphony* on a stock system without a compressor can prove to be frustrating. Just as earlier phonograph record technologies had influenced the length of music composed, the car stereo now influenced elements such as the timbre of popular music recordings.[33] Furthermore, the ability to record bass, synthesizer, and other sounds by DI (using "direct injection" to the mixing console, rather than putting a microphone up to an amplifier) provides greater flexibility in altering the sounds once they have been recorded.[34] As recording technology improved, so did the ability to tailor music to particular listening spaces.

Unlike car audio technicians, who consider the car to be a far from ideal listening environment, compared to the home,[35] many music producers speak positively of the automotive listening space. When asked by an interviewer what the ideal listening environment for a minisystem was, producer and artist Stewart Copeland commented:

> I've already got one: the car stereo—which is the first and best minisystem if you think about it. You're in this cocoon where you can have a really big sound in an enclosed environment. Then there's the fact that you're driving with scenery moving past. . . . When I record an album, I spend months listening to it in the studio. I listen to it every day going

back and forth in my car. I check it out on tiny systems. And then I hear it coming out of the radio, so I know what it sounds like.[36]

The "car test" or "car check" was and still is used in record mixing, as the car is often the first place that a mix is heard outside the studio.[37] California sound engineer Patrick Olguin states, "If I'm mixing 'unassisted' I'll check the mix in my stock system in my truck, and also check it in my custom system in my Mercedes."[38] Olguin ensures that his mix works for the majority of car owners (who have stock systems), as well as for those who enjoy the greater clarity, improved frequency response, and bass extension of a custom aftermarket system. He also mentions that "most hip-hop producers have upgraded car systems, so that would definitely be the first acid test for a mix after leaving the studio."[39] Studios normally have a number of sets of speakers for different instances of listening, selectable at the flip of a switch; some studios (such as Sony Studios in New York City) have a car speaker system built into the studio as part of their reference speaker configurations.[40] Olguin also has a wireless system, allowing him to listen to mixes through the car radio by using a radio transmitter that delivers the signal to the parking lot, in order to hear the mix as it would go through a radio station.

In addition to the car now serving as producers' listening reference, producers have also become more conscious of the idea that a recording is intended to fill a particular space, rather than to reproduce a performance accurately. Adam Krims notes a trend in new classical music recordings, which have shifted their aim from "concert realism" to an "abstract soundstage" that considers particular playback spaces. In hip-hop, the "star producer" is valued for how his or her music fills a space, such as a car or jeep, rather than what he or she can do in live performance.[41] The trademarked producer will be advertised on albums, assuring listeners that the product that they buy will fill space in a particular way.[42]

Consideration of the relatively small space of the car interior in production and mixing affects elements such as dynamic compression, how frequencies are equalized, and in particular the sound quality of low frequencies (both the aural and the tactile/corporeal elements of subwoofer playback). While the opinions of music producers are far from homogeneous, testing music mixes in the car (on both stock and custom systems) is a rarely acknowledged standard practice; if we then consider both the playback spaces and the speakers involved, we can better analyze the ecology of how a music recording interacts with the listener in particular environments.

Dr. Dre and "G-Funk"

Dr. Dre (Andre Young), the "chief architect of West Coast gangsta rap,"[43] was born in Los Angeles, California. He was a club DJ, then a producer and rapper with the groups the World Class Wreckin Cru and N.W.A. (Niggaz With Attitude). After leaving N.W.A., he spent all of 1992 producing his first solo album, *The Chronic*. What emerged was a sound that he christened "G-funk" (G for "gangsta"), inspired by the P-funk of George Clinton but also borrowing from Leon Haywood, Isaac Hayes, Curtis Mayfield, and Donny Hathaway, as well as utilizing "vocoder"-esque effects similar to those of electro-funk groups like Zapp and Cameo.[44] What results is a highly layered effect, a mix of (often high-pitched) synthesized sounds and live instruments such as guitar and bass and an added emphasis on low-end frequencies.

One example of this style is the layers of the basic beat in Dr. Dre's "Nuthin' but a 'G' Thang" from *The Chronic* (example 3.1):

Example 3.1: Transcription of Dr. Dre, "Nuthin' but a 'G' Thang"

The high synthesizer riff, derived from Leon Haywood's "I Wanna Do Something Freaky to You," has become (in both timbre and melody) an important signifier of Dr. Dre, of Southern California, and more widely of the gangsta rap or "West Coast rap" subgenre. As New York MC Mims raps of different geographical regions in "This Is Why I'm Hot" (2007), "Compton to Hollywood / As soon as I hit L.A. / I'm in that low, low / I do it the Cali way", the riff from "'G' Thang" accompanies the stanza.[45]

As opposed to East Coast hip-hop producers at the time, Dr. Dre rarely sampled directly from a record itself. He might use a 1970s record for ideas (a melody, beat, or riff), but he had live musicians rerecord the sounds that he wanted. After equalizing and sculpting particular sounds, he then can choose to put the sounds through a sampler. He often takes preexisting drum sounds from recordings, loops them, and gradually replaces each drum part with a new one. Dre then employs a bass player to record a track over the drums and other musicians to rerecord or improvise, based on various tracks. In rerecording all the material live, in addition to avoiding high copyright costs,[46] Dr. Dre has greater control over all of the individual tracks: he can detune, add more "low-end" frequency, add effects, apply dynamic compression (to help drown out road and engine noise during playback), add effects, make it sound "dirty," or equalize to his taste.[47] He often uses a Mini-Moog and synthesizers such as the Wurlitzer, Fender Rhodes, Clavinet, and Vox V-305 organ, as well as a Roland TR-808 drum machine, employed by many hip-hop producers for its kick drum bass "boom" sound.[48] This flexibility is important to Dre, often labeled a perfectionist in the studio.[49]

Dr. Dre often utilizes a number of musicians to "orchestrate" various sounds that he wants, as producer Scott Storch recounts:

> Sometimes [Dre will] have a vision for a record where he'll program a drum pattern and tell musicians such as myself what to play verbatim, and we'll emulate for him, through him. He's capable of doing a lot of the stuff, like playing piano. But he creates a little band. He's orchestrating his little orchestra. And sometimes, I'll be at the keyboard noodling, and he'll be at the drum machine noodling and we'll find each other in that way—all of a sudden, *boom*, there's a record.[50]

Jonathan Gold also writes of Dre's compositional process in the making of *The Chronic:*

> Listening to a Dre beat take shape in the studio is like watching a snow-ball roll downhill in a Bugs Bunny cartoon, taking on mass as it goes, Dre may find something he likes from an old drum break, loop it and gradually replace each part with a better tom-tom sound, a kick-drum sound he adores, until the beat bears the same relationship to the origi-nal that the Incredible Hulk does to Bill Bixby.
>
> A bass player wanders in, unpacks his instrument and pops a funky two-note bass line over the beat, then leaves to watch CNN, though his two notes keep looping into infinity. A smiling guy in a striped jer-sey plays a nasty one-fingered melody on an old Mini-Moog synthesizer that's been obsolete since 1982, and Dre scratches in a sort of surfadelic munching noise, and then from his well-stocked Akai MPC60 sample comes a shriek, a spare piano chord, an ejaculation from the first Beas-tie's record—"Let me clear my throat"—and the many-layered groove is happening, bumping, breathing, almost loud enough to see.
>
> Snoop floats into the room. He closes his eyes as if in a dream and extends both hands toward Dre, palms downward. Dre holds out his hands, and Snoop grazes his fingertips with a butterfly flourish, caught up in the ecstasy of the beat. . . .
>
> Dre comes in from the lounge, twists a few knobs on the Moog and comes up with the synthesizer sound so familiar from *The Chronic*, al-most on pitch but not quite, sliding a bit between notes.[51]

Though these journalistic sources often portray information in highly stylized ways, they nevertheless are useful in mapping out Dre's composi-tional tendencies as producer. Dre's production is a collaborative process, but he most certainly has creative control over the final product.

While the use of the drum machine was already common in hip-hop production, Dr. Dre's conspicuous use of synthesizers in the digital sam-pling era was not. The synthesizer has been a prominent feature of popu-lar music for over forty years (including 1970s groups and artists from disparate backgrounds such as Yes, Wendy/Walter Carlos, Parliament Funkadelic, Gary Numan, Sun Ra, Stevie Wonder, Kraftwerk, Genesis,

Herbie Hancock, and ABBA). Anxieties regarding the synthesizer were expressed, particularly in the 1970s, as musicians and audiences were susceptible to cultural assumptions that electronic instruments are "cold" and "inhuman," perhaps because they produce fewer overtones than other instruments.[52] Though keyboards had a mixed reception in the 1970s, Andrew Goodwin points out that a generation of 1980s popular music artists and producers grew up with the synthesized sounds of the 1970s. Goodwin, writing in the late 1980s, comments that "pop musicians and audiences have grown increasingly accustomed to making an association between synthetic/automated music and the communal (dance floor) connection to nature (via the body). We have grown used to connecting *machines* and *funkiness*."[53] He continues:

> What happened then was that the very technology (the synth) that was presumed in the 1970s to remove human intervention and bypass the emotive aspect of music (through its "coldness") became the source of one of the major aural signs that signifies "feel"! This is the sound of a bass analogue synth—often a Moog synthesizer.[54]

A number of producers have shared their proclivity for using Moog synth for bass. Producer Glen Ballard, when asked in an interview how to deal with getting the low end tight without being flabby, responded:

> Get a Minimoog! (laughs) Ninety percent of the bass I do is Minimoog. I think it's the best way to solve low-end problems—that and being real careful with the pattern of the kick drum. Because the Minimoog has three oscillators you can cover so much ground with it, and there are MIDIable versions of them now, you can sequence with them. I've always had such great luck with that as my bass, and you can get an infinite variety of sound with it—the filtering can be incredible, you can adjust the sustain. It has so many colors, and yet it's about the richest bottom end harmonic element that I've ever come across. The Minimoog is just such a workhorse for me—I can't do without it.[55]

Producer Jack Douglas has said that for bass "I like to use a subharmonic synthesizer because so many systems have subwoofers, you've gotta have stuff to feed that."[56] It is possible that the lack of overtones and the sheer power and directionality of these synthesizers are more suited to automotive technology than earlier sonic innovations. Dr. Dre's interest in synthesizers may be influenced by a nostalgia for funk music, a fascination with earlier technologies, or his general feeling that they are "warmer" than sound sampled from a record. While any attempt to locate his exact reasoning would be speculative, the timbres of synthesized sounds are strikingly compatible with car audio technology and the driving experience. Furthermore, the use of large speakers in both clubs and cars signals attention to the entire body sensations triggered by powerful, low frequencies. These often pleasurable sensations become part of the musical experience, created through subwoofer technology, the listening environment, as well as the timbres produced by synthesized sounds and their mix post-production.

At a time when the sounds of rap music were rarely discussed with any detail in journalism, media reception of *The Chronic* discussed sound, in addition to the usual topics such as rapper persona and geography. This is partly because of the familiarity of the funk music that Dre interpolates but also partly because of what he does to the sounds. One journalist described his sound as "rumbling bass lines, hyperrealistic sound effects, and beats that hit the bloodstream like a pulp fiction adrenaline shot."[57] Jan Pareles noted that *The Chronic* was

> the album that defined West Coast hip-hop with a personalized style, G-Funk, that's simultaneously relaxed and menacing. The bottom register is swampy synthesizer bass lines that openly emulate Parliament-Funkadelic; the upper end is often a lone keyboard line, whistling or blipping insouciantly. In between are wide-open spaces that hold just a rhythm guitar, sparse keyboard chords and perhaps a singalong chorus between a rapper's unhurried rhymes. It's a hermetic sound, sealed off from street noise as if behind the windows of a limousine or a jacked-up jeep; it's the sound of the player, enjoying ill-gotten gains but always watching his back.[58]

Gold wrote, "The Dre sound is clean but edgy, deeply funky, featuring slow, big-bottomed, slightly dirty beats and powered by guitar and bass work that is not sampled but re-created in the studio—so that unlike East Coast rap productions—the fidelity of the final product is not inflected by the fidelity of scratchy R&B records that have been played too many times."[59] Brendan Koerner wrote:

> Instead of merely sampling funk hits, he hired session musicians to cover their best parts on synthesizers—usually just the catchiest six to 12 notes, slowed down to stoner speed. It was as if Dre took a magnifying glass to every P-Funk classic and zeroed in on the most addictive three-second segments. The whining 10-note synth line in the chorus of "F—k Wit Dre Day," *The Chronic's* first single, in unforgettable. And unforgettable singles move albums; how many consumers bought *The Chronic* simply because they couldn't shake "F—k Wit Dre Day" from their minds?[60]

Robert Marriott wrote that G-funk was "haunted P-Funk laced with synthesized vice" and that "Dre and his collaborators gave body to the laid-back tension that characterizes the life in Los Angeles ghettos. It was depraved gospel."[61] Sound, of course, does not exist in a vacuum, and these examples of media reception indicate attention both to the character of specific sounds and to the extramusical discourses that may have influenced these interpretations. The legacy of 1970s funk music forms one recognizable influence, but the imagery from 'hood films and gangsta rap music videos (from *The Chronic*, as well as earlier videos from N.W.A., such as 1988's "Straight Outta Compton") also helped to solidify the link between synthesizers and bass extension and a "dirty" sound said to represent the ghettos of Los Angeles. *The Chronic* was advertised in 1992 in hip-hop magazines like *The Source*, with Dr. Dre standing prominently in front of his 1964 Impala, firmly establishing the link between the album and the prominence of the automobile in G-funk imagery even before the music was released (fig. 3.2).[62]

The Chronic went on to become the best-selling hardcore rap album in history at the time, and Dre helped his next production credit, Snoop Doggy Dogg's *Doggystyle*, to become the first rap album to debut at number 1 on the *Billboard* charts. This synthesized "post-funk" or "post-soul"[63] sound characterized what is known as the "G-funk era" from 1992 to 1996, emblematic of a "West Coast rap" aesthetic still influential in hip-hop production. *The Chronic* is often described as a crossroads in hip-hop historiography, the point when rap music became less about the rap itself (accompanied by unobtrusive beats) and more about how well the rapper incorporated him- or herself within the producer's beats.[64]

As the above quotations suggest, media reception of Dr. Dre's production often made the link between the wide-open spaces of the West Coast and the development of G-funk. To quote Michael Eric Dyson, "West Coast hip-hop tailored its fat bass beats and silky melodies for jeeps that cruise the generous spaces of the West";[65] the ideology of "the West" helped to create a dichotomy between G-funk's "somatic" sound (often linked with automotive listening) and the allegedly more "cerebral" East Coast sound. One writer includes pop rap artist MC Hammer (from Oakland) in this West Coast aesthetic and suggests that his sound and implied listening spaces are more conducive to mainstream success:

> In no uncertain terms, West Coast rap spelled out the acceptable and unacceptable ways to court mainstream success. On the East Coast, however, it was still just courting. New York rap often seemed deeply insular—the tricky wordsmith pyrotechnics and cryptic references of innovators like Gang Starr, Poor Righteous Teachers, and early Tribe Called Quest was much to be played on Walkmans while riding on the subway or cut up by DJ Red Alert in sweaty afterhours underground clubs. Also, much of it was interior—just listen to Rakim go back to the womb on "In the Ghetto"—as well as spiritual, frequently laden with the insider-only rhetoric of Muslim sects like the 5 Percent Nation. West Coast hip hop, in contrast, was driving music, ready-made to blare out of car windows and share with the world. And as Hammer found out with the gargantuan sales of *Please Hammer . . .* there are more pop-friendly car drivers in America than subway-riding New York rap ideologues.[66]

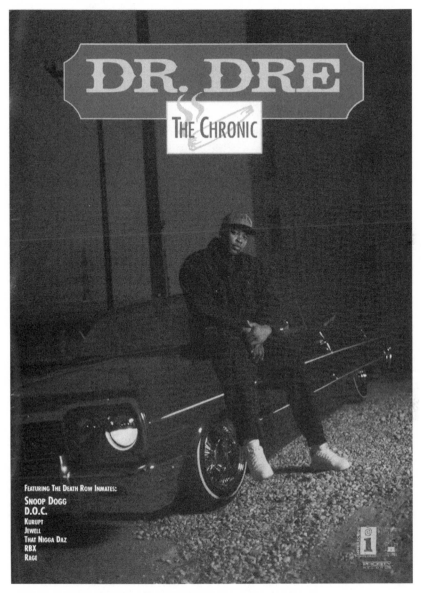

Figure 3.2: Dr. Dre, *The Chronic,* advertisement in the *Source*

This bifurcation between East and West, influenced in part by the sounds of the recordings, would have a profound influence on 1990s hip-hop.

The connection between the *sounds* of "G-funk" and their implied listening space merits investigation: Dr. Dre envisioned that the primary mode of listening would be through car stereo systems. He explained in a 1992 interview with Brian Cross:

> I make the shit for people to bump in their cars, I don't make it for clubs; if you play it, cool. I don't make it for radio, I don't give a fuck about the radio, TV, nothing like that, I make it for people to play in their cars. The reason being is that you listen to music in your car more than anything. You in your car all the time, the first thing you do is turn on the radio, so that's how I figure. *When I do a mix, the first thing I do is go down and see how it sounds in the car.*[67]

For Dr. Dre, the automotive listening space represents an idealized reference because it is reflective of the way he perceives that people listen to his music. The centrality of the car to his lifestyle can be seen in a number of Dr. Dre's music videos from *The Chronic*.[68] Dre's music video for "Nuthin' but a 'G' Thang" also features the car prominently as a crucial part of a day in the life of Compton's black youth.[69] The video opens with a close-up of Dr. Dre's car radio, with a voiceover from DJ Charmaine Champagne (actually a pornographic film star) introducing the track. During the voiceover, the camera zooms out in a crane shot similar to the famous opening of Orson Welles's 1958 *Touch of Evil* (which also features the automobile prominently in its opening sequence). The camera eventually shows Dr. Dre, exiting his car to pick up his friend Snoop Doggy Dogg at home.[70] During the music video, there is a twenty-second sequence that shows Dre and friends in their cars, driving on the freeway, going from a picnic to a party. In addition to Dre's own 1964 Chevrolet Impala (fitted with hydraulics), the video includes many other lowrider cars, as Gold recounts:

> Chugging, smoke-spewing old relics burnished to a high shine, bound-

ing and rebounding higher and higher, tossing their passengers about like so many extremely urban cowboys. If you peek into the trunk of any of these cars, you will see 14 car batteries hooked up in series and a row of hydraulic motors mounted where you'd expect to see the spare tire, but you'd better get out of the way when it starts to jump.[71]

The video ends with Dre being dropped off at the house that began the music video, creating a bookend image of the same house and automobile. Multiple gangsta rap music videos began to show the car's prominence in the Southern Californian ghetto world, such as Dr. Dre's "Let Me Ride," Ice Cube's "It Was a Good Day," Warren G's "Regulate," and Nate Dogg's "G-Funk." The association of rap music with the automobile became so ingrained that it became the source of parody, such as in an early 2000s Avis/XM Satellite Radio commercial that featured three middle-class men in business suits, white and Asian in ethnicity, commuting to work, listening and rapping along to Lumbajac's "2Gs." The lyrical topic of the song ("Make that money man . . . I gotta stack cheese")[72] fits the men appropriately, but the commercial subverts the imagined audience for the genre of music, usually depicted in myriad representations as lower-class African American youth.

The geography of California is important here, as one-half of Los Angeles is dedicated to spaces designed specifically, and often exclusively, for the automobile (i.e., freeways, roads, parking lots).[73] Southern California is the site of numerous car-culture births (hot rods, lowriders, GM's Harley Earl, the pinstriping of George Barris and Von Dutch, the car audio aftermarket),[74] helping to incorporate numerous car-inspired inventions into American life such as the drive-in, the suburban shopping mall, "cruising," the motel, drag racing, fast food, and trademarked modes of hip-hop production such as those of Dr. Dre. Krims notes that "one could certainly argue some specificity to the history of rap music in this case: Los Angeles car culture nurtured the so-called 'Jeep beats,' tracks mixed specifically for playback in car audio systems."[75] California also played a crucial role in car customization culture and the development of the subwoofer.[76] Peter Marsh and Peter Collett, in their study of the psy-

chology of the automobile, acknowledge that "the West Coast of America
has spawned more auto cults than any other part of the world."[77] The car
cultures that arose in Los Angeles became mediating cultural practices
that helped to shape Dr. Dre's music production techniques.

Los Angeles has had a long history of automobility, with the automobile central to everyday life since the 1920s. Ashleigh Brilliant writes that

> Los Angeles, as the famous architect Richard Neutra pointed out, was
> the only metropolis in America whose major expansion occurred en-
> tirely within the automobile era and was, therefore, able to incorporate
> the automobile more completely into its highly artificial landscape than
> could any already well-established city.[78]

One writer wrote in the 1920s that "if California ever adopts a new State
flower, the motor car is the logical blossom for the honor."[79] In the 1930s,
a California city planner declared that "it might be said that Southern
Californians have added wheels to their anatomy."[80] The mythologies
surrounding "the West," the frontier, and its cowboys were updated in the
automotive era, represented in the film *American Graffiti* (1973), which
depicts "cruisin'" teenagers in early 1960s California,[81] to quote the Chuck
Berry song, with "No Particular Place to Go." As Peter Wollen writes of
the film, "The soundtrack of *American Graffiti* comes straight from the
car radio, a selection of music played by the radio station's charismatic
disk jockey, Wolfman Jack"; commenting on soundtracks to films such as
Easy Rider (1969) and *Thieves Like Us* (1974), he states that "the car radio
and the roadside juke joint have taken over the role of the traditional
symphonic score."[82]

Some have theorized that the subbass frequencies central to hip-hop
and other "urban" music genres are influenced by the urban soundscape,
presenting a direct relationship between the sonic elements of an urban
environment and the music produced from it *and* for it. Producer/engi-
neer Ralph Sutton states:

> Some people have a predisposition for certain styles of music. I grew up
> in a 60-cycle domain; I was born in Chicago but we moved to the inner

part of L.A. early on, right in South Central. And there's always low frequency going on, whether it's the bus going by, the airplane flying over, the jackhammer in the background. So there are certain frequencies we are exposed to for long durations of time, and, obviously I'm not a psychologist, but I think that has something to do with it. If you grow up in an inner city where this is going on all the time, that gives you a different disposition; there's music in that noise. When you hear construction noise and something falls down, there's your boom-boom right there. A different part of that noise is your snare.[83]

His "60-cycle domain" refers to frequencies at 60 Hertz (cycles per second), according to Sutton, the frequency of a Roland TR-808 kick drum. Whether being drowned out as exterior sounds (as iPod earbuds do well) or becoming one with them, urban sounds have had a direct influence on so-called urban music genres. The automobile, as a crucial part of urban socialization, has influenced multiple forms of cultural production, including hip-hop music.

Like the car customization cultures of Southern California, Dr. Dre takes old parts and puts new features on old frameworks. Through his "replays" (Dre's term) or "interpolations," he is customizing the music for an idealized community of automotive listeners. His production style has been described as perfecting a "gangsta pop formula,"[84] the "pop" aspect most likely alluding to his use of the (usually simple) verse-chorus form and the repetitive "hooks" on the choruses (whether by synthesizer in "Dre Day" and "Nuthin' but a 'G' Thang" or by voice in "Gin and Juice"). The notion of G-funk as "gangsta pop" was influenced not only by song structure and chorus material but also by the commercial success that *The Chronic* enjoyed, demonstrating that rap music could be successful in the popular music mainstream, what hip-hop historian Jeff Chang calls the "popstream." Dr. Dre's production often crafts verse-chorus forms more familiar in non-funk-based popular music by using musical material from funk songs that do not follow this form. The finished recorded product, like the automobile, appears as a unified object but in actuality originated from numerous disparate sources. The automobile has over ten thousand parts, but car designers attempt to create the illusion of unity. Like Alfred Sloan, Dr. Dre updates the sounds of 1970s funk, what Vance Packard refers to as "the upgrading urge" of the annual model.[85] The car and Dr. Dre's productions can be seen as symbols of complexity, of hybridity, that reflect a desire to create an object with the semblance of unity.

In addition, the interplay between human and machine in the driving experience may enlighten an analysis of hip-hop (and other) recordings that embrace the hybridity of their "human" sounds (e.g., the voice) and their "synthesized" ones (e.g., the drum machine, synthesized keyboards). Rather than situate these recordings as reflecting a large-scale shift from "the human" to the "post-human" in society, as N. Katherine Hayles has suggested, it is more productive in this case to analyze how much of contemporary recorded music is a mix of the human, the synthesized, the acoustic (e.g., string, guitar, drum kit), and other electromechanical instruments that are so deeply ingrained in cultural consciousness that we give little thought to their status as "technological artifacts" (e.g., the electric guitar, the electric bass).[86] G-funk, like many rap subgenres, espouses a notion of "realness." Rather than present a case of "post-human" ventriloquism by way of cyborg-like voices (e.g., Radiohead's "Fitter, Happier"), the technology used here is derived from a funk-based lineage (Goodwin calls this "connecting machines and funkiness") that emphasizes the humanness, the *realness*, of the rapper.[87] I would argue further that Dr. Dre's emphasis on not textually signaling the borrowed material directly (i.e., not digitally sampling or making it sound sampled) helps contribute to this particular sense of realness.

An example typical of Dr. Dre's early 1990s production that demonstrates this hybridity of material and suitability for automotive listening is the Dr. Dre–produced single "Who Am I? (What's My Name?)," the debut single from Snoop Doggy Dogg's *Doggystyle* (1993). The synthesized sounds include a Roland TR-808 drum machine and a Moog synthesizer bass line derived from Tom Browne's "Funkin' for Jamaica" from the album *Love Approach* (1979). The basic beat is repeated throughout the song and changes texturally in terms of layering rather than in dynamic range, as it is likely that heavy dynamic compression was used in production to elevate the volume over the road and engine noise of a car (see the waveform in fig. 3.3) The "Snoop Doggy Dogg" line, collectively sung in the intro, is from Parliament Funkadelic's "Atomic Dog," and the second vocal line is from Parliament's "Tear the Roof Off the Sucker (Give Up the Funk)," melodically virtually the same but placed on a different harmonic backdrop/frame/chassis. Vocal line 3 is a quotation of vocal effects from "Atomic Dog": "Bow wow wow yippie yo yippie yay."[88] What I call the "guitar intro" (measures 1–2) is a sample from the Count's "Pack of Lies" from the album *What's Up Front That Counts* (1971), a two-measure excerpt with guitar and saxophones. Foregrounded lyrical textures travel among Snoop Dogg's laid-back verses, singing in the chorus, and Zapp-like vocal effects (as Zapp frontman Roger Troutman was known primarily for his use of the "talk box"). The track ends with vocals from an uncredited female voice, which sings improvisational-sounding melismas on the name "Snoop Doggy Dogg."

After the two-measure guitar intro, the basic beat begins (example 3.2). The three verses are primarily rapped by Snoop Doggy Dogg, although Dr. Dre recites a few lines at the end of the first verse. The lyrical topics of the song focus on Snoop Dogg's debut as a solo artist, bragging

(0:00–0:06)	"Guitar intro"	(2 measures)
(0:07–0:26)	Chorus	m. 3—Basic beat begins (4 measures) + Vocal line 1 (4 = 2 + 2 measures)
(0:27–0:56)	Verse 1	(12 measures)
(0:57–1:15)	Chorus 2	Vocal line 1 (4 = 2 + 2 measures) + Vocal line 2 (4 measures)
(1:16–1:46)	Verse 2	(12 measures)
(1:47–2:05)	Chorus 3	Vocal line 1 (4 measures) + Vocal line 3 (4 measures: "Bow wow wow yippie yo yippie yay" from "Atomic Dog")
(2:06–2:35)	Verse 3	(12 measures)
(2:36–3:14)	Chorus 4	(Double chorus)—Vocal line 1 (8 measures) + Vocal line 2 (8 measures)
(3:15–4:05)	Coda	twenty measures of female vocalist singing "Snoop Doggy Dogg"

TABLE 3.1. "Who am I? (What's My Name)?" Song Structure

From *Doggystyle* (1993), produced by Dr. Dre (Andre Young)

Example 3.2: Snoop Doggy Dogg "Who Am I? (What's My Name)"

about his lifestyle, the locality of Long Beach, and his collaborations with Dr. Dre.[89] Interestingly, in the music video for "Who Am I?" (directed by rapper Fab 5 Freddy), Dre's portion of the rap includes a visual of him standing next to a white car in front of a house similar to the one in "'G' Thang." Though the narrative of the music video has little to do with the automobile, "Who Am I?" still demonstrates the centrality of the automobile to Dr. Dre's lifestyle and status. In the song, each chorus always contains at least one four-measure iteration of vocal line 1 (consisting of the repeated two-measure phrase), but each chorus is slightly different, mixing multiple elements from the George Clinton songs that Dr. Dre interpolates. As was characteristic of his production style at the time, Dr. Dre borrows from multiple different songs and uses them to construct a verse-chorus form. This is a "simple verse-chorus" form,[90] in that the harmony does not change between verse and chorus, and it is noteworthy that he was able to tailor material with relatively static harmonies into a repeating four-chord pattern (bm, bm/A, G, F#7). The synthesized bass line and high-pitched synthesizers on "Who Am I?" are consistent with styles used on *The Chronic*. In fact, "F—wit Dre Day" from *The Chronic* is strikingly similar to "Who Am I?" in terms of the timbre of the bass line, its harmonic motion, and the use of high and low synthesizers.

While drum sounds and beats from funk had been used since the earliest days of digital sampling in hip-hop, these were usually drawn from the earlier funk of James Brown (e.g., "The Funky Drummer") and other recordings from the late 1960s and early 1970s, such as the Incredible Bongo Band's version of "Apache" (1972). Dr. Dre, in contrast, borrows funk music from a decade later, largely from the late 1970s and early 1980s in this example, reproducing stylistic characteristics such as synthesizers and vocal effects.

The decision to open with an early 1970s sample ("Pack of Lies") that never returns in the song may demonstrate a conscious shift in funk

Musical Phrase	Derived From
Moog bass line	Tom Browne's "Funkin' for Jamaica" (1981)
Vocal Line 1	George Clinton's "Atomic Dog" (1982)
Vocal Line 2	Parliament's "Tear the Roof Off the Sucker (Give Up the Funk)" (1976)
"Talk box"	Zapp-style (1978–80s funk band)
Low vocal effects and Vocal Line 3	"Atomic Dog" (1982)

TABLE 3.2. "Who am I? (What's My Name)?" Derivative Phrases

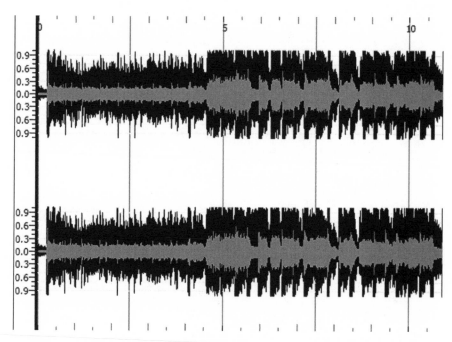

Figure 3.3: Opening of "Who Am I?" Waveform (from Sonic Visualizer). Measures 1–2 (Intro), measures 3–4 (basic beat).

sources, as Dr. Dre has expanded the hip-hop sound palette to reflect later funk developments for the rest of the song's duration. The song opening, with a digital sample quickly yielding to an unsampled basic beat, in a way authenticates this conscious shift. Richard Dyer, in his book on pastiche, includes a chapter on pastiche works within works. He cites the newsreel in *Citizen Kane* (a film within a film) and the play "Murder of Gonzago" within *Hamlet* (a play within a play). Dyer writes that the "effect of the inner pastiche is to authenticate the outer form."[91] In a way, though this "inner pastiche" occurs at the opening of the song, the purpose of the sample is to contrast with, and authenticate, the realness of the song proper.[92]

As can be heard in the contrast between measures 1–2 and measures 3–4, the basic beat of the song appears stretched so that it fills the extreme ranges of its amplitude, something that would be ideal for loud

Example 3.3: Comparison of vocal line 1: George Clinton, "Atomic Dog," and Snoop Doggy Dogg, "Who Am I?"

environments such as the rumbling noises of an automobile. The graphic representation of the audio signal in the waveform below shows the differences between the "guitar intro" and the "basic beat" (see Fig. 3.3).

In the waveform, the x-axis represents time, and the y-axis represents the voltage level of the audio output. The waveform signal shows that the overall amplitude appears expanded compared to the intro and suggests the use of dynamic range compression on the basic beat. The effect is that from measure 3 through the end the song sounds "louder" and more "filled out" than in the intro section, consistent with Dr. Dre's desire to fill the automotive listening space.

By rerecording vocal lines from preexisting sources, Dr. Dre can change the harmonic framework of phrases and adapt them to any given harmony. In vocal line 1 above, for example, the original version contains a harmonic backdrop of D for the duration, whereas the new version has a bass line that suggests a descending progression (bm, bm/A, G, F#7). This creates a different effect, one of less static harmonic motion, including relatively strong movement to the dominant before returning to the tonic every two measures. Despite the harmonic differences, the melodic line is similar enough that the allusion to "Atomic Dog" can still be easily recognized. In the Snoop Dogg version of vocal line 1, a group sings the melodic line, a quotation that directly signifies the Parliament-style, collectively sung choruses. Both versions repeat the two-measure phrase as well. Lyrically, Dr. Dre takes advantage of the dog/Dogg connection by

Parliment "Tear the roof off the sucker (Give up the Funk)" from *Mothership Connection* (1976)

"Who am I?" Second Vocal Line

Example 3.4: Comparison of vocal line 2: Parliament, "Tear the Roof Off the Sucker," and Snoop Doggy Dogg, "Who Am I?"

quoting dog references from "Atomic Dog" at multiple points in "Who Am I?" (Example 3.4 above).

A similar tailoring occurs with vocal line 2. Once again, the original from George Clinton's Parliament has a funk groove over just one chord, this time an E7. There are multiple voices singing in both examples (both shift from monophony to homophony), and the harmonies have changed to reflect the implied harmonies of the new bass line.

The contrast between the high and low synthesizer frequencies in "Who Am I?" and other examples in that style is particularly effective in car sound systems, where the highly directional tweeters can exclusively support the high-end frequencies, and the power of the subwoofer(s) produces corporeal sensations from the bassline. The "human sounds" (e.g., Snoop's rap, the collective voices, and the female voice at the end), their locus in the frequency range easiest for humans to hear (3kHz–7kHz), will be supported by woofers/midrange speakers, which require much less power than a subwoofer.

The styles utilized in G-funk (including late 1970s/early 1980s P-funk, R&B, and the simple verse-chorus form), largely pioneered in rap music by Dr. Dre and his collaborators, spread their influence over a number of subsequent groups. One example of a rap song that shares timbral style with Dre's G-funk is the song "Thuggish Ruggish Bone" by Bone Thugs-n-Harmony from their album *Creepin On Ah Come Up* (1994), which uses a mix of high synthesizer, low bass, and the singing of Shatasha Williams. Though G-funk was considered a "West Coast" style, it was also used by artists said to represent the East Coast. For example, the Notorious B.I.G.'s "Big Poppa" (1994) used a high-pitched synthesizer riff derived from the Isley Brothers' "Between the Sheets" in the style of Dr. Dre's production.

Synthesized sounds, dynamic range compression, and prominent bass frequencies are but three elements that seem to be highly compatible with the automotive soundscape. The experience of automotive listening is a synthesis of musical technology and automotive technology, which must coexist to be successful; I would argue that a certain aspect of popular music records can be analyzed through this particular, historically specific compatibility. Like the car-driver/driver-car relationship, hip-hop recordings are a mix of "human" elements and technology, a mix of human and human-made machine. Consideration of a particular listening space, the transfer function of loudspeakers and their resonant frequency, should be acknowledged as an important component of the subject position in the listening experience.[93]

As we consider the automotive soundscape in hip-hop recordings, we should allow for alternatives to traditional analysis that accommodate the way that music producers think of sound (in terms of frequency rather than pitch, in a Western notational sense).[94] Frequency, playback spaces and speakers, and the hybrid human-machine element of recordings are all undertheorized facets of popular music production and the automotive listening experience.

Conclusion

As a product of place- and space-specific urban car cultures, Dr. Dre's production techniques reflect a desire to customize and tailor sounds for the automotive soundscape. Automobile production, geographical specificity, and other mediating cultural practices such as car customization cultures have shaped Dr. Dre's and other producers' music production techniques. Perhaps car audio, like the streamlined outer appearance of many automobiles, provides the illusion of unity, sonically suturing the inconsistencies or ruptures in the fragmented bodies of culture, ideology, and subjectivity; like hip-hop music, the automobile is a unique, almost paradoxical hybrid: both public (on the road) and private (owned), a site of mastery and womblike comfort, of human and machine, symbolizing freedom and dependence (on petrol), at times transcendent and at other times suffocating, a fantasy object and the cause of trauma and nightmare, an object-cause of desire and a cause of stress (traffic jams and road rage), a "symbolic sanctuary"[95] and the cause of numerous fatalities.

Jonathan Bell, in writing of the car's influence on architecture, comments that "our experience of the city, and hence our response to architecture, is almost exclusively conducted through the medium of the automobile: the car defines our space whether we are driving, being driven, or avoiding being driven over."[96] Marsh and Collett write that "it is because the car has so much personal value that we have been, and are still, prepared to alter radically the environments in which we live in order to create societies in which the automobile can feature so centrally."[97] The automobile has had a tremendous amount of influence on many realms of life, a fact that has yet to be thoroughly researched. And if the car does indeed define the spaces in which we live, and the automotive space is largely experienced in terms of sound, then one could say that sound (as mediated through the automobile) and our sense of space mutually influence each other.[98]

There are numerous levels through which one could investigate the automobile's influence on the world's soundscapes, such as the individual experience of car drivers, the influence of the car on music production, car audio subcultures, and larger national and transnational trends.[99] In 2005, it was estimated that there were over seven hundred million cars on the world's roads;[100] this statistic suggests that automobility will continue to be a pervasive force in the decades to come, continuing the ever-shifting social, economic, and political forces that shape the automobile and the object's influence on multiple realms of societies. This chapter presents borrowing practices in hip-hop that are particularly conscious of idealized playback spaces, encouraging analysis of particular modes of listening, modes that have in turn inflected the way music recordings are produced.

CHAPTER 4

THE MARTYR INDUSTRY
Tupac Shakur, the Notorious B.I.G., and Postmortem Sampling

Posterity is to the philosopher what the hereafter is to the believer.

—DIDEROT[1]

The hero of yesterday becomes the tyrant of tomorrow, unless he crucifies *himself* today.

—JOSEPH CAMPBELL, *THE HERO WITH A THOUSAND FACES*

Picture yourself goin' out as a hero
Picture mural pictures of us painted all over street corners
Fans meet to mourn us, while we meet the coroners . . .
Biggie's back and 'Pac's, landmarks, history in rap.

—EMINEM, "IT HAS BEEN SAID," *NOTORIOUS B.I.G. DUETS:
THE FINAL CHAPTER* (2005)

Posthumous Fame, Popular Music, and Society

Featuring a number of West Coast rappers such as Ice Cube, Eminem, Snoop Dogg, Dr. Dre, and many others, the 2000 *Up in Smoke Tour* stage show included an interlude where Dr. Dre and Snoop Dogg gave tribute to a number of rappers who had passed away (e.g., Easy E, Big Pun, and Notorious B.I.G.). They saved rapper Tupac Shakur (who recorded under the name 2Pac) for last, and the audience can be seen in DVD footage standing up, cheering enthusiastically for the deceased rapper. The 2Pac song "Gangsta Party" plays over the loudspeaker as Snoop asks, "Do y'all love Tupac?" The audience responds, "Yeah." The exchange proceeds as follows:

SNOOP: Well if y'all love Tupac like we love Tupac, Boston, everybody in the muthafuckin house let me hear ya say "Tu-Pac."
AUDIENCE: Tu-Pac.
(x3) SNOOP: Say "Tu-Pac." Audience: Tu-Pac.
(x2) SNOOP: Say "we love you." Audience: We love you.
(x2) SNOOP: Say "we miss you." Audience: We miss you.

Call and response between performer and audience is quite common at
live popular music performances, but this *Up in Smoke Tour* tribute segment begins to take the character of a quasi-religious ritual. The tribute
demonstrates both the close proximity of death in gangsta rap culture
and the power of stardom functioning as a type of religion within popular music culture. As Eminem raps of stardom, "It's like these kids hang
on every single statement we make like they worship us" (1:48–1:51),[2] and
according to David Giles, who has written on the psychology of fame,
the figure of celebrity is a "conduit for a 'higher' entity' in secular culture."[3]

Posthumous stardom, particularly of artists who die young, often
constructs a more intensified aura of authority and cultural power than a
living celebrity. Memorializers intervene to create a portrait of the artist
that often involves fitting him or her into larger narratives. This is not to
say that the canonization does not begin during an artist's lifetime, but
the postmortem eulogizing and memorializing present the life and body
of work together in retrospect, looking at how the artist was a reflection
of his or her society and influenced new directions within it. For example,
Kurt Cobain was eulogized as a "spokesman for a generation," someone
who "caught the generational drama of our time."[4] Such artists' untimely
passing is of a ritualistic importance, as deaths of important figures often
become events for the media and fans as signposts of eras in their culture.[5] Journalistic memorializations that link artists with their culture
largely concern themselves with conferring on the artist a metaphorical
sense of place (into a generation, canon, history, or other tropes of the
journalistic narrative). Locating artistic identity, which often means trying to find the "real" person behind the image, seems to be of great importance to both media and fans and manifests itself in a number of ways.
While the voice of the artist becomes silenced in one sense (the fact that

Cobain cannot respond to his eulogizers or change his career makes him easier to analyze), the music is often said to "live on," becoming a symbol of the mythical artist and everything the postmortem discourse chooses him or her to represent. The romantic glorification of death in writings and the presentation of an artist's works and voice construct a complex nexus best described as a form of symbolic immortality.[6] Most important to this study is the use of this symbolic immortality by other artists through digitally sampling the voice or image of a deceased artist.

The aura from dying young surrounds figures in music as diverse as Giovanni Battista Pergolesi (who died at age twenty-six), Wolfgang Amadeus Mozart (thirty-five), Charlie Parker, (thirty-five) Jim Morrison (twenty-seven), Jimi Hendrix (twenty-seven), Kurt Cobain (twenty-seven), and the latest inductee into the "Twenty-Seven Club," Amy Winehouse. Less than two decades after the first recorded rap music, Tupac Shakur and the Notorious B.I.G. (whose real name was Christopher Wallace, also referred to as Biggie Smalls or simply Biggie) were murdered within six months of each other and became the first rap artists on whom symbolic immortality was bestowed on a large scale.[7] The media described their "feud" as a war between West Coast (represented by Tupac) and East Coast (represented by Notorious B.I.G.) rappers, which even led to speculation that Biggie was responsible for Tupac's murder and that those associated with Tupac murdered Biggie for revenge.[8] In part because of the unsolved mysteries surrounding the murders of these two rappers, their aura may be more accurately described as a mystique, one that has become a distinguished event in gangsta rap culture (and in the larger "hip-hop world" that I outline in my introduction). Journalists often invoke the "post-Biggie era" or the "post-Tupac era" or use other phrases that invoke the idea that their deaths signaled the end of one era and the beginning of another. In effect, they have become "larger than life" and, inversely, larger than death. As one author put it, alluding to the tragedy and historical moment of September 11, 2001, "2Pac and Biggie have been the twin towering martyrs of hip hop."[9] Their immortality persists while these artists are remembered and signposted, representative of a time period or social group. The UK newspaper the *Independent*, for instance, labeled Tupac Shakur on the tenth anniversary of his murder as "a hero of a generation."[10]

In the creation of a hero system in popular music, the immortality of fame coexists with artists' creations, primarily the recordings they leave behind. These recordings, which capture the "spirit" of the artist/hero, convince many that a part of the artist is still with us. Books and films about the murders of Tupac and Biggie have added to their mystique, but the other, more prominent method of keeping these artists within cultural memory has been the posthumous release of tribute albums and unreleased material from Biggie and Tupac.

As with pop artists who preceded the two rappers, their death was profitable. Alan Clayson, writing four years before Tupac's murder, said that "a death in pop sells records. Before they had a chance to dry their tears, music industry moguls would be obliged to meet the demand kindled by tragedy and rush release the product while the corpse was still warm."[11] One example of this is Jimi Hendrix, who released four albums in his lifetime and now has more than thirty official posthumous releases.[12] The publicity received from a romantic or heroic death is what leads Deena Weinstein to call it a "great career move," as critics celebrate romantic rock deaths "because they affirm the myth of the artist."[13]

Pac and Biggie were no exception to this phenomenon. In death, their popularity skyrocketed. The first posthumous Notorious B.I.G. album, *Life after Death*, released three weeks after his murder, debuted at number 1 on the Billboard 200 and was certified diamond (10 million copies sold) as of 2006.[14] In the case of Tupac, at the time of his death in 1996 he had sold 5.9 million records; after nine official posthumous releases a decade later, the number sold had increased to over 36.5 million in the United States, rendering him the best-selling rap artist in US history.[15] His first posthumous album sold more than 500,000 copies in the first week of its release, according to SoundScan.[16] The CD booklet with his second posthumous album (*R U Still Down?*) includes six pages of ads for "official 2pac gear," including t-shirts, beanies, bandanas, and commemorative phone cards.[17] Tupac iconography looms large, with his face on t-shirts, posters, and public murals all over the world. As Cheo Hodari Coker notes, "Tupac's image itself has become a symbol of cult revolution— sandwiched on the T-shirt racks between Bob Marley and Che Guevara from St. Mark's Place in Greenwich Village to the tourist shops in Paris's

Montmartre."[18] Films about Tupac have been released with such titles as *Thug Angel, Thug Immortal,* and *Tupac Resurrection.* As it became commonplace and profitable for rap artists to have clothing lines after Tupac's death, he now has one as well, Makaveli-Branded, whose website's video states, "His name is known worldwide . . . his words have inspired millions . . . and now through his clothing line Makaveli-Branded his legacy will continue to live."[19] One ad in *Vibe* magazine shows a doctored picture of Tupac on a runway wearing the clothes from his clothing line.[20] (Fig. 4.1 shows this example of visual postmortem sampling.)

Notorious B.I.G. also takes part in the institutions of tribute and memory that pervade popular culture. One of the most popular songs from 1997 was a tribute song to Notorious B.I.G. called "I'll Be Missing You," as performed by his producer, Sean "Puffy" Combs (including borrowed melodic and harmonic material from the Police's "Every Breath You Take"). The single went triple platinum after only a few weeks and was the number 1 song on the pop charts for most of the year.[21] Puff Daddy's performance of the song at the MTV Music Video Awards became an important event of remembrance:

> The September 1997 MTV Video Music Awards, the engineer of so many dramatic hip hop moments, set the stage for the most dramatic of all. With a 50-person choir dressed in white, Combs danced and bopped to the beat of "I'll Be Missing You." From a riser emerging near the front of the stage, Sting appeared, singing his original version of his Police hit "Every Breath You Take." From stage left, Faith [Evans] appeared, singing the chorus about her slain husband. Above everyone, there was a huge monitor, playing footage from Biggie videos "Hypnotize," "One More Chance," and "Juicy," among others.
>
> Four male dancers came out, spinning and dancing with Combs as he stood at the center of the stage, whipping the audience into a frenzy.
>
> "Clap your hands for Big! Clap your hands for Tupac Shakur! Clap your hands for everybody we lost!" he said, his arm stretched out as sparks rained down from the ceiling, icing the finale.[22]

Many years later, tributes continued to memorialize this respected mem-

Figure 4.1: Makaveli Branded advertisement in *Vibe* magazine (December 2006)

ber of the hip-hop community and to keep him alive in the cultural consciousness. On August 28, at the 2005 MTV Music Video Awards, Puffy
and Snoop Dogg contributed to a tribute segment to the Notorious
B.I.G. that included a full orchestra on stage, accompanying two well-
known Notorious B.I.G. raps ("Juicy" and "Warning," playing a cappella
over the loudspeakers). A month later, VH1 presented a Hip-Hop Honors Tribute to Biggie. Combs, who was B.I.G.'s producer and a shrewd
entrepreneur, was working on the next tribute album, *Duets: The Final
Chapter*, which arrived in stores in December of the same year. (The album was released by Combs's label, Bad Boy Entertainment.) As Roger
Beebe argues, music videos like Tupac's "Changes" that present stills and
films from the past create structures of mourning in hip-hop culture,
structures that are "specifically designed to encourage mourning."[23] Both
Tupac and Notorious B.I.G. are kept alive in cultural memory through
these structures of mourning, which take many forms. The production
of posthumous albums, bootleg mixtapes, films, books, and other merchandise has been part of these structures, creating a martyr industry in
hip-hop. As Lee Marshall reminds us, stars exist "because the individual
can be turned into a product."[24]

When artists die young, they become polysemous symbols that can
serve a multitude of purposes, often used as iconic of a particular culture, generation, or historical narrative. Though other figures in popular music have received a type of mythic status or sainthood after their
deaths, the pervasiveness of borrowing and collaboration in hip-hop, as
part and parcel of its aesthetic, creates a unique case of postmortem sampling. Instead of examining sampling to construct sample-based "beats,"
I intend here to look at the digital sampling of voices as a form of reception, that is, the reception of the sampled individual by the sampling
artist. Rappers who sample hip-hop martyrs such as Tupac Shakur and
Notorious B.I.G. add to the creation of new identities, tributes that often become part of new narratives within the imagined community of
hip-hop culture. The result complements the ongoing process of a triple-
voiced canonization: formulating sainthood; defining a musical canon,
which involves albums or songs that stand out in the genre; and, as part
of a Plutarchian history of great men, having sainted figures stand above

their peers as among rap's greats. Extramusical associations with the artist, such as biography, are paramount, their mystique and these associations becoming embodied in and symbolized by their voice. Using their voices in a new context, what I call "postmortem sampling," is an example of the recorded voice as relic. At the end of this chapter, I compare the similarities and distinctions of two rap contemporaries (Jay-Z and Nas) who use the voices of the slain rappers; the digital sampling of the recorded voice, used together with both the beats and new flows, comments not only on the reception of the Notorious B.I.G. and Tupac Shakur but also on each rapper's construction of and desire for a sense of place in the rap music world.

The Emergence of Tupac's Postmortem Identities

Tupac, rather than the Notorious B.I.G., has become the dominant figure of hip-hop martyrdom for a few reasons. Most obvious is that he died six months earlier, so that the memorial project for him was well under way when the latter significant tragedy occurred. Tupac had also been a star for longer; his image was prevalent in a variety of films and music videos; and he had had a slightly longer recording career. Though there is some consensus in academic literature that, on a technical basis, Biggie Smalls was the better rapper,[25] Neil Strauss explains that "Shakur was a better star, a more charismatic presence, a more gifted actor, a bigger lightning rod for trouble, a more complex visionary."[26] This complexity has been the source of the scale and variety of his myth-making. George Kamberelis and Greg Dimitriadis make the point that much of the myths have to do with details of Tupac's biography and with songs like "Dear Mama" and "Keep Your Head Up" about personal struggles, to which youth could relate; they observe that the people they interviewed "were much less invested in Biggie's life."[27] Tupac's films, music videos, and media coverage have provided an image (and a charismatic bodily presence) to accompany the variety of topics discussed in his lyrics, providing the quasi-sacred texts and philosophies for dissection and symbol creation.

It is important to note that a large part of Tupac's postmortem identity was created while he was still alive by Tupac himself. Though it is not uncommon for rap artists to engage in a discourse of death, ruminating on their own death in rap lyrics in particular, he may have been obsessed more than others.[28] With tracks entitled "Death around the Corner," "How Long Will They Mourn Me?," "If I Die 2 Night," "Wonder if Heaven Got a Ghetto," and "So Many Tears" (in which he raps "I'm having visions of leaving here in a hearse"), Tupac was aware of his mortality. Being shot five times in 1994 also fostered his awareness, along with the relatively low life expectancy for African Americans and those involved in gang violence in inner-city America. On one track, "Never B Peace" from *Better Dayz*, he raps, "How the fuck can you have a childhood when you at the funeral every weekend?" The culture of death was prevalent in the ghettos of America, and the gangsta rap genre often tries to depict the harsh realities of ghetto culture. Tupac was a product of this death culture and one of its most vocal narrators.

So when the early death seemingly foretold by Tupac became real, there was plenty of material for tributes, myth-making, and canonization. Two days after his death, Death Row Records released the single "I Ain't Mad at Cha" (from *All Eyes on Me*), which was particularly appropriate for tribute, because the visual images of the music video (recorded months earlier) depicted Tupac shot down, delivering his message of forgiveness in heaven among other canonical black musicians (Jimi Hendrix, Louis Armstrong, Miles Davis, and Nat King Cole, to name a few). Album sales of *All Eyez on Me* (released seven months before his death) tripled within one week of the shooting, and it climbed from number 69 to number 6 on the Billboard 200 in the course of two weeks.[29] His first posthumous album, *The Don Killuminati: The Seven Day Theory* (released under the pseudonym Makaveli), was released by Death Row Records eight weeks after his death. The cover features a cartoon of Tupac being crucified. (Tupac explained the album cover prerelease in one interview by saying, "I'm on the cross bein' crucified for keepin' it real.")[30] The iconography is striking, no doubt adding to the notion that Tupac was a hip-hop martyr.[31]

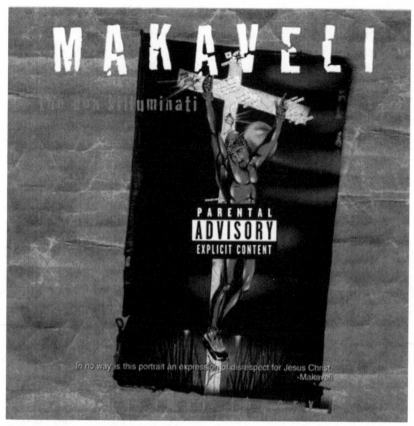

Figure 4.2: Makaveli (Tupac), *The Don Killuminati: The Seven Day Theory*, cover (Death Row/Interscope, 1996)

Michael Eric Dyson, in *Holler if You Hear Me: Searching for Tupac Shakur*, writes on martyrdom, and his thoughts are worth quoting at length:

> At least four notions are crucial to the conception of martyrdom: embodiment, identification, substitution, and elevation. The martyr's death embodies, and in some cases anticipates, the death of those who follow. It may be that his death signifies the manner in which his followers, adherents, or comrades could die. The martyr is identified by and with the

community that follows him. He is identified as the leader of a group of believers or followers who identify with him as a member of their own tribe or community. The martyr's death often substitutes for the death of his followers, he dies in their place, at least symbolically. For instance, when [Martin Luther] King died, his death changed the black political future in this nation. He died in the place of millions of blacks, since it could easily have been one of them who perished from racial violence. Finally, the martyr is elevated to a high status, even as he elevates the condition of his followers through his death, drawing attention to their hidden or overlooked suffering.[32]

The idea that the martyr dies in the place of his or her followers is a crucial point and perhaps explains why pop martyrs are said to represent a particular generation or culture. It is highly suggestive of how cultures deal with the death anxiety, as well as of the functions of ritual sacrifice, symbolic or otherwise, in a given society. It is this elevation to a high status that popular artists who die young are able to attain, and the martyr's aura informs both their previous recordings and their new ones. The iconic status of an artist, partly shaped by the music (both musical figures and lyrical content) and partly shaped by extramusical mythologizing, is the result of an interplay crucial to studies of music reception.

Tupac's compositional process and quantity of output are worth noting because they contribute to the memorialization process. As of this writing, nine official posthumous albums have been released,[33] featuring commercially unreleased material (not to mention the dozens of bootlegs and remixes, which would provide plenty of material for another study). Accounts of Tupac as workaholic frequently pervade writings on him.[34] Many describe Tupac running from studio to court appearance to film set, and there are anecdotes of Tupac still working after others had gone to bed. Dyson's research points to one oft-told anecdote: "Notorious B.I.G. said that when he once visited Tupac, the latter went to the bathroom, and when he emerged, he had penned two songs."[35] Tupac's bodyguard wrote that he recorded six tracks in one night after he got out of prison and wrote songs in the movie trailer that he would record later the same night.[36] One journalist writes, "Pac was a studio prodigy, more

like a one-take jazz musician than a punch-me-in rapper."[37] The number
varies concerning how many tracks he recorded after he left prison, but
it is usually placed in the 100–200 song range. One article comments
that Tupac had recorded 150 unreleased tracks, which his mother, Afeni
Shakur, had to go to court to obtain from Death Row Records owner
Suge Knight.[38] The ferocity with which he worked, and the multitude
of his rap topics, contributed to the range of his characterizations. And
with an unknown number of songs still unreleased, the mystique of the
unknown is again prevalent; fans hope that he still has more to say.

One reason for the high amount of material on Tupac is that he can be
fit into multiple traditions and frameworks, both academic and popular.
One of these includes Tupac Shakur the revolutionary,[39] as Afeni Shakur
most famously was a member of the Black Panther party and was preg-
nant with her son while in prison.[40] His poverty and struggles, such as
having a crack-addicted mother, are circumstances frequently recounted
in Tupac biography, reflecting the romantic concept of the mythologized
artist who battles extraordinary circumstances to create art that tran-
scends its time and place.[41] Others have written of Tupac as following
a lineage of Black Panthers, asserting that his more political rap lyrics
reflect this, along with his intense style of rap delivery or flow.[42] One
church in Kansas City now includes a mural that depicts Martin Luther
King, Malcolm X, and Tupac together on the same wall.[43] In addition to
Tupac as black revolutionary, his gangsta rap mystique also places him
within a larger tradition of black outlaws (the Shine and Stackolee myths
in particular).[44]

Tupac's religious references in rap lyrics and interviews are also used
by authors to varying effects. Essay collections such as *Noise and Spirit:
The Religious and Spiritual Sensibilities of Rap Music* locate the Christian
messages of rap songs, and this book in particular includes a full chapter
on Tupac.[45] One book entitled *Jesus and the Hip-Hop Prophets: Spiritual
Insights from Lauryn Hill and 2Pac*[46] uses Bible verses and various lyrics to
convey messages that correspond to teachings of Jesus. For Tupac, there
are separate chapters on songs like "Dear Mama," "Brenda's Got a Baby"
(about teenage pregnancy), and "Changes," which is about the need to be
socially active to make a change in the world. This book was written by

two religious hip-hop fans who seek to translate the teachings of their religion into a language that they hope better communicates their message. Theresa Reed's *The Holy Profane* deals with elements of the sacred within black popular music. Reed is particularly interested in Tupac, showing examples in his lyrics to make the point that God, death, redemption, and the afterlife are common themes in tracks like "God Bless the Dead" and "Black Jesuz." Discussing "Hail Mary," she notes that "references to Christ in this rap are salient because the rapper connects Christ's suffering to his own."[47] Important to this comparison, Susan Sontag has written that the artist has now replaced the saint as exemplary sufferer in modern Western society, the figure "to whom we look to be able best to express his suffering."[48] Tupac can be theorized either through a religious lens or through a more secular "suffering artist" role, as he was also one of the first rappers to present (presumed) inner psychological thoughts and feelings within his raps.

The positive messages from selected Tupac songs such as "Dear Mama," as well as many of his culturally literate musings, have facilitated Tupac's extensive use in the academy (including Dyson's book and others I have already cited).[49] One of the first instances of Tupac's receiving national press for academic analysis was the class offered at the University of California at Berkeley entitled "History '98: Poetry and History of Tupac Shakur," taught by Arvand Elihu;[50] five years later, a conference was held at Harvard University entitled "Tupac Shakur and the Search for a Modern Folk Hero." Participants discussed his book collection (including *Catcher in the Rye*, *Moby-Dick*, and works by Alice Walker and Shakespeare), and Mark Anthony Neal presented a paper portraying Tupac as an "organic intellectual," a concept articulated by Antonio Gramsci.[51]

Tupac the intellectual has been represented visually with images of him wearing glasses. The album cover of *Loyal to the Game* (shown in fig. 4.3) shows Tupac in a suit wearing glasses, a contrast to more common photos of him with his shirt off, showing off tattoos, one on his abdomen famously saying "Thug Life" (see his image on the cover of *Rolling Stone* in fig. 4.4). The third chapter of Dyson's *Holler if You Hear Me* focuses on Tupac's hunger for knowledge. According to Dyson, who interviewed a number of people close to Tupac, he read Kurt Vonnegut,

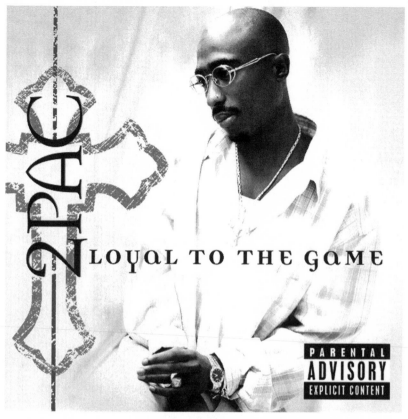

Figure 4.3: Tupac *Loyal to the Game*, cover (Aurora/Interscope, 2004)

Teilhard de Chardin's *Phenomenon of Man*, Maya Angelou, Sigmund Freud, and George Orwell. He could quote Shakespeare and listened to many genres of music (including Kate Bush, Eric Clapton, Muddy Waters, Don McLean, Sarah McLachlan, and the soundtrack to *Les Misérables*). He enjoyed the art of Van Gogh, writing a poem dedicated to Van Gogh entitled "Starry Night".[52] He saw Kabuki theater in San Francisco, watched Japanese movies, wrote plays from the age of six, and was an actor before he was a rapper. Most of his biographies note that Tupac spent the beginning of high school at the Baltimore School for the Arts, where he was exposed to much of this artistic culture.

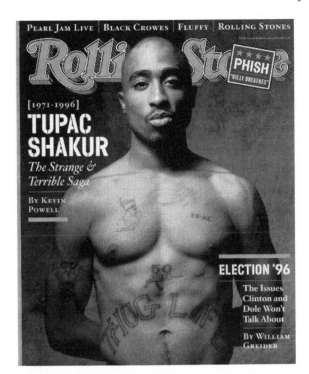

Figure 4.4: Rolling Stone's Tupac cover (issue 746, October 1996)

This portrayal of Tupac the intellectual is, as one DVD title puts it, of the "hip-hop genius."[53] He has had two books of poetry published since his death, *The Rose That Grew from Concrete*, first published in 1999 (from poems written between 1989 and 1991), and *Inside A Thug's Heart*, edited by Angela Ardis, containing letters and poems from their correspondence when Tupac was in jail in 1995.[54] In the case of *The Rose That Grew from Concrete*, Tupac's mother wrote the preface, which opens, "I thank God and all my ancestors for the Artistic Tupac, for the Poetic Tupac."[55] One side of each page contains his original handwriting, the other side a typed version of a given poem. This gives the work a sense of authenticity, as well as cultural elevation, the printed book offering intellectual priority over the sound recording or website (not to mention the facsimile of his original handwriting). Putting Tupac's message in a book rather than on a "rap record" changes its packaging significantly.

Considering Tupac as a poet rather than rapper offers a terminological ploy worth considering. Thomas Swiss, in writing about singer-songwriter Jewel's media coverage regarding her book of poetry, notes, "Simply to name something 'poetry' or 'music,' in fact, is already to invoke someone's values—values that are in some part constructed culturally and dependent on who is doing the naming and for whom."[56] Using the term *poetry*, like associations with "chamber music" in classical worlds, connotes intimacy and a privacy that audiences demand to invade.[57] Labeling Tupac a poet elevates his status, and the label has been used by academics, in part, to legitimize a problematic and complex icon and his music—and I acknowledge that my own study of him is a part of the academic trend I discuss.

Tupac Shakur, a hero with a thousand faces, provides himself as a placeholder for a number of purposes. His large compositional output (in itself an aspect of the mythology: Tupac the workaholic) allows those who study him to identify the messages on which they wish to focus. Some include Tupac the revolutionary, Tupac the saint, Tupac the Romantic, Tupac the martyr, Tupac the sufferer, Tupac the poet, Tupac the genius, and 2Pac the gangsta rapper. I have noted his connection to the black revolutionary tradition; his religious nature; the positive messages in his songs; Tupac as a Romantic artist who suffered in order to bring his message to the people; and his literacy, which makes him a poet representative of the hip-hop intelligentsia. His multifaceted and chameleon-like (some exaggeratedly say schizophrenic) nature allows for political reading, religious reading, academic reading, and a quasi-Romantic reading by journalists, academics, and fans who wish to frame him within particular narratives. The prevalence of his image in films (*Juice, Poetic Justice, Above the Rim*) and television (on MTV and BET, as well as in interviews and footage of his many court cases) adds to this cultural status. The idea of the mythic narrative has always been important to society, and the life and lyrics of Tupac have provided ample material to elevate him to mythic status in the rap music and hip-hop worlds. Perhaps the most telling physical symbol that Tupac has achieved a level of heroic immortality is the seven-foot-high gold statue that now stands at the Tupac Amaru Shakur Center for the Performing Arts in Georgia.[58]

Musician Biography and the Narrative Mediation of Music Reception

The varied portrayals of Tupac Shakur summarized share two common characteristics: each facet of Tupac has rap lyrics that can be interpreted to support it, and there is an aspect of his life story that will also correspond to the particular portrayal. As Steve Jones writes regarding posthumous fame:

> To a great extent, the performer's presence, once mediated, provides sufficient material with which ongoing construction of celebrity can proceed. Consequently, in the realm of the symbolic construction of celebrity, the performer's "real" presence is only necessary insofar as the performer may provide additional grist (mediated or otherwise) to add to the potential pool of symbolic material already in the mill.[59]

Kamberelis and Dimitriadis see Tupac's biography as crucial to collective memory, a process they call "narrative mediation": "Narratives (especially cultural narratives) are centrally involved in the creation and perpetuation of remembering, especially collective remembering."[60] Knowledge of an artist's life has always had an effect on interpretation of his or her works. In the case of rap music, the artists' lives (or perceived lives) are often embedded in the recordings as intramusical discourse. More specifically, aspects of artist biography often can be found in their rap lyrics, an integral part of the intramusical discourse. This is not to say that extramusical factors such as album covers, liner notes, websites, and music videos are no longer relevant to interpretation, but within the song, there exist both sonorities and linguistic text that give rise to an identity, in combination with extramusical forces.

In "The Domestic *Gesamtkunstwerk*; or, Record Sleeves and Reception," Nicholas Cook notes that the record sleeve and the music work together, or more generally, that the "visual image and musical sound circulate indivisibly, and are consumed together."[61] In other words, the record sleeve, considered an "optional accessory" by nineteenth-century absolute music ideology, inevitably contributes to musical meaning. This applies to the liner notes, as well as existing music videos. In addition to these extramusical factors, the nineteenth-century program notes or the twentieth-century liner notes now manifest themselves as embedded in the rap lyrics: contributing just as strongly to musical meaning as these earlier examples if not more so.

This is enhanced by rap's consumption as autobiographical rather than as fictional narrative. What Kodwo Eshun refers to as the "nauseating American hunger for confessional biography" is satisfied in many rap lyrics, interviews, music videos, and films.[62] Perhaps Sontag puts it best when she writes of the desire to read writers' journals: "It is the author naked which the modern audience demands, as ages of religious faith demanded a human sacrifice."[63] She continues that "we are interested in the writer's soul because of the insatiable modern preoccupation with psychology, the latest and most powerful legacy of the Christian tradition of introspection."[64] In addition, we have not escaped the Romantic assumption that the composer's life is embedded in the notes he or she writes (or in this case, the rap's lyrical content). To listeners, this is an authentic ("coming from the heart") musical expression of the life of the artist.

While these postmortem recontextualizations in hip-hop most overtly involve the creative task of placing previously recorded raps with a new musical complement, this practice concurrently forces a recontextualization of interpretation on the part of the listener. The sometimes unavoidable influence of perceived artist biography (or biographical mediation) affects audience reception of the text, as well as of the musical structures. In other words, after Tupac's murder (or Cobain's suicide, or Lennon's assassination), we listen to Tupac in a new context, influenced by new media discourse that elevates him to iconic status. It is hardly convincing to state that listening to a recording of Tupac in 1995 is the same as listening to the same recording in 1997. Or to use a quote from another artist's biography: "Cobain commits suicide, a suicide which gives his anguished lyrics a new *frisson*."[65] Or consider the change in audience interpretation after the death of Karen Carpenter:

After Karen's death, songs such as this ["When It's Gone"] were often reread in a much more complex and sympathetic light. Rather than a little girl fumbling for the words to express her loss, she became instead a deeply introspective and psychologically complex artist. . . . After Karen's death, much of the Carpenters' work was revived within the cultural memory because suddenly Karen had an artistic depth not attributed to her in life.[66]

This rereading of and recontextualization of interpretation of Cobain's and Carpenter's music illustrate precisely my point: extramusical biography, as a type of narrative mediation, has a profound effect on the way we hear music.

Postmortem Sampling: Definition and Examples

Culturally speaking, borrowing the voice of a deceased hip-hop artist seems less conspicuous than using artists from other genres. Using a Notorious B.I.G. rap seems to be more in concert with the borrowing ethos of hip-hop than it would if another genre that promotes the cult of originality used the voice of Kurt Cobain or Elvis Presley as extensively. Pragmatically speaking, one reason is that it is easier to mould a rap than a melody to a new song or sampled beat, but also the practice is part of hip-hop's tradition of digitally sampling and borrowing sounds. Thus, when the voice of a deceased rapper is used in a new context, the voice (the timbre of the flow and its nexus of signifieds), the semantic parameters of the text itself, and the musical features of the beat/flow interaction all provide meaning.

Another reason why postmortem sampling in hip-hop seems less conspicuous than in other genres is that the use of multiple voices/collaborators on one hip-hop track is not uncommon. The Sugar Hill Gang, Run-DMC, N.W.A., and the Wu-Tang Clan are only a few of the well-known examples of commercially successful groups that have multiple MCs, not to mention the number of single-MC albums that include a plethora of guest artists. The MC persona or the famous producer can successfully coexist with other MCs or producers on the same album. In other words, to use another person's voice (dead or alive) is aligned with the already existing collaborative ethos in hip-hop (including its intertextual traditions that lie at the heart of this book).

A third reason for rap's hospitality to postmortem sampling has to do with traditions of DJing and bootleg mixtapes in rap music. Hip-hop's foundational use of two turntables has allowed the beat-and-flow dichotomy to be mixed from the earliest days of the genre. While one record could be used for its breakbeat, the other record could have an a cappella rap, creating an infinite number of combinations of beat and flow. This same concept could be applied in the form of bootleg mixtapes. Though bootlegs are common to many genres of music, this DJ concept of beat and flow as separate parts of the "puzzle" has produced tapes doctored to feature artist's raps over beats with which the artist did not originally rap. As technology made it more common for people to have studios at home, the process became easier. After Tupac died, there was a slew of bootleg mixtapes out on the underground market, varying in quality but nevertheless in high demand (early posthumous mixtape titles included *Makaveli 2 and 3, Pac 4 Ever: Last Messages,* and *The Last Words of Tupac Shakur*).[67] It is important to note, therefore, that the commercial releases I discuss are part of the DJing and mixtape phenomena; Jay-Z's and Nas's sampling of the voices of Tupac and Biggie, for example, only produced legal versions of existing practices.

Before presenting examples of the postmortem sampling of Tupac and Biggie, it is worth explaining precisely what I mean by the term *postmortem sampling*. Postmortem sampling is the digital sampling of the voice or image of an artist after he or she has died, in a new context. The artist now has an aura or mystique, perhaps regaining the aura lost in mechanical reproduction. Though many pop music figures have some element of aura that accompanies celebrity and fame, the artist as spirit seems to trump more earthly beings or at least to penetrate the culture differently. Though the artist mystique is difficult to measure quantitatively, I would use the measuring stick of cultural consciousness (visibility in the "public eye") to gauge the extent of an artist's aura. It is crucial to this phenomenon that the sampled artist(s), and their aura, be recognized.

The other important aspect of postmortem sampling is the authenticity that comes from using a genuine recording of the artist. Postmortem sampling does not include Elvis impersonators, because though they borrow a style, it is not an image of the real Elvis.[68] One could mimic a dance step or two from Gene Kelly in *Singing in the Rain*, but it would not be "authentic" unless it were actually the filmic image of him, as his image has been used, manipulated by computers, to breakdance to a remixed version of "Singing in the Rain" for a Volkswagen Golf commercial. It is one level to imitate, parody, or allude to the artist; postmortem sampling is at the level of direct quotation, even if the quote is manipulated to a certain extent. The closest thing to a literary analogy would be if one were writing something and, in order to quote a given author, made a copy of his or her quote in his or her *actual handwriting*. Perhaps this is why Cobain's journals and Tupac's poetry books are published in their own handwriting, giving the sense of unmanipulated authenticity. In this age of recording, our idea of authenticity reaches the level of the recorded voice and image. Because of digital technology, recordings can be easily manipulated, an ethical issue for many but tangential to their definition. The key to postmortem sampling is the authority and aura from the actual recording (whether it be sound or image) used in the updated version or hypertext. Seeing *how* the use of mystique is framed in postmortem sampling is the focus of the rest of the chapter. First, however, I would like to illustrate my point with a few musical examples of postmortem borrowing.

One of the highest-selling, most acclaimed, and most critiqued albums of 1991 was Natalie Cole's *Unforgettable: With Love*. It capitalized on the connection with Cole's famous father, Nat King Cole, featuring the songs he made famous, such as "Route 66," "Mona Lisa," "Smile," and "Nature Boy." The hit single from the album was a duet of "Unforgettable" Cole performed with her father; producer David Foster mixed her father's old recording of the song with Natalie's newly sung performance. Any potential hostility toward inauthenticity seemed to be absent in media reception, presumably because of the recording's "family moment" nature. The music video, directed by Steve Barron, juxtaposes a set of present live images, Natalie Cole singing, with images of the past, her father in black and white singing on television. There is a dialogue here, of nostalgia and of past and present fused together in music. The album won the Grammy for Album of the Year and was one of the first instances of showing the possibilities of studio manipulation to the imaginations of popular music fans. Rather than being critiqued for the lack of authenticity in the "duet," the single was a novelty that the fans could feel they were "in on."

One of the main selling points of the 1995–96 *Beatles Anthology* three-volume CD collection was that the release contained new material, a Beatles "reunion" of sorts, because the three members alive at the time had recorded songs from old John Lennon demos. Two such singles were released, each with a music video, "Free as a Bird" on the first volume of the *Anthology* and "Real Love" on the second. Gary Burns's "Refab Four: Beatles for Sale in the Age of Music Video" notes the Beatles' "quasi-religious" function, as well as aspects of the band that help give them mythological status (such as the magical nature of the *Magical Mystery Tour* and *Yellow Submarine* films and the drugs and mysticism of their Indian influences).[69] The Beatles *Anthology* and its music videos use postmortem sampling as tribute and history at the same time, particularly "Free as a Bird," which goes though the Beatles' lifespan in a flying bird's-eye-view collage of images. A similar reunion was constructed for the 1995 Queen album *Made in Heaven*, though Queen's lead singer, Freddie Mercury, had been dead for three years.

Other digital duets that involve portmortem sampling include Lauryn Hill with Bob Marley on "Turn Your Lights Down Low," on *Chant Down Babylon* (1999); Celine Dion with Frank Sinatra on a version of "All the Way"; and Tony Bennett with Billie Holiday for "God Bless the Child" on Bennnett's album *Tony Bennett on Holiday* (1997), which won a Grammy for Best Traditional Pop Performance.[70] Digital duets can also include instrumental soloists, such as soprano saxophonist Kenny G on an updated version of Louis Armstrong's "What a Wonderful World," a duet that received much criticism in the jazz world, most vociferously from guitarist Pat Metheny.[71]

Whether it is Natalie Cole recording with her father, the spirit of Elvis in Vegas in a ZZ Top video, or John Lennon's demo resurrected, each case exemplifies postmortem sampling. And in many cases, the memorial project becomes more than just tribute, homage, or pastiche; the aura of the postmortem artist can be used to the benefit of the sampling artist. The construction of a postmortem identity, in this case the rapper as martyr or saint, constructs the existing rap voice as relic. The meanings located in the voice signify aspects of artists' "biographies," their images and identities.

The power of the human voice to arouse emotion may suggest why using the voice of an artist may be more powerful than simply using an image. The voice has been theorized extensively in film theory and in popular music studies, the latter often citing Roland Barthes's influential "The Grain of the Voice": "The 'grain' is the body in the voice as it sings, the hand as it writes, the limb as it performs."[72] Michel Chion, in *The Voice in Cinema*, notes that Lacan placed the voice "in the ranks of '*objet (a)*,' these *part objects* which may be fetishized and employed to 'thingify' difference.'"[73] And the earliest scientific writings on the phonograph reasoned that speech had now become immortal; recordings had the ability to transcend death.[74]

Jason Toynbee writes of the voice as central in popular music as "the building block of musical possibility."[75] And Marshall, writing about Bob Dylan, says that the meaning of Dylan's songs is not "in the words" but "in the voice" and that great singers have authoritative voices.[76] These voices have distinct personalities that contribute to their popularity and recognizability. Marshall's observation regarding the "authoritative voice" in popular music is important to the rapping as well as the singing voice, as great rappers can be said to have authoritative voices. Mikhail Bakhtin, in his essay "Discourse in the Novel," makes the distinction between two types of discourse that can be assimilated by another's speech: "authoritative" (e.g., reciting by heart) and "internally persuasive" (e.g., retelling in one's own words). In postmortem sampling the voice of a famous artist seems an intensification of the "authoritative word," a word that is connected to the past with its authority already attached. Bakhtin's authoritative discourse, in the context of the novel, is useful here, as Bakhtin writes that it "demands, so to speak, not only quotation marks but a demarcation even more magisterial, a special script, for instance."[77] Borrowing in the digital era means that a magisterial script is not necessary to convey the voice's authoritative discourse; the words are simply re-presented as they were spoken in the past.[78]

In addition to the voice signifying the authoritative figure speaking, the voice can symbolically represent a number of places, eras, genres, or other ideas. For one, the voice could represent a specific place and time, in the case of Tupac the early-to-mid-1990s West Coast rap world. But on another level, the postmortem voice is able to transcend time and place because it presently belongs to neither, an *acousmêtre* that takes on a ghostly presence in the right context.[79]

It is the authenticity and authority of the recorded voice (with its extramusical associations, connotations, and resonances) that become a symbol of the postmortem mystique that Tupac Shakur and the No-torious B.I.G. have attained within rap culture. They simultaneously represent nostalgia for a specific place-time and a transcendent, almost sublime status. The status of iconic artists who die young is formed by a synergistic process; the symbolic immortality of posthumous fame is the product of numerous elements greater than the sum of its individual contributions.

In the following examples, the voices of Tupac and Biggie, recogniz-able by fans, provide symbolic presence while contributing to new iden-tities. It is the distinctive sound of the borrowed and borrowing artists' delivery (their "flow"), their biographies as narrative mediator (including image, raps, media), musical aspects of the "beat," and the act of inter-preting them that give rise to these new meanings.

Jay-Z's "A Dream" and Nas's "Thugz Mansion": A Comparison of Postmortem Sampling

The third official posthumous 2Pac album, the double album entitled *Better Dayz* (2002), includes two versions of a track entitled "Thugz Mansion." The song is about a utopian place that exists beyond the after-life, a place where Tupac can escape the hardships of life. The version of the track on the second CD (called "Thugz Mansion—7 Remix") is what could be characterized as fairly typical of Tupac's brand of hip-hop: it contains a synthesized hip-hop beat produced by Seven Aurelius (produced by Johnny Jackson in the original sessions) with guitar and keyboard; it includes three verses by Tupac and a chorus sung by Anthony Hamilton. But the beat to the "Thugz Mansion" that ends the first disc (called "Thugz Mansion—Nas Acoustic") is drastically different from anything Tupac had ever recorded: the beat includes only an acoustic guitar, as played by Michael "Fish" Herring. There is, in fact, no drum track at all, only the guitar. Produced by Herring and Claudio Cueni, the chorus features a small male choir, sung with close harmonies and overdubbed by J. Phoenix. MCing in the second verse, instead of Tupac, is well-established New York rapper Nas (Nasir Jones). His rap mourns the recent passing of his mother, Anne Jones: "My love goes to Afeni Shakur / Cause like Anne Jones, she raised a ghetto king in a war / And just for that alone, she shouldn't feel no pain no more / 'Cause one day we'll all be together, sipping heavenly champagne" (2:11–2:20). He makes comparisons between himself and Tupac, simultaneously placing himself within the same utopia described by 2Pac and the same canonical space.

The sound of "Thugz Mansion—Nas Acoustic" is worth noting. It is almost as if the instruments used, only voice and acoustic guitar, produce an "Unplugged" aesthetic that could be interpreted, given the postmortem context, as the sonic construction of a utopian heaven.[80] This image of heaven described by Tupac is strikingly similar to the heaven portrayed by Tupac in the "I Ain't Mad at Cha" video, as his rap includes canonical figures in African American culture (e.g., Malcolm X, Billie Holiday, Marvin Gaye). Furthermore, not having some sort of drumbeat makes it extremely conspicuous in its genre. The Seven Aurelius "remix" version uses a more densely layered effect, received as a more "authentic" Tupac beat, something that one could dance to or that at least could accompany a public space. The "acoustic" version would not be something traditionally played in a club or any typical public setting. It is asking to be listened to closely (as opposed to as background or foreground party music). The paucity of instrumentation and the lack of layering give priority to the vocals and the message that Tupac presents.[81] The acoustic guitar, in the words of Philip Auslander (from Baudrillard), represents

Example 4.1: Transcription of 2Pac, "Thugz Mansion—7 Remix"

Rhythmic strumming over this basic chord progression

Example 4.2: Transcription of 2Pac/Nas, "Thugz Mansion— Nas Acoustic"

a "Sign of the Real," representative of an authentic live performance.[82] The distinction between these two beats, both on the *Better Dayz* album, seems to suggest the difference between music for a private space versus music for a public space.

Rapper Nas (Nasir Jones) used the "Thugz Mansion" acoustic version beat on his album *God's Son*, released a month after *Better Dayz*, on

December 17, 2002. Instead of his MC persona "Nas" for this album, he used his real name, Nasir Jones. The cover of the album shows him from the waist up, with no shirt on (fig. 4.5 below). The use of his real name and the seminudity on the album cover again present an authenticity of intimacy, suggesting Sontag's notion that the "author naked" is what the audience demands, both literally and metaphorically.[83] As in the acoustic version on *Better Dayz*, the use of acoustic guitar also plays on a cultural reference to intimacy on the *God's Son* version. The main difference between the "Thugz Mansion" on *God's Son* and "Thugz Mansion—Nas Acoustic" is that, on the former, Nas replaces Tupac's opening lines and

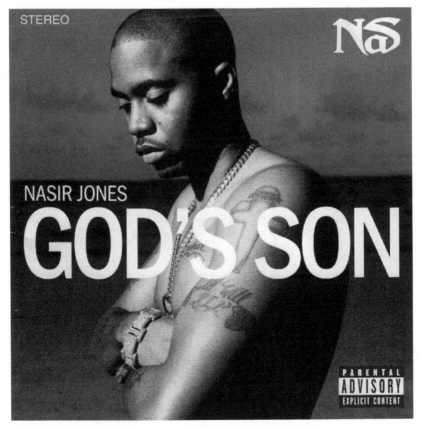

Figure 4.5: Nas, *God's Son*, cover (Ill will/Columbia, 2002)

first verse with a completely new rap from himself. This difference in framing the track affects its aesthetic effect: on *Better Dayz*, the song form becomes |Tupac intro| |Tupac verse 1| |Nas verse 2| |Tupac verse 3|, and on *God's Son*, the scheme is |Nas intro| |Nas verse 1| |Tupac verse 2| |Nas verse 3|, with the chorus from Phoenix between the verses on both versions.

Nas's exchange of the first verse and intro with his own quickly changes the implied ownership of the song. While the acoustic guitar and Tupac's verse act as a memorial structure, Nas's opening to the song without reference to Tupac makes it his. Instead of the original Tupac intro, "Shit, tired of getting shot at / Tired of getting chased by the police and arrested / Niggaz need a spot where we can kick it / A spot where we belong" (0:10–0:16), we now have Nas: "I want you to close your eyes and envision the most beautiful place in tha world / if you in the hood, the ghetto street corner, come on this journey, the best journey, it's a mansion / acres of land, swimming pools and all that, check it out" (0:13–0:33). Whereas Tupac was looking for a place to end his suffering, Nas's opening defines Nas as the storyteller. Through narration, this becomes Nas's song.

The one verse of Tupac that Nas decides to use is the third one from the "Thugz Mansion—7 Remix," which becomes the second verse of "Thugz Mansion—Nas Acoustic" on both *Better Dayz* and *God's Son*. It is in the aforementioned verse that his narration is from heaven (again, an aural complement to the visual imagery of his "I Ain't Mad at Cha" music video):

> Dear momma don't cry, your baby boy's doin good
> Tell the homies I'm in heaven and they ain't got hoods
> Seen a show with Marvin Gaye last night, it had me shook
> Drinking peppermint Schnapps with Jackie Wilson and Sam Cooke
> Then some lady named Billie Holiday sang
> Sittin there kickin it with Malcom, 'til the day came. . . .
> Just think of all the people that you knew in the past that passed on
> They in heaven, found peace at last
> Picture a place that they exist, together

There has to be a place better than this, in heaven
So right before I sleep, dear God, what I'm askin
Remember this face, save me a place, in thug's mansion.
    "Thugz Mansion (7 Remix)," *Better Dayz*, 2:35–3:20
    "Thugz Mansion (Nas Acoustic)," *Better Dayz*, 2:45–3:29
    "Thugz Mansion (N.Y.)," *God's Son*, 1:40–2:23

Following this verse from Tupac is the third verse from Nas. At this point, he is no longer narrator or storyteller but has now included himself in the suffering: "Cuz I feel like my eyes saw too much sufferin' / I'm just 20 some odd years, I done lost my mother" (3:07–3:11). Both the death of his mother and his highly publicized feud with rapper Jay-Z were elements of his biography known to fans, the feud played up in the media and in songs from both artists.

In addition to placement, the "heaven verse" in Nas's album is different in one other crucial respect: Tupac's vocals are doubled as two separately recorded layers. One has to be knowledgeable of Tupac's behaviour in the studio for a greater understanding of this: he often went into the recording booth with his written rap and would record it twice or three times to create a layered effect. Shock G (Greg Jacobs) told this anecdote about Tupac in the studio:

He's gasping for air, he's got a joint in his hand and he was smoking weed and cigarettes and Newports all night. So he's missing words here and there. So the way he would do it was like a dotted line principle. When he would gasp for air and miss a line, on this track, maybe it caught that word. So he would triple his vocals to make sure every word was said.[84]

Ta-Nehisi Coates writes, "From 1993's *Strictly 4 My N.I.G.G.A.Z.* to 1996's *All Eyez On Me*, he would hit the track with his voice perpetually doubled over and in perfect time with the beat, stressing syllables until they bled."[85] Another observation in the studio from 1994 is recalled by journalist dream hampton: "Tupac likes to add effects to his vocals: Chuck D-style reverbs and echoes that give his voice that godly quality."[86] This effect can be utilized in these memorial recordings to evoke a sense

Song Title	Thugz Mansion—Remix	Thugz Mansion—Nas Acoustic	Thugz Mansion (N.Y.)
Artist Album Producer	2Pac *Better Dayz* (2002)—Disc 2 Seven Aurelius	2Pac *Better Dayz* (2002)—Disc 1 Michael Herring and Claudio Cueni	Nasir Jones *God's Son* (2002) Michael Herring and Claudio Cueni
Song Form	Intro: 2Pac Verse 1: 2Pac Verse 2: 2Pac Verse 3: 2Pac (heaven)	Intro: 2Pac Verse 1: 2Pac Verse 2: Nas Verse 3: 2Pac (heaven)	Intro: Nas Verse 1: Nas Verse 2: 2Pac (heaven) Verse 3: Nas

TABLE 4.1. Comparison of Three "Thugz Mansion" Versions

of omnipresence and a "larger-than-life" quality. Tupac's voice doubled, contrasted against Nas's single track in this context, creates the distinction between an earthly voice and one with more aura (a "sonic halo").

This was not the first time Nas had used the voice of Tupac for one of his singles. In the song "Ether" from the 2001 album *Stillmatic* (which is a brutal comeback against Jay-Z's "Takeover"), Nas samples a slowed-down 2Pac saying "Fuck Jay-Z" (from "Fuck Frienz" on *Until the End of Time*) three times before Nas commences his rap. Nas states later in the song, "Who's the best? Pac, Nas and Big." (Jay-Z evokes a similar canon in 1997 in his song "Where I'm From": "I'm from where niggas pull ya' card . . . And argue all day about who'se the best MC: Biggie, Jay-Z, or Nas?") When Nas calls on Tupac to aid with the "diss" (as in disrespect) track and puts himself within the canon between two hip-hop martyrs— and when 2Pac raps with Nas—it is not the 1996 bodily Tupac as collaborator, but rather the transcendent, resurrected, and immortal Tupac as symbol that Nas uses. Tupac is an (unwilling) ally to Nas, and using Tupac on *God's Son* the following year strengthens such an alliance.[87] The implicit assumption when two rappers perform on the same single is that they are allies of some sort; the gang mentality of gangsta rap seems to promote this idea. In addition, reverence toward Tupac by Nas could represent acknowledgment of the canon of historical figures within rap's culture and help define it. According to Todd Boyd, Nas is said to have a tendency to "embrace history at the cost of all else,"[88] which is part of a larger self-conscious historicism in hip-hop (see chap. 1). Both "Thugz

Mansion" and "Ether" use the iconic symbol of Tupac to give legitimacy to a rapper concerned with his own place in the rap music canon.

Turning to Jay-Z: the first track from his *The Blueprint 2* (2002) is entitled "A Dream." In the song, he recounts a conversation he had with the Notorious B.I.G. in a recent dream, which includes a chorus sung by B.I.G.'s former wife Faith Evans.[89] The second verse of "A Dream" is the opening rap of Notorious B.I.G.'s "Juicy" from his debut album *Ready to Die* (1994), but with a new beat (produced by Kanye West). Though both Jay-Z and Nas utilize postmortem sampling for the second verse, unlike the case of Nas's "Thugz Mansion," Jay-Z uses a rap fragment that would have been known by all Notorious B.I.G. fans: "Juicy" was the lead single of his debut album *Ready to Die,* a single that debuted at number 5 on the Billboard rap chart and received heavy radio and music video rotation.[90] The single and album received a tremendous amount of press at the time for shifting the focus back on New York after many years of California rap dominance; "Juicy" would have been deeply engrained in the consciousness of listeners.[91]

While 2Pac has arguably received more attention in the wider mainstream, Notorious B.I.G. has received a tremendous amount of respect within hip-hop communities for his skills as rapper.[92] Accounts of his studio practices recall his ability to freestyle his lyrics and to rap material without having to write anything down.[93] While borrowing in hip-hop is primarily known for sampling breakbeats, the voice of Notorious B.I.G is often sampled by other rappers, before and after his death (examples include Lil' Kim, Method Man, Smitty, Big Pun, and Bossman).[94] One writer comments that "that unmistakable voice coupled with a gut busting wit has made Biggie as sample-able as any break."[95] Like the use of Tupac, the use of Biggie's voice can signify a number of things, depending on the specific narratives that mediate one's listening experience: representing supreme rap skills, East Coast rap's return to prominence, mid-1990s rap culture, or Biggie himself as a canonical figure in rap history. Notorious B.I.G. is certainly in an elite canon of "great rappers," and the tragedy of his death mediates the reception of his voice, mutually influencing those who sample his voice and his own posthumous reputation.

Jay-Z (and producer Kanye West) uses the first verse from "Juicy" as the second verse of "A Dream." Its musical features largely characterize the song as a rap lament: its repeated, descending tetrachord ostinato and the presence of a female voice facilitate expressions of mourning within the song. The lament, which became common in Baroque opera, was, as *Grove Music Online* defines it, "usually, a vocal piece based on a mournful text, often built over a descending tetrachord ostinato."[96] These four chords would be in a minor key and follow the progression i–VII–VI–V. (The classic example is "Dido's Lament" from Purcell's *Dido and Aeneas*.) Susan McClary has mentioned this type of chord progression as a pattern "deeply inscribed in our cultural memories,"[97] discussing the pattern in reference to Tupac's song "Tradin' War Stories," from *All Eyez on Me*. She notes that the progression in the song (i–VII–VI) has "no sense of arrival," considering that it never finishes the pattern to the dominant. ("the point of relative stability," as McClary calls it). It always swiftly moves back to the i chord from the VI. McClary concludes, "The power and the cultural memory of these patterns is harnessed and with that truncation of it every time, there's a sense that we cannot grieve properly within this music. That we're constantly flipped back to the beginning."[98] This particular interpretation could partly be influenced by Tupac's postmortem identities, because one potential problem theorizing its association with grieving is that the song comes from an album recorded and released when Tupac was still alive.

McClary's contention, however, works much better for Jay-Z's "A Dream." In Kanye West and Jay-Z's construction of a lament, their tribute to the dead is intertwined with encouragement of mourning or at least of an emotional response. It is important to note here that the original "Juicy" is actually in a major key (sampling Mtume's "Juicy Fruit"), and "A Dream" is in a more common (for rap at this time) minor key. Though the song is not a typical Baroque lament in the sense of a descending tetrachord ostinato, its progression is cyclical and centers on the first three descending chords of a lament. The difference lies in the fourth chord, which returns to the VII. In other words, instead of the Baroque lament's i-VII-VI-V, the progression goes as follows: i-VII-VI-VII. Though this progression never reaches the dominant, it is possible to "grieve properly" in the tribute, not only because the VII often acts in place of a dominant in popular music in minor modes but also because there are enough lament structures in place that encourage mourning: the song uses a descending bass line, repeated ostinato, strings (particularly the cello, though synthesized), and female vocals from B.I.G.'s widow (particularly vocal "wailing" and mournful "ohs" throughout the beat of the song, in addition to her singing "Was it all a dream?" in the chorus). In addition to the fragment from his popular single "Juicy," there are plenty of musical codes of mournfulness that contribute to the song as a rap lament.[99] James Porter writes that "the ritual character of laments embodies notions of transitions to another state or world and the possibility of symbolic renewal,"[100] and both "A Dream" and "Thugz Mansion" seem to also serve this function: to suggest musically the transition into immortality.

As in the case of Nas's "Thugz Mansion (N.Y.)," a distinction is made between the voice of the deceased artist and that of the current recording artist. Reverb and echo are added to B.I.G.'s voice, which are not present in the original recording of "Juicy," digitally creating the aura of symbolic

Example 4.3: Transcription of Jay-Z, "A Dream"

immortality. Also, the tempo is slightly slower than that of the original ("Juicy" originally at 93–94 BPM and "A Dream" at 86 BPM). Heavy echo on the words "Starski" and "good," of "it's all good," fills the space between rap phrases. Both Tupac and B.I.G. are digitally manipulated in the studio to become larger than life, in some ways analogous to the use of the "slapback delay" echo effect for Elvis on his recordings for Sun Records.[101] As Richard Middleton writes in the context of blues recordings, "The link between disembodied voice (as in echo, for example) and supernatural power is an anthropological commonplace, are totemic ritual masks designed to enable the actor to represent godlike authority not only visually but also vocally."[102] Like Nas, Jay-Z contrasts his own voice with the reverb and echo of B.I.G. (similar to church acoustics), sonically representing the heavenly qualities of a hip-hop saint.

The layering of the track is also worth noting in "A Dream": it is significantly denser than "Thugz Mansion—Nas Acoustic" or B.I.G.'s original "Juicy." Jay-Z/West's version includes a heavy drum beat, along with overdrive-effect guitars, guitars playing arpeggiated chords, record scratching, and synthesized piano and 'cello. Its key is somewhere between f#m and gm, lying between two tonal worlds.[103] Midway through each of the two verses, through the sudden omission of overdrive and arpeggiating guitars, the piano becomes more prominent. The voice of B.I.G. along with the piano line invokes the past, utilizing the "romantic" reference of the piano to evoke emotion. One journalist describes the guitar chords as "somber" and notes "Faith Evans's impassioned vocals supplying the dramatic backdrop."[104] Another reviewer writes:

> Kanye ditches his trademark soul sound for this tribute to Mr. Frank White [Notorious B.I.G.], instead opting for an epic-sounding apocalyptic jawn with full-on ominous piano, bomb-boogie bass, distorted guitar and some sick Premier-type scratching courtesy of the ROC's [Jay-Z] other super-producer, Just Blaze.[105]

The layering adds to the "epic-sounding" quality, along with the reverb and echo added to B.I.G.'s voice. If the acoustic guitar in "Thugz Mansion" invokes intimacy, then the beat of "A Dream" suggests urgency. The beat, with its heavy layering, is what contributes to the song's descriptions as "somber," "dramatic," "epic-sounding," and "apocalyptic." Both the musical structures of mourning and Biggie's postmortem narrative contribute to these song descriptions.

It is noteworthy that the song only contains two verses, one from Jay-Z and one from Biggie. The scratching, prominent during the last double chorus (2:59), samples B.I.G.'s first phrase "It was all a dream" (though the scratching and the phrase occur throughout the song). The scratching could evoke a similar nostalgia that Biggie had for the 1980s, as scratching was then a prominent feature of the rap mainstream. Even more so, the way the scratches are used, in this instance, evokes the evanescence of Biggie's voice. The scratches over the double chorus use Biggie's voice but chop it up to the point where it becomes unrecognizable. It shortens to one syllable ("all"), and as the scratches repeat this syllable in a regular rhythm, its pitch descends (an effect similar to the batteries dying during boom box playback, causing the tape to slow down and the pitch to lower). Just like the dream Jay-Z describes, Notorious B.I.G. returns for a fleeting moment, only for us to be reminded that he is only here in spirit. As the beat finishes after the double chorus, Jay-Z ends by repeating the last few lines of his first verse a cappella:

> I see I said, jealousy I said
> Got the whole industry mad at me I said
> Then B.I. said, "Hov' remind yourself
> Nobody built like you, you designed yourself"
> I agree I said, my one of a kind self
> Get stoned every day like Jesus did
> What he said, I said, has been said before
> "Just keep doin' your thing," he said, say no more. (3:45–4:11)

Jay-Z's final verse, with no accompaniment whatsoever, becomes an exposing gesture perhaps even more intimate than Nas with acoustic guitar. Furthermore, the repetition of this verse gives it greater focus, and after the voice of Biggie fades into nothingness (along with the music), Jay-Z is the last man standing.

Form	"A Dream"
Chorus	Faith Evans (B.I.G.'s widow)
Verse 1	Jay-Z
Chorus	Faith Evans
Verse 2	Notorious B.I.G. "Juicy"
Chorus	F.E. with scratching and strings
Verse 3	Jay-Z (a cappella), lyrics from verse 1

TABLE 4.2. "A Dream" Song Form

In recounting the dream he had of Notorious B.I.G., Jay-Z raps of B.I.G. as mentor, not so much giving advice as providing authoritative approval of his career ("'Just keep doin' your thing,' he said, say no more"). Like Nas, Jay-Z also speaks of his own suffering ("Got the whole industry mad at me . . . Get stoned every day like Jesus did"). When the line "It was all a dream" is exclaimed on the chorus, Biggie's voice and Jay-Z's say it together (with added echo on Biggie's voice), making even more explicit the presentation of an alliance between these two rappers. And just as in the example of "Thugz Mansion (N.Y.)" on *God's Son*, Jay-Z's raps bookend himself in relation to Biggie. This places the deceased artist as the emotional climax of the song. Jay-Z, in a manner akin to Nas's implied ownership, has the first word and the last.

Conclusion

Both Nas and Jay-Z use the voices of Tupac and Biggie, respectively, as tribute but also as an appeal to authority to reinforce their own status as dominant rappers. As Jay-Z raps on Missy Elliot's "Back in the Day," "Post-Biggie and 'Pac I gotta hold down the city,"[106] many rappers invoke these names, creating a number of effects: as boasting, as attempting to include oneself in the canon, and as reinforcing key events in the history of hip-hop culture. These voices function as powerful relics, a reference to a "higher" figure with symbolic immortality. Nas and Jay-Z also immortalize Tupac and the Notorious B.I.G. to a further extent by surrounding their rhymes with lamenting soundscapes; at the same time Nas and Jay-Z immortalize themselves in association with a canon of great rappers, a canon formed before their tributes but nevertheless made more powerful by their inclusion. The strong sense of historical identity and the frequency of musical borrowing in hip-hop help to facilitate such instances of postmortem sampling. "Thugz Mansion" and "A Dream" have a shared purpose, to use the iconic symbols of Tupac and Notorious B.I.G. to give legitimacy to rappers still concerned with their own legacies.

CHAPTER 5

BORROWING AND LINEAGE IN
EMINEM/2PAC'S *LOYAL TO THE GAME* AND
50 CENT'S *GET RICH OR DIE TRYING*

In the previous chapter I was able to demonstrate the emergence of various postmortem identities for Tupac and Notorious B.I.G., using two
examples of postmortem sampling from their contemporaries, Jay-Z
and Nas. Nas's "Thugz Mansion" and Jay-Z's "A Dream" digitally sample
the voices of 2Pac and Notorious B.I.G. respectively, creating tributes
through structures of mourning and intimacy while simultaneously including the artists in a canon of great rappers. The topic of this chapter
also involves sampling the voices of Tupac and Biggie, but by rappers
associated with the "next generation,"[1] those who rose to prominence (to
quote Jay-Z) "post-Biggie and Pac." This chapter focuses on Eminem
(Marshall Mathers III) and 50 Cent (Curtis Jackson), two rappers who
were not well-known artists in the hip-hop world until after 1997. While
tributes from Jay-Z and Nas suggest a shared canon of great contemporary rappers, later artists such as Eminem and 50 Cent participate in studio "collaborations" that suggest the construction of lineage within their
own hip-hop world. As hip-hop culture is often historically conscious,
this lineage helps to mark particular eras in gangsta/reality rap history,
as well as the "great men" who define them (the "history in rap" to which
Eminem alludes in "It Has Been Said"). The examples that follow fuse
the concept of intrageneric borrowing (chap. 1) with postmortem sampling (chap. 4) to create something greater than the sum of its parts.

   Hip-hop media discourse, in its historical self-consciousness, has categorized its world into a number of eras (e.g., "Old School," "Golden Age,"
"Gangsta Era," etc.), defined in part by the rise of iconic figures who cause

or embody stylistic shifts in image, music, topics, and so on.[2] Eminem could be said to represent the microgeneration that follows 2Pac and Notorious B.I.G. (1997–2003), and 50 Cent the generation after him (2003–), though all these rappers share generic space; they are all commercially successful rap icons who belong to the "reality rap" subgenre of rap music, as Adam Krims's genre system defines it.[3] Eminem-produced albums such as *Loyal to the Game* (2004) and singles such as 50 Cent's "Patiently Waiting" help to construct Eminem within a gangsta rap lineage, with Tupac as his ancestor, Dr. Dre his father, and 50 Cent as his heir/protégé.

The postmortem sampling of Biggie and Tupac as lineage construction forms the subject of this chapter, a phenomenon that revisits many of the themes from the previous chapter: the close proximity of death and memorial in hip-hop culture, the cultural aura attached to "Biggie and Pac" and their narrative mediation of these songs, the borrowing and collaborative ethos in hip-hop, the ease of digitally sampling the voice to be added to new musical compliments, and legal/commercial versions of already existing mixtape traditions.[4] Through extra- and intramusical discourse, Eminem and 50 Cent are integrated into a lineage, a centuries-old practice in the musical world, now updated in the digital era for hip-hop music.

Lineage and Tradition

As Robert P. Morgan reminds us, musical and artistic lineage is not a natural occurrence, but largely a social construction: "One chooses the tradition one wants, or even creates a unique tradition for one's own personal requirements. The past is not forced upon the composer, handed down by decree (or 'testament'); he shapes it himself."[5] Morgan quotes Stravinsky from *Poetics of Music:* "The artist imposes a culture upon himself and ends by imposing it upon others. That is how tradition becomes established."[6] Hip-hop culture is no exception to this, as its historical self-consciousness contributes to the constructions of continuity and tradition within the hip-hop world.[7]

While the composer is often responsible for the promotion of him-

or herself into a lineage, it is important to add that tradition is also constructed by a complex web of other influences, including fans and the media. To use one example, in 50 Cent's "Patiently Waiting," Eminem raps the lyric:

> Take some Big and some Pac and you mix 'em up in a pot
> Sprinkle a little Big L on top, what the fuck do you got?
> You got the realest and illest killas tied up in a knot
> The juggernauts of this rap shit, like it or not. (2:09–2:21)[8]

I will return to this song in more musical detail later in the chapter, but a cursory reading of the lyrics shows that Eminem is using some of hip-hop's "ancestors" (Big, Pac, and Big L) to describe and promote 50 Cent as "the realest," not an uncommon gesture in the bragging and boasting traditions of rap music.[9] A well-established rap star's promoting 50 Cent lends an aura of stardom to him as part of the exchange of symbolic capital found in mentor-student relationships.

The above lyric opens an article by Lynne D. Johnson entitled "Hip-Hop's Holy Trinity."[10] She draws a parallel between the Dr. Dre, Eminem, and 50 Cent triumvirate and the claim that Albert Ayler proffered that John Coltrane, in his song "The Father, Son, and Holy Ghost," was referring to himself as father, Pharoah Sanders as son, and Ayler as the Holy Ghost.[11] Johnson explicitly confirms the lineage by describing 50 Cent as the "next Biggie and Tupac rolled into one."[12] In this case, lineage is constructed through the lyrics of the song (intramusically) and by media articles such as "Hip-Hop's Holy Trinity" (extramusically), and the two processes mutually shape one another. Like posthumous fame, lineage is constructed through media, audience, and the works/recording themselves.[13]

The construction of musical lineage extends further than Albert Ayler and jazz.[14] Multiple musicians, for example, have mentioned blues icon Robert Johnson in their lyrics, another artist who died young and is said to exemplify his genre. His posthumous fame helps solidify his legend as one of the classic masters of the blues guitar, and he is mentioned in lyrics by Steve Earle, John Fogerty, Lucinda Williams, and Eric

Clapton, the last of whom recorded an album of his songs entitled *Me and Mr. Johnson* (2004).[15] Pete Frame's *Rock Family Trees* provides an example of constructed lineage in rock music.[16] Jazz historiography has used the trope of a continuous history of great men and stylistic periods that emphasize continuity and direct transmission between these musical generations, just as a linear trajectory purportedly pervades Western art music history, a view exemplified in the writings of Arnold Schoenberg.[17] Paula Higgins convincingly finds earlier cases of intertextuality that emphasize the student-mentor lineage (what she deems "creative patrilineage") between composers in early laments, particularly in laments for the fifteenth-century French composer Johannes Ockeghem.[18]

The most striking parallel of lineage construction to the figures in this chapter, however, may be that of Mozart, Haydn, and Beethoven. Tia DeNora's *Beethoven and the Construction of Genius: Musical Politics in Vienna 1792–1803* looks at what she sees as the construction of "serious music" around the characters of Mozart, Haydn, and Beethoven. The story begins, in many ways, with the death of a young Mozart:

> Any gap that may have been felt during Mozart's lifetime between his over-learnedness and his more popular works was quickly bridged, however, after his death. During the early 1790s and later, Mozart was hailed (initially in the Prague press) as "immortal Mozart" whose "death came too soon both for [his widow] and for Art"—as Constanze Mozart herself put it in the announcement of a benefit concert published in the *Weiner Zeitung* on 13 December 1794. . . . This posthumous rediscovery of Mozart revolved around imagery of the composer culled from his life before his genius had reached its fullest flower. The precise genus and species of that flower became the object of dispute, however, as Mozart's posthumous prestige became a resource for the reputations of potential musical heirs. *In other words, association with Mozart became a way of articulating status claims.*[19]

DeNora writes of the public and symbiotic student-teacher relationship between Beethoven and Haydn in Vienna and notes that Beethoven's forged connections with patrons and other members of society helped him to be perceived as the musical heir to Mozart. The well-known fare-well letter from Count Waldstein, as Beethoven left to study with Haydn in Vienna in 1792, asserts that "with the help of assiduous labor you shall receive Mozart's spirit from Haydn's hands."[20] DeNora writes that oth-ers were looking for the heir to the "immortal Mozart"; after Beethoven's success, people began to fabricate stories of how Mozart had actually heard a young Beethoven play, Mozart allegedly commenting that he was the "man to watch."[21] DeNora traces the creation of an identity in a spe-cific time and place, the evolution of "serious music" in late eighteenth-century Vienna. Memorial processes surrounding the premature death of Mozart provided him with an auratic symbolic immortality, prompt-ing patrons to speculate on the next great artist to take his place.

Though this example is from over two hundred years ago, it parallels the desire of current fans and journalists to find and label an "heir" to an "immortal" figure in music, as well as the apotheosis of that figure fol-lowing premature death. In *Classic Material: The Hip-Hop Album Guide*, Kris Ex writes of a post-Tupac rap world: "And even at this early date, there's no shortage of would-be heirs to the throne of Thug Immortal."[22] The digital sampling of 2Pac's and Biggie's voices contributes to the artis-tic posturing of Eminem and 50 Cent as part of a gangsta rap lineage. As the associations of Mozart, Haydn, and Beethoven helped to solidify the notion of "serious music" in Vienna, the association of Tupac Shakur, the Notorious B.I.G., Eminem, and 50 Cent constructs and reinforces par-ticular time- and place-specific identities within mainstream rap music.

Eminem's Constructed Identities

"White rapper" Eminem's rise to stardom in late-1990s media discourse emphasized the constructed lineage between him and his mentor/pro-ducer Dr. Dre, in addition to controversies surrounding his race and the misogyny and homophobia of his lyrics. Dr. Dre was featured in Eminem songs and music videos such as "My Name Is" and "Guilty Conscience," and Eminem was a guest rapper on Dr. Dre's *Chronic 2001* (1999), on "What's the Difference" and "Forgot about Dre." Early tours featured

Eminem rapping Dre's early solo hit "Nuthin' but a 'G' Thang," which would segue to Eminem's first single, "My Name Is."[23] In 1999, Eminem's MTV Music Video Awards performance debut featured a medley of "My Name Is," "Guilty Conscience," and "Nuthin' but a 'G' Thang," Eminem performing on stage with Dr. Dre and Dre's earlier protégé Snoop Dogg.[24] The relationship between the two was mutually beneficial: through Dre, Eminem was able to gain a certain level of rap credibility, and through Eminem, Dre could be in a mentor role and flaunt his longevity in a genre whose rappers had little longevity.[25] Todd Boyd writes:

> Hip hop has always been a movement interested in history, particularly its own. When considering that many rappers come and go with increased regularity, be it from poor record sales, incarceration, or in some cases, death, Dr. Dre's long tenure in the game makes him stand out. . . . He can endorse Em and provide for him the cultural credibility that would not necessarily be available to Em on his own.[26]

In the song "Crazy in Love," Eminem emphasizes the link between himself and Dre with a list of comparisons: "You're the Kim to my Marshall, You're the Slim to my Shady, the Dre to my Eminem" (2:53–2:57). Dre also mentored Eminem in music production techniques, as Eminem's own production style resembles Dre's in the heavy use of synthesizers and the utilization of "pop-style" choruses. Both artists often invoke the name of the now-iconic Tupac Shakur: Dr. Dre, on "The Watcher," states, "I ain't a thug, how much Pac in you you got?" (1:16–1:17), and Eminem, on "Soldier," raps, "I'm like a thug with a little bit of Pac influence" (2:28–2:30).[27] These references provide intertextual significations that represent an earlier rap era, one of its canonical star figures, and one of countless and often exaggerated associations that the utterance of the name "Pac" might accompany.

While Eminem's early career has been the subject of much journalistic and other discourse, I focus here on his career post-2002, the year he starred in his quasi-biopic *8 Mile*. The popularity of this film gave Eminem a certain level of legitimization in the mass media and among mainstream youth audiences.[28] Biographer Anthony Bozza writes:

As with film reinterpretations of classic literature or world history, *8 Mile* became, for those who weren't already fans, the story of Eminem. It accomplished what Eminem had been trying to do all along: show the world where he came from so that everyone would understand who he was and, maybe, why he felt the way he did. In short, it focused the story for those who couldn't see it through the music.[29]

Like Tupac Shakur, Eminem used tropes of the suffering artist, as seen in his dysfunctional trailer home life in the film and in autobiographical songs like "Cleanin Out My Closet": "Have you ever been hated or discriminated against, I have / I've been protested and demonstrated against . . . Just try to envision your momma poppin' prescription pills in the kitchen / Bitchin' that someone's always going through her purse and shit's missin' / Going through public housing systems / Victim of Munchausen's syndrome" (0:33–0:37; 3:04–3:15). And like Tupac, Eminem has frequently rapped about his mortality, such as in the opening line of the chorus to "When I'm Gone": "And when I'm gone just carry on / don't mourn, rejoice every time you hear the sound of my voice." At the end of his 2004 album *Encore*, Eminem shoots himself, mirroring the Notorious B.I.G., who stages the same gesture at the end of his first album, *Ready to Die* (1994).[30]

After *8 Mile*, Eminem produced three songs for the soundtrack to the documentary film *Tupac Resurrection* (2003). Tupac's mother, Afeni Shakur, subsequently gave him permission to use more material to create an entire 2Pac album, *Loyal to the Game* (2004). Eminem and 2Pac never met each other, as Eminem's professional career began after 2Pac's death, but Eminem has acknowledged his admiration for the rapper in a number of interviews and discussed his debt to Tupac, speaking of what he learned from him:

> There's a lot of things about Pac that stood out. Personality. I guess no matter what color you was or where you came from, you felt like you could relate to him. He made you feel like you knew him. I think that honestly, Tupac was the greatest songwriter that ever lived. He made it seem so *easy*. The emotion was there, and feeling, and everything he was

trying to describe. You saw a picture that he was trying to paint. That's what I picked up from him, making your words so vivid that somebody can picture them in their head.[31]

Notice that Eminem uses the term *songwriter,* as opposed to rapper. Using the term *songwriter* to describe Tupac invokes an authenticity from earlier folk styles that were later adapted by rock. In other words, Tupac's "author function" for Eminem differs little from ideologies of the "rock star" or "singer-songwriter." Marshall's ideological distinction between live performer and the mythical stardom of the songwriter is useful here: "The singer may be in front of us, but the songwriter is from another lifetime."[32]

Unlike Tupac, Notorious B.I.G., Jay-Z, or Nas, Eminem produces many of his own "beats."[33] Eminem has emerged as a successful producer over the years, creating a distinctive sound for himself that can be found on many albums, including his own.[34] For *Loyal to the Game,* Eminem "updates" the production to reflect his own personal style and includes raps by himself and others associated with him (50 Cent, Obie Trice, Lloyd Banks, etc.). According to one article in *Rolling Stone,* Eminem spent three days and nights in September of 2004 obsessed with making the album.[35] It is noteworthy that Eminem's own album *Encore* was released on November 16, 2004, and *Loyal to the Game* was released one month later, on December 14, 2004; two projects released one month apart, produced by the same person, will most likely share similar stylistic characteristics. As I will show, Eminem's "sonic signature" as producer adds a crucial authorial element to his collaborations.

Eminem constructs himself into a hip-hop lineage in a number of ways. The most obvious is the linkage created by rapping with his "ancestor" on record. An overt example of this is the morphing from Eminem's to 2Pac's voice on "One Day at a Time." Eminem's verse ends with "And we continue growin', one day at a time" (2:11–2:17); during this line the vocal morphing from Eminem to Tupac occurs, representing a lineage through vocal effect in the music.[36]

Perhaps not as overt a gesture, but nevertheless recognizable by rap fans, is the construction of lineage through Eminem's "sonic signature" as producer. A sonic signature, as developed in the work of Mark Gillespie, refers to the number of ways a producer or a producer's style can be identified in a recording: literally saying his or her name, recognizable sounds, rhythmic patterns, structural elements, orchestration and timbre, sound-effects, or phonographic staging.[37] Many rap fans are knowledgeable enough to identify producers' sonic identities on rap albums: star producers such as Timbaland, Kanye West, and Pharrell Williams espouse what Krims has identified as branding in recent music trends, as there often exist elements of a sonic signature recognizable by fans (and sometimes imitated by other producers), and consumers will purchase these albums based on the producer-brand.[38] Producer Scott Storch expresses the importance of creating an identifiable production style in reference to Eminem:

> People say that his music sounds the same or whatever but anybody can make a beat, the thing they need to realize is you need to create a signature beat so that every time you hear a beat you automatically think "yeah Lil Jon or Dr. Dre or Just Blaze."[39]

To demonstrate the use of elements associated with Eminem's sonic signature, I will discuss the song "Ghetto Gospel" from *Loyal to the Game*. It is worth reiterating that Eminem released his own album, *Encore*, in 2004 as well, and there are tracks that stylistically match each other on the two albums ("Drips" on *Encore* and "Hennessy" on *Loyal*, for example). For "Ghetto Gospel," Eminem samples and sequences lines from Elton John's "Indian Sunset" from the 1971 album *Madman across the Water*; the sampled material is represented by boxes around the lyrics below. The choice of song is apt for a memorial, as it tells the tale of a Native American warrior who dies in despair, knowing his tribe faces extinction at the hands of the white man. The voice of Elton John also attaches significations of mourning and loss; as mentioned in the previous chapter, John's "Candle in the Wind '97" is associated with the funeral of Princess Diana as a mass cultural event and is the best-selling single of all time (thirty-seven million copies).[40]

Elton John—"Indian Sunset"

From Madman across the Water *(1971)*

Verse A1[41]**:** As I awoke this evening with the smell of wood smoke
    clinging
    Like a gentle cobweb hanging upon a painted teepee
    Oh I went to see my chieftain with my warlance and my woman
    For he told us that the yellow moon would very soon be leaving
    This I can't believe I said, I can't believe our warlord's dead
    Oh he would not leave the chosen ones to the buzzards and the
    soldiers guns

Verse A2: Oh great father of the Iroquois ever since I was young
    I've read the writing of the smoke and breast fed on the sound of
    drums
    I've learned to hurl the tomahawk and ride a painted pony wild
    To run the gauntlet of the Sioux, to make a chieftain's daughter
    mine

Verse A3: And now you ask that I should watch
    The red man's race be slowly crushed
    What kind of words are these to hear
    From Yellow Dog whom white man fear

[Interlude 1]

Verse B1: I take only what is mine Lord, my pony, my squaw, and my
    child
    I can't stay to see you die along with my tribe's pride
    I go to search for the yellow moon and the fathers of our sons
    Where the red sun sinks in the hills of gold and the healing waters
    run

Verse B2: Trampling down the prairie rose, leaving hoof tracks in the
    sand
    Those who wish to follow me I welcome with my hands
    I heard from passing renegades Geronimo was dead
    He'd been laying down his weapons when they filled him full of lead

[Interlude 2]

Verse C1: Now there seems no reason why I should carry on
In this land that once was my land I can't find a home
It's lonely and it's quiet and the horse soldiers are coming
And I think it's time I strung my bow and ceased my senseless
running
For soon I'll find the yellow moon along with my loved ones
Where the buffaloes graze in clover fields without the sound of guns
And the red sun sinks at last into the hills of gold
And peace to this young warrior comes with a bullet hole.

"Ghetto Gospel" chorus (0:06–0:29):
(B2, line 2) Those who wish to follow me,
I welcome with my hands
(C1, line 8) And the red sun sinks at last into the hills of gold
(C1, line 9) And peace to this young warrior
(C1, line 7) without the sound of guns

The excerpt chosen for the chorus of "Ghetto Gospel" discusses the "warrior," who could be interpreted in this context as a reference to 2Pac. John's original consists of verses and no chorus, a conspicuous example in light of the songwriter's oeuvre, but in Eminem's version, the original material is sampled and sequenced into a chorus. The framing of the Elton John source material as chorus in "Ghetto Gospel" is also an important signature of Eminem's style, as manipulated large portions of pop-rock songs are used as a chorus in singles such as "Sing for the Moment," "Runnin," and "Crazy in Love." The sampling of such a large portion of material is what Gillespie terms "syntagmatic sequencing," the source unfolding temporally (with important melodic and harmonic components), as opposed to "morphemic sequencing," which organizes isolated discrete sounds.[42] The chorus is also sped up from its source tempo (John's being in e minor and Eminem's in f minor), a technique frequently used by Kanye West, but a style not as widespread when 2Pac was alive. "Ghetto Gospel"'s form is composed of intro-chorus-verse-chorus-verse-chorus-outro, and its use of contrasting verse-chorus form still stands out in rap music but is also consistent with Eminem's productions (and those of his mentor Dr. Dre). The verse uses a driving pedal point of repeated quavers, what Allan Moore calls a "driving pattern" in rock, albeit at a slower tempo than most examples from rock music.[43] This musical gesture is audible in many Eminem productions (see examples 5.1, 5.5, 5.6, and 5.7).[44]

Example 5.1—"Ghetto Gospel" (0:29–0:53)
Examples 5.2–5.4: "Driving patterns" in rock music
Examples 5.5–5.7: "Driving pattern" in other Eminem productions

Example 5.1: Transcription of 2Pac, "Ghetto Gospel"

Example 5.2: Transcription of Deep Purple, "Smoke on the Water"

Example 5.3: Transcription of Black Sabbath, "Paranoid"

Example 5.4: Transcription of Megadeth, "Symphony of Destruction"

Example 5.5: Transcription of 50 Cent, "Patiently Waiting"

Example 5.6: Transcription of The Game, "We Aint"

Example 5.7: Transcription of Eminem, "Crazy in Love"

What Gillespie calls an "abstract sound signature" is present in the emphasis on the rhythm in "Ghetto Gospel" (example 5.8) as well, perhaps not as immediately identifiable as a "discrete sound signature" (e.g., "tolling bell" sounds or Eminem's synthesizer choices) but nevertheless found in a number of his beats (including "Thug 4 Life," "Crazy in Love" in the bass above, "Mockingbird," "One Day at a Time," and Dr. Dre's "The Watcher," albeit all at different tempos and sometimes resembling the figure in example 5.9).[45]

Example 5.8   Example 5.9

The following shows the "Eminem rhythm" as abstract sonic signature:

Example 5.10: Transcription of Eminem, "It Has Been Said"

Example 5.11: Transcription of Eminem, "Runnin"

Example 5.12: Transcription of Eminem, "Mockingbird"

Example 5.13: Transcription of 2Pac, "Thug for Life"

Example 5.14: Dr. Dre, "The Watcher"

An "orchestral sonic signature" (by definition a characteristic style of orchestration) is also present, as the highly synthesized sound of Eminem's
production (largely pioneered by his mentor, Dr. Dre) includes recognizable sound patches from keyboards and drum machines.

For "Ghetto Gospel," Eminem takes as his first line of the chorus
"Those who wish to follow me I welcome with my hands," followed by
the last two lines, which constitute the musical climax of the song; but
instead of "comes with a bullet hole," he uses the last phrase from the
penultimate stanza, "without the sound of guns." The resulting last line
of Eminem's chorus reads, "And peace to this young warrior, without the
sound of guns." Those who look solely at the lyrics may be compelled to
try to discover reasons that Eminem would change "with a bullet hole"
to "without the sound of guns," since the original arguably works better
as a memorial.

For a possible answer to this, one needs to look at the harmonic
structures of the two examples. In Elton John's final verse (verse C1), the
descending harmonic progression takes on characteristics of a lament, in
concert with the semantic topic of the final verse:

Verse C1: em–D–C–G/B–am–G/B–C–D (x5)

The progression descends from a minor i chord, through a series of passing chords, to the relative goal of "a minor (iv)" before ascending back to
"e minor (i)."[46] The last line of the chorus ("peace to this young warrior
comes with a bullet hole") accompanies the progression am–G/B–C–
em, with the final e minor chord on the word "hole," which occurs on the
downbeat as the drums enter. Elton John sings a high G (G5) with the e

minor chord on the downbeat ("hole"), an octave jump from the lower G he sings on "with a bullet," and the moment occupies the position of the song's climax in terms of register and dynamic intensity. For the material to function as chorus, Eminem requires a more cyclical end phrase, hence borrowing "without the sound of guns," which accompanies the VI–VII chord pattern, ideal for repetition back to the tonic minor in this context. Below is a harmonic comparison of the two versions, and for purposes of comparative analysis, both versions are in the Eminem f minor (see Example 5.15).

Eminem has also added lower bass notes at the beginning of the two phrases in the chorus, a Db on the first Ab chord and a Db on the f minor that begins the second half of the chorus. The effect is again harmonically cyclical, making the move to f minor in the verse more grounded, toward the "focused intensity" of the one-note driving pattern on f (see example 5.1).

The musical symbolism involved in this track thus achieves a high level of complexity: the chorus uses a voice now associated with memorial; the verse features Tupac Shakur, a canonized rapper with an iconic mystique; and the beat is produced by Eminem. Though Eminem does not rap on "Ghetto Gospel," the *sound* is clearly his. "Ghetto Gospel" has a similar song structure, framing, function, orchestration, and manipulation of sample to the singles "Sing for the Moment" and "Crazy in Love." These similarities are not lost on listeners, as demonstrated in media reception of the album:

> Em is more noticeable on this album than Pac himself, as everywhere is Em, either singing a hook, rapping a verse, or just behind the boards. . . . He also proves he cannot sample without making it into some fake epic confessional, as the Elton John collabo "Ghetto Gospel" sounds much like "Sing for the Moment" and "Runnin."[47]

Another reviewer writes, "I thought I was going to be listening to 2Pac, but I was sorely disappointed because it is nothing more than another Eminem release. When Eminem was introduced to 2Pac's a cappellas for

"Indian Sunset" (transposed up a half-step):

Ab: I	V6	vi	fm: VII	VI	VII		i	VII
Ab	Eb/G	fm	Eb	Db	Eb		fm	Eb

Those who wish to follow me,   I welcome with my hands

i	VII	VI	III6
fm	Eb	Db	Ab/C

And the red sun sinks at last into the hills of gold

iv	III6	VI	i
bbm	Ab/C	Db	fm

And peace to this young warrior [comes with a bullet hole]

VI	VII
Db	Eb

[without the sound of guns]

"Ghetto Gospel" Chorus:

VI (add 9)	VII6	i	VII	VI	VII		i	VII
Ab/Db	Eb	fm	Eb	Db	Eb		fm	Eb

Those who wish to follow me,   I welcome with my hands

VI (add6)	VII	VI	III6
fm/Db	Eb	Db	Ab/C

And the red sun sinks at last into the hills of gold

iv	III6	VI	VII
bbm	Ab/C	Db	Eb

And peace to this young warrior, without the sound of guns

Example 5.15: Harmonic comparison of "Indian Sunset" and "Ghetto Gospel" this release, I believe he forgot whose album *Loyal to the Game* was, since every song sounds like something off *The Eminem Show* or his latest release *Encore*."[48] Many of the reviews did not find Eminem capable of producing beats that reflect the "real classic sound of Tupac," strongly disagreeing with the use of Elton John and Dido samples on the album and with Eminem's own rapping and singing on the album.[49]

Despite these unfavorable reviews, the album was commercially successful, reaching number 1 on the Billboard Top 200, selling one million units within three months of its release;[50] the single "Ghetto Gospel" reached number 1 in the UK. Despite this, however, the album has been perceived as a "failure" by many for what I locate as three important reasons: authenticity/originality, responses to death and mourning, and racial identity.

Most of the negative album reviews express arguments of intentionality and authenticity: Tupac was not alive when it was made, Tupac would not have liked Eminem and his crew, and other opinions that reflect and fetishize a notion of the "composer's intentions." Reviews and commentators find fault with the time stretching of 2Pac's voice (on "Ghetto Gospel" and others), though this is also common on earlier 2Pac mixtapes. Another frequent criticism is of Eminem's digital manipulation of Tupac's rap syllables to say things that he had not previously said, like referring to the year "2005" and "G-Unit," the group of rappers who are associated with 50 Cent. In hip-hop it is not uncommon to shout the year, one's name, or the names of others whom one wants to honor at the end or beginning of a rap song. But many critics seem to have a problem with Eminem's manipulating Tupac to reference those he did not even know. While this is a fair criticism with regard to historical accuracy and reflects a drive for authenticity that may privilege live performance over studio manipulations, there is a subtle irony in criticizing such manipulations within a genre that constantly digitally manipulates its source material (and whose practitioners/fans praise the practice). The notable difference, here, is that reviewers may be more angered by the use of a person's *voice* (and its associations) rather than by a drum sample or other sound. Hip-hop has thrived on using and manipulating previously existing material for three decades, but some fans now find fault with the practice when one of their own is used to the same ends.[51] This may be simply because Romantic notions of stardom have seeped into hip-hop culture (particularly with Tupac Shakur and the Notorious B.I.G.); various reviewers are using notions of authenticity found and debated in rock and other journalism but now applied to rap icons.

A second reason for the negative reviews involves cultural rituals of death and mourning. Though the use of Elton John encourages structures of mourning, the album overall is an updated 2Pac album, not a tribute per se. Previous tributes in films, books, and music videos such as "Changes" and "I Ain't Mad at Cha" (and the Jay-Z and Nas tributes discussed in chap. 4) have memorialized 2Pac and placed him in the past, but this album, with current production techniques, keeps him "alive," so to speak.[52] As Douglas J. Davies writes of ritual, "Even in secular contexts, rites are performed to locate the dead firmly in the past and in memory."[53] Because of the "updating" of 2Pac, we lose the Lacanian/ Žižekian "second death," the symbolic death that resolves the disruption caused by the first "real" death.[54] The inability to mourn 2Pac musically on this album is complicated by the fact that knowledgeable listeners *do* know that he is dead. Thus, the album may create some sort of rupture without the promise of closure or synthesis. Eminem's album does not put Tupac in the past in a traditional, ritualistic way, and this is what may make critics uncomfortable or even hostile.

Lastly, the hostility toward the album may involve an element of racial prejudice. One reviewer describes an Eminem beat on the album as a "red-neck style of music,"[55] something that less likely would be said of an African American producer. It is one thing to accept a successful white rapper, an issue highlighted in the racial debates surrounding Eminem's debut album; it is another to accept a white man into such a prominent place in gangsta rap genealogy, as heir to 2Pac. To make a parallel to lineage in another place in music history, one reason that Higgins has used the term *creative patrilineage* for fifteenth-century composers is that it emphasizes the exclusion of women at the time.[56] Eminem, as a white male, may suffer from a level of exclusionary hostility as he tries to insert himself into a primarily African American rap music lineage.

50 Cent

Another prominent figure who emerged in post-1997 gangsta rap is New York rapper 50 Cent (Curtis Jackson). Much of the hype began for 50 Cent when he was shot nine times in 2000, before his debut album on Columbia could be released. He had been featured on a number of bootlegs previously, including one underground hit in 1999 called "How to Rob," with lyrical content that insulted a number of well-known rappers. The album was shelved, and he began to have underground success with mixtapes, which caught the attention of Eminem, culminating in a joint label deal between Dr. Dre's Aftermath Records and Eminem's Shady Records. Both Dr. Dre and Eminem did not hesitate to promote their new find, and Eminem, in particular, allied his new artist with the immortal martyrs of hip-hop, telling *Rolling Stone* magazine:

> One of the things that excited me about Tupac was even if he was rhymin' the simplest words in the world, you felt like he meant it and it came from his heart. That's the thing with 50. That same aura. That's been missing since we lost Pac and Biggie. The authenticity, the realness behind it.[57]

Eminem used 50 Cent as guest rapper on a number of productions, including the *Tupac Resurrection* soundtrack and *Loyal to the Game*, and he produced a number of songs on 50 Cent's major-label debut album *Get Rich or Die Tryin'* (2003).

In the first single, "In Da Club" (produced by Dr. Dre), there is the overt recognition of a constructed mentor-student relationship among Dr. Dre, Eminem, and 50 Cent. The music video takes place at the sign-posted "Shady/Aftermath Artist Development Center," where 50 Cent is shown being conditioned in gym training, at a shooting range, and partying in a club while Dr. Dre and Eminem watch through a two-way mirror, wearing lab coats. Lynne Johnson comments on the music video for "In Da Club":

> Displaying Dre and Eminem in white coats watching the doctors from

above as they reengineer and reenergize 50 on the operation table not only symbolizes the gods watching down from the sky ideal, but also represents that in fact 50 Cent has post-human qualities.[58]

His survival from being shot was always an element of his media-disseminated biography, an important instance of the narrative mediation of his music recordings and music videos. The single has a prominent one-note-riff driving pattern (like that of "Ghetto Gospel") as a component of its basic beat (occurring at 00:59–1:52 and 2:24 to the end), played by a guitar. The synthesizer rhythm is Eminem's signature rhythm, described earlier (his "abstract sound signature," to use Gillespie's terminology), but displaced one eighth-note earlier.

Example 5.16: 50 Cent, "In Da Club"

Though this pattern is more often associated with Eminem productions, Dr. Dre and Eminem have overlapping stylistic qualities that make it difficult to differentiate between them. Lyrically, 50 Cent not only mentions his producers but also alludes to both his mentors and his gangsta rap "ancestor":

> Niggas heard I fuck with Dre, now they wanna show me love
> When you sell like Eminem, and the hoes they wanna fuck . . .
> In the hood then the ladies sayin "50 you hot"
> They like me, I want them to love me like they love 'Pac.
>
> (0:43–0:48, 1:00–1:03)

Media accounts of 50 Cent are rife with comparisons to Tupac, rather than to Dr. Dre or Eminem, citing 50 Cent's use of religious lyrics, his having been shot, the frequency of death as his lyrical topic, and his ongoing "beefs" with other artists (most prominently with rapper Ja Rule).[59] As one reviewer writes, "Like his Kevlar-wearing predecessor and idol, Tupac Shakur, 50 has charisma up the muzzle-hole"; the same reviewer also states that 50 Cent shares Tupac's work ethic, having written sixty tracks for his twenty-two song album *The Massacre* (2005).[60] A similarity is also apparent in the iconography of the rappers, as both adopt menacing postures, while flaunting their tattooed, shirtless bodies. Perhaps S. Craig Watkins sums it up best when he writes, "The marketing of 50 Cent came straight from the script that guided 2Pac's meteoric rise and tragic fall."[61] Stars often fit familiar frames: as Lee Marshall writes, "Despite the emphasis on uniqueness, stars' stories are never unique."[62] 50 Cent has noted his debt to Tupac and Biggie, writing in *Rolling Stone* that "every rapper who grew up in the Nineties owes something to Tupac";[63] he sees both Tupac and Biggie as a source of inspiration: "Sometimes I build one CD with Tupac's best songs, and one with Biggie's best songs. Then I listen and get ready to go into my next project."[64]

50 Cent's postmortem sampling of Tupac Shakur and the Notorious B.I.G. also reinforces his identity as an authentic successor to Tupac and Biggie. Two examples, "The Realest Killaz" and "The Realest Niggaz," will demonstrate this lineage construction. Using the tapes of a cappellas from Afeni Shakur, Eminem had producer Red Spyda produce a song entitled "The Realest Killaz" for the *Tupac Resurrection* soundtrack. The first line of the chorus features 50 Cent singing, "Till Makaveli returns it's all eyes on me," a possible reference to Tupac as messiah figure (referencing the cover of the Makaveli album), to the 1996 2Pac album *All Eyez on Me*, and also to 50 Cent's egotism. In the last part of the introduction, 50 Cent says, addressing rival Ja Rule:

> Tupac cut his head bald, then you wanna cut yo' head bald
> (You pussy nigga)
> Tupac wear a bandana, you wanna wear a bandana
> [2Pac singing: What do we have here now]

Tupac put a cross on his back, you wanna put crosses on yo' back
Nigga, you ain't Tupac, this is Tupac. (0:17– 0:30)
[2Pac verse begins]

The song form consists of an introduction, a Tupac verse, a chorus, a 50 Cent verse, and then a double chorus, and it is generally agreed in the rap community that the song is a response to a Ja Rule song entitled "Loose Change" (dissing 50 Cent). The beat incorporates chimes reminiscent of those in "Hail Mary" from *The Don Killuminati* (and Eminem's "The Way I Am"), including other bells, gunshot sounds, and synthesized string sounds. When interviewed about the track, 50 Cent said:

> That was me and Tupac. I took Tupac vocals, actually, the producer Red Spyda had um, produced the track around the vocals. . . . The production on the track was a little dated 'cause Pac had recorded it so long ago that we re-did the production. And it was like, exciting. I enjoy that record more than I enjoy some of my solo records because I got a chance to work with him.[65]

It is worth reflecting on his comment about the production's sounding "dated"; rather than concern himself with any sort of authenticity toward the time period in which Tupac recorded, 50 Cent and producer Red Spyda wanted to update the sound and fit 50 Cent into the equation. Just as Eminem puts his "composer voice" onto *Loyal to the Game*, Red Spyda uses a more contemporary sound, both referencing 2Pac by using his voice and "updating" the production, inserting 50 Cent in the canonical web of gangsta rap history.

In the same year, the *Bad Boys II* soundtrack contained a track entitled "The Realest Niggas" (also produced by Red Spyda), which features 50 Cent and samples raps from Notorious B.I.G.'s "NIGGAS" (originally produced by Tony Dofat), from the album *Born Again* (1999). As in "The Realest Killaz," the deceased artist opens the first verse of the rap, and 50 Cent sings the hook; Biggie raps the first two verses, and 50 Cent raps the last verse. The single, for many listeners, was an important introduction to 50 Cent, a shrewd marketing plan to include the single in a film the summer of his debut album. Coker writes of a similar version ("Niggaz") from a mixtape:

> In the summer and fall of 2002, 50 Cent generated a New York City wide street buzz more notorious than any artist since Biggie himself. So it's only fitting that the controversial Queens MC would "duet" with Big for one of his now-legendary mixtape albums. Though it recycles Big's performance on "Niggas" from *Born Again*, "Niggaz" makes a whole lot better use of it. The production from Miami-based boardsman Red Spyda is punchier, G-Unit's faux Last Poets style ad libs gleefully interact with Big, and 50 freely flaunts his outlaw-come-favored-son status.[66]

So with "The Realest Killaz," "The Realest Niggaz," and other bootlegs, from early in his commercial career, 50 Cent was heard rapping with the martyrs of hip-hop.[67] As opposed to the cases of Jay-Z and of Nas, whose tributes distance the immortalized voice by adding effects such as doubling, reverb, and echo, Red Spyda creates an authenticity with the aural illusion that 50 Cent could have been rapping in the same room with Biggie and Tupac.

50 Cent's "Patiently Waiting" contains the Eminem passage that I cited earlier in the chapter:

> Take some Big and some Pac and you mix 'em up in a pot
> Sprinkle a little Big L on top, what the fuck do you got?
> You got the realest and illest killas tied up in a knot
> The juggernauts of this rap shit, like it or not.[68]

The track was produced by Eminem, and this excerpt comes from his rap in the middle verse of the song. (50 Cent raps on verses 1 and 3.) In "Patiently Waiting," I would argue, the crux of the song, musically and lyrically, is the moment when Eminem says "Take some Big and some Pac," which accompanies the addition of another layer in the song's beat. Apart from the beeping sounds at the beginning of Eminem's rap,[69] this

Example 5.17: 50 Cent, "Patiently Waiting"

is the first point at which these higher-pitch notes are introduced in the basic beat. These notes, which match the rhythm of the flow and put emphasis on the names "Big" and "Pac," demand attention from the listener, and they are similar to the rhythmic figures in Eminem's other productions.

The new layer begins at the moment that Eminem mentions Big and Pac; in fact, the accents on the words "Big" and "Pac" correspond to the accented rhythms in the new layer. The highest pitches in the texture are in consonance with the lyric "take some Big and some Pac," and this layer strongly emphasizes its accompanying lyric, as John Sloboda has emphasized that there is a "general psychological tendency to focus on the top line of any musical texture."[70] This moment is a consonance of beat and flow that solidifies the relationship between Eminem and 50 Cent while including them in a web of slain gangsta rap artists.[71]

The examples discussed in this chapter share a number of common themes and ideas: postmortem sampling, peer reference, and elements of Eminem's "sonic signature" such as the framing and function of samples and synthesized orchestration. The acts of Signifyin(g) and intertextuality discussed in this chapter are similar to the two primary instances of Signifyin(g) in James Brown's "Superbad" as identified by David Brackett: intertextual referentiality and the repetition with variation of small musical figures.[72] These examples link with "Superbad" in that they are consistent with these frequently cited tropes of African American music making, but they are updated to reflect digital technology and the complex hybridization that occurs within more current African-based popular music identities (e.g., the "driving pattern" of rock music and the "rock star" status attributed to Tupac Shakur). And the intertextuality located in these examples constructs and reinforces notions of canon and lineage that have been apparent in artistic cultures for centuries, albeit in their own temporally and historically specific situations.

Conclusion

Zygmunt Bauman writes in *Mortality, Immortality, and Other Life Strategies* that "future immortality will grow of today's recordings. Tomorrows' immortals must first get hold of today's archives."[73] Eminem's postmortem sampling of Tupac Shakur's voice and his sonic signature on *Loyal to the Game* contribute to his artistic posturing as part of a gangsta rap lineage; his "discovery" of a rap protégé in rapper 50 Cent extends the genealogy further. Eminem-produced 50 Cent songs such as "Patiently Waiting" include a number of intertextual references to Tupac, Eminem, and Dr. Dre, forming a "constellation" of gangsta rap icons: Tupac as ancestor God, Dr. Dre as father, Eminem as star, and 50 Cent as heir/protégé. These constellations or networks include a sense of historical self-consciousness in which creative patrilineage plays a part. In the creation of a tradition, as Lois Parkinson Zamora has written in the context of fiction of the Americas, one finds a "usable past" from which to draw. For Eminem, this "usable past" is the voice of Tupac Shakur, endowed with a cultural aura and signifying a number of emotive meanings. In other words, Tupac represents a mythology, a bio-mythology (to invoke Barthes's discourse on Beethoven) signified by his voice as relic. The notion of myth here suggests a quote regarding blues musicians from Samuel Floyd's *The Power of Black Music*:

> The figures and events of African-American music making connect the individual and the group to the realm of cultural memory, to the realm of

spirit and myth. And it is myth that privileges the figures and metaphors that validate the blues musicians' music making and their place in the culture. It's all a circle.[74]

Loyal to the Game and *Tupac Resurrection* arguably inform us about Eminem's and 50 Cent's identity construction more than anything about the albums' title star—Tupac Shakur. The coexistence of myth (cultural memory) and artistic validation (canon) has been a centuries-old practice and now finds itself in a digital guise within selected gangsta rap recordings. *Loyal to the Game* and similar albums demonstrate that memorial processes, lineage, and canon formations are manifest in mainstream gangsta rap recordings.

CONCLUSION

Through a range of examples, from A Tribe Called Quest to 50 Cent, it is clear that borrowing is a central feature of the aesthetics of hip-hop music. Intertextuality in hip-hop recordings can take the form of autosonic digital quotations as well as allosonic ones; this can occur in the lyrics, the "flow" of the MC, and the "beat." Furthermore, intramusical discourses (e.g., the sonic signature, musical gestures such as the "driving riff," harmonic progressions such as the lament, quotations, cover art) can work together with extramusical factors (media reception, interviews, codes from other genres, and wider cultural signifiers) to add meaning within the hip-hop world. Borrowing in hip-hop is not simply "digital sampling," but a vast network of processes, strategies, and modes of expression, among which digital sampling comprises but one method. Hip-hop embraces borrowing traditions from both African-based and European-based musics yet is also a product of its sociohistorical and technological situation. Hip-hop, like blues and jazz, is an "open source" culture, and this particular character of these musical cultures is crucial to their aesthetics.[1]

I would argue that one element that differentiates hip-hop from other open source cultures of the past is the sheer density and variety of intertextualities, in part influenced by what Paul D. Miller calls "the electronically accelerated culture of the late 20th Century."[2] The internet has no doubt influenced the way that people think about and discuss music, and Miller argues that the world wide web is a legacy from the way DJs looked for information decades earlier: "Look at the role of the search engine in web culture as a new kind of thoroughfare, and that role is expanded a million fold—the information and goods are out there, but you stay in place."[3] Lee Marshall cites a similar analogy from an email about Bob Dylan's album *Time Out of Mind*: "The album is also like a website full of hypertext links to the history of blues and folk, with lots of references all the way."[4] What Miller calls "the crowded spaces of info-modernity" demonstrate that advanced societies are perhaps more referential than they have ever been,[5] copyright law permitting, reflecting an intensification of the intertextualities and modes of borrowing in hip-hop culture.

Furthermore, how borrowing functions in hip-hop is largely dependent on the particular context and the interpretive lens one utilizes in reception. For example, borrowing from hip-hop's past can demonstrate a "historical authenticity," borrowing sonic codes from another genre such as jazz can influence its reception, borrowing and mixing for particular listening spaces can affect the sonic qualities of the recordings, sampling the voice postmortem can align an artist in a canon or lineage, and borrowing musical phrases such as Eminem's "driving riff" sonic signature can create a linkage with the rappers who collaborate with him. These codes and references in the musical text of the recordings have provided a glimpse of the highly varied modes of musical borrowing in hip-hop. At the same time, though this project has been bounded by hip-hop's imagined communities quite deliberately, the interplay between intra- and extramusical discourses has highlighted and developed themes that reflect wider cultural processes than simply within hip-hop culture.

This book is the tip of an enormous iceberg, and there are many other examples involving musical borrowing in hip-hop that I could have pursued. In addition to a comparative analysis and taxonomies of borrowing in multiple hip-hop "elements" (graffiti, breakdancing, turntabilism, etc.), numerous avenues still lie untraveled in studies of rap music borrowing. For example, in addition to borrowing from the jazz genre, I could have chosen borrowing from Bollywood films and its connection with exoticism and Orientalism. The use of electric guitar in Rick Rubin's productions of Run-D.M.C. and the Beastie Boys as signifying rock music as genre synecdoche, a crossover strategy tangled with issues of race, and borrowing from popular Broadway musicals could also have been potential topics. Newer collage and mash-up artists such as Girl Talk (Gregg Michael Gillis) and DJ Danger Mouse (Brian Burton) seem to extend a tradition of digital sonic collage made famous by artists such as the Bomb Squad, Prince Paul, John Oswald, and Negativland in the 1980s.

While I have primarily dealt with US-based mainstream hip-hop, the landscape of international hip-hop has become a formidable force in the past ten to fifteen years. Countries like Japan and Germany have had long-standing engagement with the genre, and the United Kingdom (my current residence) has taken hip-hop influences in new directions. This is not to mention hip-hop in Senegal, France, Spain, Cuba, Korea, Russia, and China, of which studies are starting to emerge. Intertextuality takes a most interesting direction in these cases as there often seems to be a counterpoint in references to the US mainstream (its products distributed internationally since at least the early 1990s, when the majors bought up hip-hop labels) and to local identities. In other words, what some call the "glocal" in various cultures is demonstrated within the intramusical discourses of international hip-hop.

In the interest of keeping the book focused on music analysis and intertextuality, I have arguably given less attention to issues such as political, legal, racial, and gender contexts. My case studies are based on the compatibility between specific musical examples and issues such as history, genre (and class), space, death, and lineage, as both the examples and the topics that I have selected have received less scholarly attention in the field of hip-hop studies than, say, race or gender. Race and gender are most certainly relevant and important to the case studies here, but I chose to open less explored hermeneutic windows in the interest of expanding the interpretive vantage points in hip-hop studies. For example, one could certainly engage in a psychoanalytic reading of the pleasures of automotive listening, not least pointing to the nameless female voice that features at the end of "Who Am I?" Or an attempt could be made to label certain semiotic musical codes as gendered (in McClary fashion), thus adding to notions of identity for sampling artists/groups.

In addition to invoking the historical authenticity of the 1970s Bronx, I could have chosen borrowing from the so-called hip-hop music Golden Age (1986–92), as both time periods are strong cases of intrageneric borrowing and strongly defined moments within the genre. Gangsta rapper The Game is an important figure in light of chapters 4 and 5, a highly intertextual artist who continues the Dre-Eminem-50 Cent lineage that I constructed. Other potential research directions include borrowing in the "Bling Bling" era; a study of hip-hop cover versions (both within and outside the hip-hop genre); global cover versions of internationally distributed US rap music; borrowings in Christian rap; and collage styles in albums such as *Endtroducing, Paul's Boutique,* and *Fear of a Black Planet.* Some of these may become future scholarly endeavors, but this extensive list of possibilities is intended to demonstrate that at present this book opens a space that could be filled limitlessly.

I would like to conclude by returning to Samuel Floyd, whom I reference in the conclusion of the previous chapter. Cultural memory, or myth, helps to bind a community together, additionally providing a sense of continuity in a fragmented, disjointed world. Floyd identifies this continuity in the history of African American music: "a compelling cultural and musical continuity exists between all the musical genres of the African-American cultural experience—a continuity that can be seen and traced from the musical characteristics of the ring into the most recent music making of black Americans."[6] This history of the "ring shout" as theorized by Sterling Stuckey, or Signifyin(g), or "the changing same," binds these communities together across generations.

In the introduction to this book, I emphasize the importance of investigating how much a given musical culture values the concept of individual originality or collective creation. This is perhaps the thread that most connects hip-hop intertextuality to its artistic lineage. In Zora Neale Hurston's 1934 essay "Characteristics of Negro Expression," she writes, "It has been said so often that the Negro is lacking originality that it has almost become a gospel. Outward signs seem to bear this out. But if one looks closely its falsity is immediately evident."[7] She argues that what is really meant by the concept of "originality" is "masterful revision," considering that all great art reworks previous art to varying degrees.[8] Since African American culture has little concealed its imitations and influences, it has been subject to such criticism, not to mention the potential racist assumptions involved. Hip-hop will always belong to two communities: its African-based heritage, as explained by Hurston, Gates, Floyd, Stuckey, and others; and its own intrageneric imagined community, with its constantly shifting values and signs. In the same way that I hope authors can cease feeling the need to justify hip-hop as a field for scholarly inquiry, I hope we can start to emphasize global and local hip-hop communities on their own terms to begin to understand just how complex and powerful hip-hop is.

Nevertheless, if we shift the focus to the communities themselves, there is much at stake in the discussion of historical continuity: not only artistic and cultural validation but also escaping or denying a culture's "death," so to speak. In the context of national communities, Benedict Anderson suggests that nationalism serves the same purpose as religion in that it can turn fatality into continuity.[9] The postmortem use of the symbolically immortal rappers Tupac's and Notorious B.I.G.'s voices is one way to create continuity, but this is also a symptom of a larger desire for continuity in hip-hop and other musical cultures and communities. Hip-hop as an imagined community, a hip-hop nation with origins, sub-genres, and landmarked events and icons, maintains its health through the borrowing strategies that I have presented and discussed.

Foundational and integral to hip-hop culture, borrowing and sampling solidify communities in a number of ways: creating history and lineage, immortalizing icons, creating links with other genres, forging links with an African American musical past (as in the case of jazz), solidifying subgenres (such as gangsta rap), and updating older sounds for newer playback technology (such as car sound systems). Importantly, the creation or imagining of a community lends its members a continuity also offered by previously dominant institutions such as religion, monarchy, nationalism, and sport. In this way, the hip-hop nation reflects society at large, with its members trying to make sense of a fractured world while simultaneously striving to belong to a community that will last longer than their individual lifetimes. Canons, lineage, and other traditions, formed in part by borrowing practices, are one particular way in which to celebrate an imagined community and ensure its vitality. Thus, borrowing is hip-hop culture's most widespread, and arguably most effective, way of celebrating itself.

NOTES

Introduction

1. Joseph G. Schloss, *Making Beats: The Art of Sample-Based Hip-Hop* (Middletown: Wesleyan University Press, 2004), 33.

2. Bill Brewster and Frank Broughton, *Last Night a DJ Saved My Life: The History of the Disc Jockey* (London: Headline, 2006), 267.

3. For a more detailed history of sampling, see Hugh Davies, "A History of Sampling," *Organised Sound* 1, no. 1 (1996): 3–11; and Gavin Kistner, "Hip-Hop Sampling and Twentieth Century African-American Music: An Analysis of Nas' 'Get Down' (2003)," M.Mus. dissertation (Université Laval, Quebec, 2006), 26–72.

4. I do not deal with issues of copyright at any great length because its impact is largely tangential to my aims, as I choose to focus on the aesthetics of hip-hop recordings and their reception. I would argue that copyright clearance has been extremely influential, and in many instances limiting, on what can be produced in mainstream hip-hop, but that is another book-length project too large in scope to be included here. See Kembrew McLeod, *Owning Culture: Authorship, Ownership and Intellectual Property Law* (New York: Peter Lang, 2001), in particular chapter 3, "Copyright. Authorship and African-American Culture" (71–99); Jessica Litman, *Digital Copyright* (Amherst, NY: Prometheus Books, 2001); Joanna Demers, *Steal This Music: How Intellectual Property Law Affects Musical Creativity* (Athens: University of Georgia Press, 2006); Simon Frith and Lee Marshall, eds., *Music and Copyright*, 2nd ed. (London: Routledge, 2004); Siva Vaidhyanathan, *Copyrights and Copywrongs: The Rise of Intellectual Property and How It Threatens Creativity* (New York: New York University Press, 2003); Lawrence Lessig, *Free Culture: The Nature and Future of Creativity* (Harmondsworth: Penguin, 2005); Richard L. Schur, *Parodies of Ownership: Hip-Hop Aesthetics and Intellectual Property Law* (Ann Arbor: University of Michigan Press, 2009).

5. For a description of the linkage between timbre and genre in the context of jazz fusion, see Steven F. Pond, *Head Hunters: The Making of Jazz's First Platinum*

Album (Ann Arbor: University of Michigan Press, 2005), 147–49. This is not to say that these 1970s sounds stay entirely intact within hip-hop; these timbres can be, and often are, manipulated in the studio to differing effect.

6. The Nas version uses primarily the top voice of "Für Elise" and is rhythmically modified for the new context. An even more ubiquitous breakbeat in hip-hop is James Brown's "The Funky Drummer" (1969), specifically the instrumental break from James Brown's drummer Clyde Stubblefield. See Mark Katz, *Capturing Sound: How Technology Has Changed Music* (Berkeley: University of California Press, 2004), in particular chapter 7, "Music in 1s and 0s: The Art and Politics of Digital Sampling" (137–57).

7. This "basic beat" can be defined as a structural layer or core layers of the musical complement that change little for a significant duration of the song. Though I do not go as far as to locate an *Ursatz* in a given hip-hop song, and I would argue that Schenker's theories are ill suited to African-based musics, layering forms an important structural component in hip-hop. For theorizations approaching such foundational rhythmic structures in popular music, see Robert Fink's concept of the tonic rhythm in the context of Motown's "four-on-the-floor" patterns: Robert Fink, "Analyzing Rhythmic Teleology in African American Popular Music," *Journal of the American Musicological Society* 64, no. 1 (2011): 198–99. The concept of a "basic beat" is strongly indebted to Adam Krims, in particular his discussion of layering and analysis of Ice Cube's "The Nigga Ya Love to Hate." See Adam Krims, *Rap Music and the Poetics of Identity* (Cambridge: Cambridge University Press, 2000), 93–122.

8. Recent exceptions include Felicia M. Miyakawa, *Five Percenter Rap: God Hop's Music, Message, and Black Muslim Mission* (Bloomington: Indiana University Press, 2005), chapter 5, "Sampling, Borrowing, and Meaning" (100–122); and Katz, *Capturing Sound*.

9. Joanna Demers, "Sampling the 1970s in Hip-Hop," *Popular Music* 22, no. 3 (2003): 41–56.

10. See Serge Lacasse, "Intertextuality and Hypertextuality in Recorded Popular Music," in *The Musical Work: Reality or Invention?* ed. Michael Talbot (Liverpool: Liverpool University Press, 2000).

11. Russell A. Potter, *Spectacular Vernaculars: Hip-Hop and the Politics of Postmodernism* (New York: State University of New York Press, 1995), 42. Other examples of hip-hop studies utilizing frameworks of postmodernism include Richard Shusterman, "The Fine Art of Rap," in *Pragmatist Aesthetics: Living Beauty, Rethinking Art* (Oxford: Rowman and Littlefield, Inc., 2000), 201–35; and Cheryl L. Keyes,

"At the Crossroads: Rap Music and Its African Nexus," *Ethnomusicology* 40, no. 2 (1996): 239–40.

12. Potter, *Spectacular Vernaculars*, 44.

13. Signifyin(g), as Gates writes, is derived from myths of the African god Esu-Elegbara, later manifested as the trickster figure of the Signifying Monkey in African American oral tradition. For a summary of the tale of the Signifying Monkey, see Henry Louis Gates Jr., *The Signifying Monkey: A Theory of African-American Literary Criticism* (Oxford: Oxford University Press, 1989), 55–56; and Potter, *Spectacular Vernaculars*, 83. Ingrid Monson, David Metzer, and Gary Tomlinson use the concept of Signifyin(g) effectively in jazz contexts: Ingrid Monson, "Doubleness and Jazz Improvisation: Irony, Parody, and Ethnomusicology," *Critical Inquiry* 20, no. 2 (1994): 283–313; David Metzer, "Black and White: Quotations in Duke Ellington's 'Black and Tan Fantasy,'" in *Quotation and Cultural Meaning in Twentieth Century Music* (Cambridge: Cambridge University Press, 2003), 47–68 (chapter 2); Gary Tomlinson, "Cultural Dialogics and Jazz: A White Historian Signifies," *Black Music Research Journal* 22 (2002): 71–102. David Brackett uses the concept in his analysis of James Brown's "Superbad": David Brackett, *Interpreting Popular Music* (Berkeley: University of California Press, 2000). In hip-hop studies, notable applications of Signifyin(g) include Demers, "Sampling the 1970s in Hip Hop"; Kistner, "Hip-Hop Sampling"; Katz, *Capturing Sound*; Imani Perry, *Prophets of the Hood* (Durham: Duke University Press, 2004); and Mickey Hess, *Is Hip Hop Dead?* (London: Praeger, 2007), 98–101.

14. Potter, 27.

15. In addition to the trickster figure, the figure of the griot is also important here, the West African poet/musician who is responsible for retaining the cultural memory of a community and passing it along through oral tradition. The connection between a community and its cultural memory will be exemplified in chapter 1, on borrowing from the internal history of the hip-hop world.

16. Schloss believes, as does Miyakawa, that political and symbolic motivations for sampling are largely overstated by scholars as compared to aesthetic reasons. He writes that "symbolic meaning is almost universally overstated by scholars as a motive for sampling"(*Making Beats*, 146). He argues convincingly for his group of producers that "the hip-hop discourse is primarily concerned with aesthetics. Simply put, sampling is not valued because it is convenient, but because it is beautiful" (65).

17. Chris Cutler, "Plunderphonia," in *Audio Culture*, ed. Christoph Cox and Daniel Warner (London: Continuum, 2004), 149. See also Katz, *Capturing Sound*, 139.

18. Though writing on digital sampling has largely been in the context of hip-hop music, it is important to note that the sampler was first used in rock and pop music and continued to be used alongside hip-hop production. Wayne Marshall points out that the first "authentic" hip-hop sample (authentic in that it digitally sampled a funk song) was actually from the progressive rock band Yes, which sampled Kool and the Gang's "Kool is Back" for "Owner of a Lonely Heart" in 1984: Wayne Marshall, "Giving Up Hip-Hop's Firstborn: A Quest for the Real after the Death of Sampling," *Callaloo* 29, no. 3 (2006): 887. Digital samplers were often used for ease and cost-effectiveness, such as for using a guitar or horn line instead of hiring musicians, and producers Pete Waterman and Hugh Padgham have admitted to using samplers to these ends. Earlier tape-based "samplers" such as the Mellotron were used by bands such as King Crimson as early as the 1960s. See Mark Cunningham, *Good Vibrations: A History of Record Production*, 2nd ed. (London: Sanctuary, 1998), 313, 329. See also Andrew Goodwin, "Sample and Hold: Pop Music in the Digital Age of Reproduction," in *On Record: Rock, Pop, and the Written Word*, ed. Simon Frith and Andrew Goodwin (London: Routledge, 1990), 270–71.

19. Katz, *Capturing Sound*, 140–41.

20. Tricia Rose makes a similar point in her groundbreaking *Black Noise: Rap Music and Black Culture in Contemporary America* (Middletown: Wesleyan University Press, 1994), 64. Imani Perry argues that with hip-hop, technology was simply used to reproduce sounds already aesthetically pleasing to an African American audience (*Prophets of the Hood*, 13).

21. The term *instrumental hip-hop* is defined by Michael D'Errico as "hip-hop that intentionally leaves out the rap element," using examples such as DJ Shadow, Madlib, and Flying Lotus. His thesis is one of the most useful pieces of work for investigating technology and hip-hop compositional practice, including information on Akai MPC samplers, software such as Ableton Live, and the MPD. See Michael D'Errico, "Behind the Beat: Technical and Practical Aspects of Instrumental Hip-Hop Composition," MA thesis (Tufts University, 2011), 5.

22. For a more thorough explanation of differences between "rap music" and "hip-hop music," see Krims, *Rap Music*, 10–11.

23. Joseph Schloss, *Foundation: B-Boys, B-Girls, and Hip-Hop Culture in New York* (New York and Oxford: Oxford University Press, 2009), 67.

24. It is important to emphasize that I am using the term *text* throughout the book in terms of the recording as text, rather than simply text as written hip-hop lyrics. I use the term *flow* for the delivery of rap lyrics and the term *lyrics* to discuss the semantic aspects of the lyrics.

25. It is important to note that the beat encompasses not only percussive elements of a rap song, but the entire complement to the rapper's flow (i.e., delivery of lyrics). Schloss defines a *beat* as "musical collages composed of brief segments of recorded sound" (*Making Beats*, 2). I will extend this terminology to encompass all sounds that are not the flow, including non-sample-based material.

26. This sentiment reflects Krims's observation that music is mediated but itself acts as a mediator: Adam Krims, *Music and Urban Geography* (London: Routledge, 2007), xxxvi.

27. Jonathan Lethem, "The Ecstasy of Influence: A Plagiarism Mosaic," in *Sound Unbound: Sampling Digital Music and Culture*, ed. Paul D. Miller (London: MIT Press, 2008), 28–29. Lethem's essay is particularly noteworthy because his endnotes reveal that every sentence from the essay has come from a different source, either directly quoted or paraphrased.

28. To quote Katz at length: "As a form of musical borrowing, the roots of digital sampling reach back more than a millennium. Consider just the Western musical tradition: medieval chants freely incorporated and adapted melodic patterns from earlier chants; dozens of Renaissance masses were based on the melody of the secular song 'L'homme armé'; a similar craze raged centuries later when composers such as Berlioz, Liszt, Rachmaninoff, Saint-Saëns, and Ysaÿe 'sampled' the chant *Dies irae* ('The Day of Wrath') in their instrumental works; Bach reworked Vivaldi's music; more than a century later Gounod returned the favor, adding a new melody to Bach's Prelude in C Major and calling it *Ave Maria*; Mahler cannibalized his own earlier vocal works in several of his symphonies; Ives quoted George M. Cohan's 'Over There' in his song 'Tom Sails Away'; Bartok parodied Shostakovich's *Leningrad* Symphony in his Concerto for Orchestra; and so on and so on" (*Capturing Sound*, 139–40).

29. Heather Dubrow, in terms of the novel, has described genre as a contract between reader and audience, and the idea of a "generic contract" has been developed most fully in musicology by Jeffrey Kallberg. See Jim Samson, "Genre," in *Oxford Music Online* (formerly *Grove Music Online*), www.oxfordmusiconline.com (accessed Aug. 10, 2009); Heather Dubrow, *Genre* (London: Taylor & Francis, 1982); and Jeffrey Kallberg, "The Rhetoric of Genre: Chopin's Nocturne in G Minor," *Nineteenth-Century Music* 11 (1987–88): 238–61.

30. Catherine Grant, "Recognizing Billy Budd in *Beau Travail*: Epistemology and Hermeneutics of Auteurist 'Free' Adaptation," *Screen* 43, no. 1 (2002): 57, quoted in Christine Geraghty, *Now a Major Motion Picture: Film Adaptations of Literature and Drama* (Plymouth, UK: Rowman and Littlefield, 2008), 3.

31. Richard Dyer actually does consider hip-hop as pastiche but includes it in

what he calls a *pasticcio* form, a "combination pastiche" as opposed to an "imitation pastiche." Certainly not all hip-hop music could accurately fit as *pasticcio* as he defines it, but a number of examples do. Dyer is most likely narrowly considering collage-style hip-hop production such as the Bomb Squad in his categorization, as he considers combination pastiche as combining "things that are typically held apart in such a way as to retain their identities": Richard Dyer, *Pastiche* (London: Routledge, 2007), 21. Other *pasticcio* forms he includes are Brazilian Tropicalism, *cento*, *contrafactum*, *capriccio*, and photomontage.

32. The "birth" of rock 'n' roll and bebop are described in some histories as radically new, as musics that marked a radical break from previous practices rather than borrowing, extending, and Signifyin(g) on them. In other words, the extramusical discourse conceals their borrowings to a certain extent. For a critique, see Chris McDonald, "'Rock, Roll and Remember?': Addressing the Legacy of Jazz in Popular Music Studies," *Popular Music History* 1, no. 2 (2006): 126–42. To use an inverse example, the subgenre of "Theme and Variations" is unconcealed through its title and arguably textually signaled through its format.

33. For audio examples and an explanation of fragmentation versus unity in hip-hop music, see Justin A. Williams, "Beats and Flows: A Response to Kyle Adams," *Music Theory Online* 15, no. 2 (2009), http://mto.societymusictheory.org/issues/mto.09.15.2/mto.09.15.2.williams.html.

34. Daphne Keller writes, "Human culture is always derivative, and music perhaps especially so. New art builds on old art": Daphne Keller, "The Musician as Thief: Digital Culture and Copyright Law," in Miller, *Sound Unbound*, 135. Lethem writes, "Any text is woven entirely with citations, references, echoes, cultural languages, which cut across it through and through in a vast stereophony. The citations that go to make up text are anonymous, untraceable, and *yet already read*; they are quotations without inverted commas. The kernel, the soul—let's go further and say the substance, the bulk, the actual and valuable material of all human utterances—is plagiarism" ("Ecstasy of Influence," 43).

35. Howard Becker, *Art Worlds* (Berkeley: University of California Press, 1982).

36. Schloss, *Foundation*, 3–4.

37. Benedict Anderson, *Imagined Communities: Reflections on the Origin and Spread of Nationalism*, 2nd ed. (London: Verso, 1991), 6. Schloss also mentions Anderson's book in *Making Beats* (4).

38. Anderson, *Imagined Communities*, 6.

39. Touré, "I Live in the Hiphop Nation," in *Never Drank the Kool-aid* (New York: Picador, 2006), 334–35. Other articles include Christopher John Farley,

"Hip-hop Nation," *Time*, Feb. 8, 1999, http://www.time.com/time/magazine/article/0,9171,990164,00.html; and Neil Strauss, "The Hip-Hop Nation: Whose Is It?; A Land with Rhythm and Beats for All," *New York Times*, Aug. 22, 1999. See also Potter, *Spectacular Vernaculars*, 56.

40. Oliver Wang, "Trapped in Between the Lines: The Aesthetics of Hip-Hop Journalism," in *Total Chaos*, ed. Jeff Chang (New York: Basic Civitas Books, 2006), 167.

41. See J. Peter Burkholder, "Borrowing," in *Grove Music Online*, ed. Laura Macy, http://www.oxfordmusiconline.com/subscriber/article/grove/music/52918?q=Borrowing&search=quick&pos=1&_start=1#firsthit (accessed Sept. 16, 2007).

42. One example is Beethoven, who in 1798 denied knowing Mozart's operas, though he had written several variations on Mozart arias years earlier. See Christopher Alan Reynolds, *Motives for Allusion: Context and Content in Nineteenth-Century Music* (Cambridge: Harvard University Press, 2003), 102.

43. Raymond Knapp, "Review of *Motives for Allusion* by Christopher Reynolds and *Quotation and Cultural Meaning in Twentieth-Century Music* by David Metzer," *Journal of the American Musicological Society* 58, no. 3 (2005): 740.

44. See LeRoi Jones, "The Changing Same (R&B and New Black Music)," in *Black Music* (London: MacGibbon and Kee, 1969), 180–211.

45. Jean-Jacques Nattiez, *Music and Discourse: Toward a Semiology of Music*, trans. Carolyn Abbate (Princeton: Princeton University Press, 1990), 11–15.

46. Reynolds, *Motives for Allusion*, 182.

47. Metzer, *Quotation and Cultural Meaning*, 6–7. Knapp's review of the Metzer and Reynolds books makes the point that the two books' "differing approaches could benefit from 'talking' to the other": Raymond Knapp, "Review of *Motives for Allusion*," 747.

48. Metzer, *Quotation and Cultural Meaning*, 6–9.

49. Stanley Fish, *Is There a Text in This Class? The Authority of Interpretive Communities* (Cambridge: Harvard University Press, 1980), 14.

50. Album sales as a measure of popularity could certainly be used to support the idea that a sample source will be recognized. For example, in choosing a popular (in the sense that it sold a large number of units) song from the past (the use of "Superfreak" for MC Hammer's "U Can't Touch This" and, more generally, Will Smith songs and Puff Daddy's choice of sample material), one could assume that the source will be more recognized than an obscure or highly transformed sample.

51. Monson, "Doubleness and Jazz Improvisation," 291. Gates also uses these two songs as an example of Signification (*Signifying Monkey*, 63).

52. One example of a complex song genealogy is the long and varied history of the "Apache" break in hip-hop and other electronic musics. See Michaelangelo Matos, "All Roads Lead to 'Apache,'" in *Listen Again: A Momentary History of Pop*, ed. Eric Weisbard (Durham: Duke University Press, 2007), 200–209. This was posted with examples on Oliver Wang's blog Soul Sides, Apr. 19, 2005, http://www.soulsides.com/2005/04/all-roads-lead-to-apache.html.

53. Elizabeth A. Wheeler, "'Most of My Heroes Don't Appear on No Stamps': The Dialogics of Rap Music," *Black Music Research Journal* 11, no. 2 (1991): 200.

54. In addition to Wheeler, other examples include Katz, *Capturing Sound*, 140–41; Rose, *Black Noise*, 64; Andrew Bartlett, "Airshafts, Loudspeakers, and the Hip Hop Sample: Contexts and African American Musical Aesthetics," *African American Review* 28 (1994): 639–52; Nelson George, "Sample This," in *That's the Joint: The Hip-hop Studies Reader*, ed. Murray Forman and Mark Anthony Neal (London: Routledge, 2004): 437–41; Portia K. Maultsby, "Africanisms in African American Music," in *Africanisms in American Culture*, ed. Joseph Holloway, 2nd ed. (Bloomington: Indiana University Press, 2005), 326–55; See also Demers, "Sampling the 1970s in Hip-Hop."

55. Monson, "Doubleness and Jazz Improvisation," 303, 305.

56. Shusterman, "Fine Art of Rap," 202.

Chapter 1

1. While boundaries between internal and external dynamics of a culture are by no means impermeable, I outline these two hermeneutical methods because they are often utilized by academics, fan cultures, and the media to investigate and construct particular artistic cultures.

2. Sarah Thornton writes, "Authenticity is arguably the most important value ascribed to popular music. . . . Music is perceived as authentic when it *rings true* or *feels real*, when it has *credibility* and comes across as *genuine*": Sarah Thornton, *Club Cultures: Music, Media and Subcultural Capital* (Middletown: Wesleyan University Press, 1996), 26.

3. James A. Snead, "On Repetition in Black Culture," in *Out There: Marginalization and Contemporary Cultures*, ed. Russell Ferguson et al. (London: MIT Press, 1990), 215. For praise of artistic lineages, see Sterling Stuckey, *Slave Culture: Nationalist Theory and the Foundations of Black America* (New York and Oxford: Oxford University Press, 1987); Gates, *Signifying Monkey*; Samuel A. Floyd Jr., *The Power of*

Black Music: Interpreting Its History from Africa to the United States (New York and Oxford: Oxford University Press, 1995); Demers, "Sampling the 1970s"; Michael Eric Dyson, *Know What I Mean? Reflections on Hip Hop* (New York: Basic Civitas Books, 2007); and William Jelani Cobb, *To the Break of Dawn: A Freestyle on the Hip Hop Aesthetic* (New York: New York University Press, 2007).

4. Lois Parkinson Zamora, *The Usable Past: The Imagination of History in Recent Fiction of the Americas* (Cambridge: Cambridge University Press, 1997), ix.

5. Zamora, *Usable Past,* 5.

6. Historical authenticity could be applied to a number of genres, from blues, to jazz, to the "historically informed performance" (HIP) movement in classical and early music. It is best defined as the belief that a musical form was more authentic and of greater value at some idealized earlier point in its internal history. For the purposes of narrowing my argument, I choose the period of prerecorded hip-hop (1973–79), early 1980s hip-hop performance cultures that were said to extend/ continue these earlier practices, and their recorded representations (e.g., *Wild Style,* "Grandmaster Flash on the Wheels of Steel").

7. One can theorize many reasons why artists feel the way they do about their racial, national, musical, and artistic histories, but this is beyond the scope of this chapter.

8. Concern with this early time period is what Anthony Kwame Harrison has called the "formative line of argument" for hip-hop authenticity, which "is based on the idea that there is a bounded period of time in which what we now consider hip hop was initiated and crystallized": Anthony Kwame Harrison, *Hip Hop Underground* (Philadelphia: Temple University Press, 2009), 91. Harrison spends a few pages discussing this issue in the context of debates surrounding the racial authenticity of the culture. In other words, because hip-hop's founders were primarily African American (and Puerto Rican), they have true claim to the authenticity of hip-hop today. Passing references to contemporary invocations of earlier rap artists occur in both Schloss (*Making Beats*) and Miyakowa (*Five Percenter Rap*), while Imani Perry spends a few pages on nostalgia and homage to hip-hop's "old school": Imani Perry, *Prophets of the Hood: Politics and Poetics in Hip Hop* (Durham: Duke University Press, 2007), 54–57.

9. Nineteenth-century German historian Leopold von Ranke wrote in his first historical work that the role of history is simply to show what actually happened— "Wie es eigentlich gewesen": Leonard Krieger, *Ranke: The Meaning of History* (Chicago and London: University of Chicago Press, 1977), 4.

10. Herc recounts, "I was smoking cigarettes and I was waiting for the records to

finish. And I noticed people was waiting for certain parts of the record": quoted in Jeff Chang, *Can't Stop Won't Stop: A History of the Hip-Hop Generation* (London: Ebury Press, 2005), 78–79. This was the birth of the "breakbeat," as Grandmaster Flash defined it, as the "best part of a great record," the moment when "the band breaks down, the rhythm section is isolated, basically where the bass guitar and drummer take solos" (as told to Rose, *Black Noise*, 73). David Toop writes, "In the Bronx, however, the important part of the record was the break—the part of a tune in which the drums take over": David Toop, *Rap Attack 2* (London: Serpent's Tale, 1992), 14. Many of these accounts of the breakbeat can be found in Schloss, *Making Beats*, 31–32; Chang, *Can't Stop Won't Stop*, 78–79; Rose, *Black Noise*, 73; Toop, *Rap Attack 2*, 12–14, 60; Nelson George, *Hip-Hop America* (Harmondsworth: Penguin Books, 1998), 17–18; Anthony Bozza, *Whatever You Say I Am: The Life and Times of Eminem* (New York: Three Rivers Press, 2003), 129; John Leland, *Hip: A History* (New York: Harper Perennial, 2005), 297–327; S. H. Fernando, *The New Beats* (New York: Anchor Books, 1994), 4–5, Brewster and Broughton, *Last Night*, 227–46; Jim Fricke and Charlie Ahern, eds., *Yes Yes Y'all: The Experience Music Project Oral History of Hip-Hop's First Decade* (Oxford: Perseus Books Group, 2002); and Johan Kugelberg, *Born in the Bronx: A Visual Record of the Early Days of Hip Hop* (New York: Rizzoli International Publications, 2007).

11. Toop, *Rap Attack 2*, 60.

12. Brewster and Broughton, *Last Night*, 230.

13. Bambaataa defines this concept: "Break music is that certain part of the record that you just be waiting for to come up and when that certain part comes, that percussion part with all those drums, congas, it makes you dance real wild. You just let all your feelings go, but that break is so short in the record, you get mad, because the break was not long enough for you to really get down to do your thing. As soon as the break part comes, boom, the singing or music part comes right back and the break part is gone": quoted in Leland, *Hip*, 322.

14. It is said that Bambaataa obtained records by groups like Kraftwerk from the "record pools" that were organized among DJs from other genres. See Brewster and Broughton, *Last Night*, 246.

15. Quoted in Schloss, *Making Beats*, 32.

16. For an example, see Leland, *Hip*, 327.

17. Schloss, *Making Beats*, 33.

18. Luis Manuel Garcia, "On and On: Repetition as Process and Pleasure in Electronic Dance Music," *Music Theory Online* 11, no. 4 (2005), 5, http://www.music-theory.org/mto/. His typology of pleasure, adapted from Karl Bühler, in-

cludes three types of pleasure: satiation pleasure, function pleasure, and pleasure of creative mastery.

19. Herbert Gans, *Popular Culture and High Culture: An Analysis and Evaluation of Taste*, 2nd ed. (New York: Basic Books, 1999), 102.

20. Richard Middleton, *Studying Popular Music* (Milton Keynes: Open University Press, 1990), 287–89.

21. Polyculturalism, as explained by Chang, describes generally how multiple cultures influence one another (*Total Chaos*, xv). The term was coined by Robin D. G. Kelley and became a central topic in Vijay Prashad's book on cultural exchange between African and Asian cultures: Vijay Prashad, *Everybody Was Kung Fu Fighting: Afro-Asian Connections and the Myth of Cultural Purity* (Boston: Beacon Press, 2002).

22. Herc's first MCs were Coke La Rock and Clark Kent. Grandmaster Flash first had MCs Cowboy and Melle Mel, both later part of his Furious Five. Bambaataa had Soulsonic Force, the Jazzy Five, and Planet Control. DJ Breakout had Funky Four +1, Cold Crush Brothers worked with DJ Charlie Chase, and Grandwizard Theodore would become DJ for Fantastic 5. See Brewster and Broughton, *Last Night*, 250.

23. For a more detailed account of these conditions, see Rose, *Black Noise*, 30–34; Chang, *Can't Stop Won't Stop*.

24. Quoted in Kugelberg, *Born in the Bronx*, 16.

25. *The Freshest Kids*, dir. Israel, 94 min. (QD3 Entertainment, USA, 2001; DVD, 2002), 30:07.

26. Fab 5 Freddy was an important artist and cultural intermediary on the 1980s hip-hop scene. He was a rapper, graffiti artist, and music video director who brought hip-hop to a larger audience in the early 1980s. In 1988, he became host of *Yo! MTV Raps*, the first show on MTV dedicated to rap music. He directed such music videos as Nas's "One Love" and Boogie Down Productions' "My Philosophy." He made connections in the early 1980s with the downtown art scene to feature works by graffiti artists such as Jean-Michel Basquiat, conceiving of and collaborating with Charlie Ahern to make *Wild Style*.

27. "Rapper's Delight," the first rap hit single, used live musicians to rerecord Chic's "Good Times" as the sonic backdrop to the raps performed by the Sugar Hill Gang. Many see "Rapper's Delight" as the moment when hip-hop became "commercialized" and therefore inauthentic. Flash, in returning to the original source (and he may have been playing this record pre–Sugar Hill Gang), may have been trying to reclaim the music, regardless of the associations it now had with "Rap-

per's Delight," which by then had substantial baggage as a successful rap commodity.

28. Charlie Ahern, *Wild Style: The Sampler* (New York: Powerhouse Books, 2007), 2.

29. Ahern, *Wild Style: The Sampler*, 197.

30. Interview with Lee Quinones, on *Wild Style*, DVD Extras.

31. Thornton, *Club Cultures*, 26.

32. David Shumway, "Rock 'n' Roll Sound Tracks and the Production of Nostalgia," *Cinema Journal* 38, no. 2 (1999): 36–51.

33. Neil Kulkarni, "Kurtis Blow and 'The Breaks,'" in *Hip-Hop Bring the Noise: The Stories behind the Biggest Songs* (London: Carlton Books, 2004), 29.

34. Kodwo Eshun, *More Brilliant than the Sun: Adventures in Sonic Fiction* (London: Quartet Books, 1999), 14.

35. Chang, *Can't Stop Won't Stop*, 127.

36. See Nelson George, "Introduction," in Fricke and Ahern, *Yes Yes Y'all*, iv.

37. There were a number of important women in the early hip-hop scene: Sha-Rock of the Funky Four +1; the all-female MC crew Sequence, who were on Sugarhill Records, featuring Angie B, who became Angie Stone; Wanda D; MC Lisa Lee; Little Lee; Sweet and Sour; Debbie D; Pebblee Poo; DJ Wanda Dee; the Zulu Queens B-Girl Crew; graffiti artist Sandra Fabra (Lady Pink); and breakdancer Daisy Castro (Baby Love). Blue (later Kool Lady Blue) organized events at Club Negril and Wheels of Steel Night at the Roxy and was the manager of the Rock Steady Crew. It is not that women in hip-hop left; it is just that mainstream hip-hop in the 1990s focused on objectifying women in music videos and rap lyrics, something that early hip-hop did much less of. For one article on the role of women in early hip-hop, see Nancy Guevara, "Women Writin' Rappin' Breakin'," in *Droppin Science: Critical Essays on Rap Music and Hip Hop Culture*, ed. William Eric Perkins (Philadelphia: Temple University Press, 1996), 49–62.

38. For example, early flyers show that most of the parties cost money to enter, though artist profit can be said to be significantly different from corporate profit, at least in scale.

39. Thornton, *Club Cultures*, 30.

40. These posters are in the style of Buddy Esquire and Phase 2, who are known for designing the flyers advertising early hip-hop parties. See Kugelberg, *Born in the Bronx*.

41. Ahern, *Wild Style: The Sampler*, 33.

42. Krims, *Music and Urban Geography*, 7.

43. Murray Forman, *The 'Hood Comes First: Space, Race and Place in Rap and Hip-Hop* (Middletown: Wesleyan University Press, 1992). See also Krims, *Music and Urban Geography*.

44. Krims, *Music and Urban Geography*, 17.

45. Brewster and Broughton, *Last Night*, 228.

46. The acknowledgment of a "breakbeat canon" exists in a number of hip-hop writings, including Cobb, *To the Break of Dawn*, 28.

47. See Schloss, chap. 2, "History, Community, and Classic B-Boy Records," in *Foundation*, 17–39. Not surprisingly, the "b-boy" canon includes many songs from the hip-hop DJ breakbeat canon, including "Apache," "Give It Up or Turnit a Loose," "It's Just Begun," and "The Mexican."

48. The "Apache" break was used early on in hip-hop recordings by Grandmaster Flash for his "Adventures of Grandmaster Flash on the Wheels of Steel"; by the West Street Mob for "Break Dancin': Electric Boogie"; and by the Sugar Hill Gang for their version of "Apache." For an extensive history of the "Apache" song and breakbeat, see Matos, "All Roads Lead to 'Apache.'"

49. Toop, *Rap Attack 2*, 114.

50. Will Hermes, "All Rise for the National Anthem of Hip-Hop," *New York Times*, Oct. 29, 2006, http://www.nytimes.com/2006/10/29/arts/music/29herm.html?ex=1319774400&en=601060e59bd8f7ee&ei=5088&partner=rssnyt&emc=rss.

51. Hermes, "All Rise."

52. Brian Coleman, *Check the Technique: Liner Notes for Hip-Hop Junkies* (New York: Villard Books, 2007), 401. DMC, in relation to the use of Bob James's "Take Me to Mardi Gras," which was used on "Peter Piper," said, "We had been rhyming over that loop before rap records was even made. We always used to just freestyle over those beats, but for the album song we wrote those lyrics down, while we was on the road" (B. Coleman, *Check the Technique*, 400).

53. Rose wrote of "Walk This Way" in a footnote, commenting: "After expressing frustration over the coverage of 'Walk This Way' as a crossover strategy, Run describes his motivation: 'I made that record because I used to rap over it when I was twelve. There were lots of hip-hoppers rapping over rock when I was a kid.'" Run is cited from Ed Kierch, "Beating the Rap," *Rolling Stone*, Dec. 4, 1986. See Rose, *Black Noise*, 195.

54. Keyes, "At the Crossroads," 239–40.

55. Wheeler, "Most of My Heroes," 195.

56. Other pop artists have collaborated with notable hip-hop producers, such

as Christina Aguilera did with DJ Premier. Their single "Ain't No Other Man" uses samples that include the hiss and pop of the records.

57. The use of a live DJ for tours seems to be of importance for a number of artists, even those who utilize primarily sample-based hip-hop on their studio albums. I recall one concert of Kanye West and Talib Kweli at Brixton Academy (London) in Nov. 2004; both artists had a DJ as well as a featured interlude in the set to display his or her virtuosic talents—similar to jazz, in which a bandleader might let the drummer take a ten-to-fifteen-minute solo.

58. W. Marshall, "Giving Up Hip-Hop's Firstborn," 871.

59. W. Marshall, "Giving Up Hip-Hop's Firstborn," 873.

60. Miyakowa, *Five Percenter Rap*, 120.

61. "Premier" is a reference to the producer DJ Premier.

62. The single is from Nas's second album, *It Was Written*, and is discussed as a "radio friendly" crossover piece produced by the Trackmasters. One review is from Mark Coleman, *Rolling Stone*, Sept. 19, 1996, http://www.rollingstone.com/artists/nas/albums/album/301203/review/6068277/it_was_written.

63. The beat (and keyboard line) is derived from "Friends," by Whodini (1984).

64. All transcriptions in the book are my own. It is worth mentioning that most hip-hop studies take a sociological or historical approach rather than a musicological one. In fact, the use of musical notation is, more often than not, seen as exclusionary and elitist by many who do academic work on hip-hop music and culture. My intention in including musical examples is primarily to emphasize the importance of the musical detail, the features of the intramusical discourse on hip-hop recordings, which has agency and all too often goes unexplored in hip-hop scholarship.

65. Alan Light, "Beastie Boys: White Dudes in the House," in *Spin: 20 Years of Alternative Music*, ed. Will Hermes and Sia Michel (New York: Three Rivers Press, 2005), 81.

66. Ahern, *Wild Style: The Sampler*, 200.

67. See Detlev Rick, aka DJ Rick Ski, "Die Entstehung des Albums Watch Out for the Third Rail der Band LSD," in *Samples: Online-Publikationen des Arbeitskreis Studium Populärer Musik*, 2010, Ralf von Appen, André Doehring, Dietrich Helms, and Thomas Phelps, http://aspm.ni.lo-net2.de/samples/ (accessed July 15, 2011).

68. Pharcyde, "Return of the B-Boy." Group member Tre recounts: "We were trying to re-create old-school style on that one. I didn't do too well at it [laughs]. But everyone else did" (quoted in B. Coleman, *Check the Technique*, 332).

69. Krims, *Music and Urban Geography*, 49–50.

70. Tom Breihan, "Jurassic 5: Feedback," *Pitchfork Media*, July 28, 2006, http://www.pitchforkmedia.com/article/record_review/37529-feedback.

71. Breihan, "Jurassic 5: Feedback."

72. Shumway, "Rock 'n' Roll Sound Tracks," 38.

73. Brewster and Broughton, *Last Night*, 228.

74. Quoted in Chris Wilder, "A Tribe Called Quest: Abstract Attitude," *Source*, no. 26 (1991): 25.

75. Francis Grasso, described as the first modern DJ, was said to play "In-A-Gadda-Da-Vida" in the late 1960s at clubs like the Haven in New York. See Brewster and Broughton, *Last Night*, 145–46. Nas used the Incredible Bongo Band's cover of the Iron Butterfly song for his "Thief's Theme" from *Streets Disciple* (2003). It is not unlikely that this version was played at early hip-hop parties since we know DJ Kool Herc had the record.

76. Michel Foucault, "Nietzsche, Genealogy and History," in *Language, Counter-memory, Practice*, ed. Donald F. Bouchard (Ithaca: Cornell University Press, 1977), 143.

77. Schloss, *Foundation*, 131–32. For an example from blues, see Leland, *Hip*, 131–33.

78. Foucault, "Nietzsche, Genealogy and History," 142.

79. *Freshest Kids*, 1:00.

80. Quoted in Schloss, *Foundation*, 91.

81. Harrison, *Hip Hop Underground*, 91.

82. Zamora, *Usable Past*, 127.

Chapter 2

1. Quoted in Danyel Smith, "Gang Starr: Jazzy Situation," *Vibe*, May 1994, 88.

2. Considered by historians to begin in the mid- to late 1980s and ending in 1993, this "golden age" began with Run-D.M.C.'s rise to popularity and ended with what Jeff Chang calls "the big crossover" in Dr. Dre's *The Chronic*. In this era, a diversity of artists and groups such as N.W.A., Ice Cube, Public Enemy, and 2 Live Crew coexisted in the rap mainstream with Jungle Brothers, KRS-One, De La Soul, A Tribe Called Quest; women such as MC Lyte and Queen Latifah; and pop rap artists MC Hammer and Vanilla Ice. Writers and critics lament the loss of this "golden age" in light of the post-1992 hegemony of gangsta rap in the mainstream. See Chang, *Can't Stop Won't Stop*, 420; and Cobb, *To the Break of Dawn*, 47.

3. Krims, *Rap Music*, 65–70.

4. Lawrence Levine, *Highbrow/lowbrow: The Emergence of Cultural Hierarchy in America* (Cambridge: Harvard University Press, 1988).

5. Krims, *Rap Music*, 92.

6. Krims, *Rap Music*, 55.

7. The term *neo-classical* conservative jazz is used by Gary Giddins, "Introduction: Jazz Turns Neoclassical," in *Rhythm-a-ning: Jazz Tradition and Innovation in the '80s* (New York: Oxford University Press, 1985). The idea of jazz as an elite art form was, admittedly, supported by a select number of critics and writers well before the bebop era, particularly in France and often centering on the work of Duke Ellington.

8. Robert Walser notes that "by the 1980s, jazz had risen so far up the ladder of cultural prestige that many people forgot it had ever been controversial." He cited a 1987 resolution by the US Congress that declared jazz had "evolved into a multifaceted art form" and that the youth of America needed "to recognize and understand jazz as a significant part of their cultural and intellectual heritage": Robert Walser, ed., *Keeping Time: Readings in Jazz History* (Oxford: Oxford University Press, 1999), 332–33.

9. For a more complete description, see Stuart Nicholson, *Jazz: The 1980s Resurgence* (New York: Da Capo Press, 1995), vi.

10. A popular single from the soundtrack of *Mo' Better Blues* was "Jazz Thing" by the hip-hop group Gang Starr (MC Guru and DJ Premier). The song tells a selective history of jazz, uses a number of jazz samples from across jazz's history, and includes characteristic turntable scratching styles from DJ Premier. The single and accompanying music video use stock footage from older jazz performances such as those from Duke Ellington and Charlie Parker. "Jazz Thing" brought the group national attention, though Gang Starr as a group subsequently tried to distance themselves from any jazz rap categorization. See *Mo' Better Blues,* dir. Spike Lee. 130 min. (Universal Pictures, USA, 1990; DVD, 2004).

11. Other jazz films of the 1980s worth mentioning are the Chet Baker documentary *Let's Get Lost,* dir. Bruce Weber, 120 min., VHS (Little Bear Productions, USA/West Germany, 1989), and the biopic *Thelonious Monk: Straight No Chaser,* dir. Charlotte Zwerin, 90 min. (Warner Brothers Pictures, USA, 1989; DVD, 2001); a number of jazz musicians were also writing film scores at the time (e.g., Terence Blanchard, Mark Isham, and Lennie Niehaus).

12. Christopher Harlos, "Jazz Autobiography: Theory, Practice, Politics," in *Representing Jazz,* ed. Krin Gabbard (Durham: Duke University Press, 1995), 132–33.

13. The show ran from 1984 to 1992 and was the number-one show in America for five consecutive years.

14. These films include *Boyz n the Hood,* dir. John Singleton, 107 min. (Columbia Pictures, USA, 1991; DVD, 2001); *South Central,* dir. Steve Anderson, 99 min. (Warner Brothers Pictures, USA, 1992; DVD, 1999); *Juice,* dir. Ernest R. Dickerson, 95 min. (Paramount Pictures, USA, 1992; DVD, 2001); and *Menace II Society,* dir. Albert Hughes and Allen Hughes, 97 min. (New Line Cinema, USA, 1993; DVD, 1997). Juxtapositions of the black middle class and a lower class were not new; for example, such a distinction was made during the Harlem Renaissance in the 1920s. For more on the black middle class, see William Julius Wilson, *The Declining Significance of Race* (Chicago: University of Chicago Press, 1978); Mary Patillo, *Black Picket Fences* (Chicago: University of Chicago Press, 1997); and Karyn Lacy, *Blue-Chip Black* (Berkeley: University of California Press, 2007).

15. See Krin Gabbard, "Introduction: The Jazz Canon and Its Consequences," in *Jazz among the Discourses,* ed. Krin Gabbard (Durham: Duke University Press, 1995), 1–2; see also Krin Gabbard, *Jammin at the Margins: Jazz and the American Cinema* (Chicago: University of Chicago Press, 1996), 102; and Richard Cook, *Blue Note Records: The Biography* (London: Secker and Warburg, 2001), 182.

16. One example can be found in *Rolling Stone* 565, Nov. 16, 1989, 1.

17. *Rolling Stone* 600, Mar, 21, 1991, 2. This was part of a larger GAP campaign entitled "Individuals of Style," which featured Dizzy Gillespie, Miles Davis, Maceo Parker, Courtney Pine, and others. See John McDonough, "Jazz Sells," *Downbeat,* Oct. 1991, 34.

18. This includes methods taught by Jamey Aebersold, Jerry Coker, and David Baker. For a more detailed account of these developments in jazz education, see "Jazz 'Training': John Coltrane and the Conservatory," in David Ake, *Jazz Cultures* (Berkeley: University of California Press, 2002), 112–45.

19. Grover Sales, *Jazz: America's Classical Music* (New York: Da Capo Press, 1992), 219.

20. Francis Davis, "The Right Stuff," in *In The Moment: Jazz in the 1980s* (New York: Da Capo Press, 1996), 29. See also Stuart Nicholson, chap. 2, "Between Image and Artistry: The Wynton Marsalis Phenomenon," in *Is Jazz Dead? (or has it moved to a new address)* (London: Routledge, 2005), 23–52.

21. Cook, *Blue Note Records,* 212–13.

22. Perhaps the most exemplary document of his views at the time can be found in an article Marsalis wrote for the *New York Times* (July 31, 1988) entitled, "What Jazz Is—and Isn't," subsequently anthologized in Walser, *Keeping Time,* 334–39.

For more on cultural intermediaries, see Keith Negus, "The Work of Cultural In-termediaries and the Enduring Distance between Production and Consumption," *Cultural Studies* 16, no. 4 (2002): 501–15.

23. There were multiple forms of jazz in the 1980s, with a number of ideological connotations. Two worth mentioning are more avant-garde streams of jazz, exemplified by John Zorn and Anthony Braxton, and smooth jazz, which was a lighter version of fusion from the 1970s. Smooth jazz artists such as Kenny G and David Sanborn are often the focus of criticism from jazz purists, but their albums were commercially successful in the 1980s and helped to form their own significant jazz subgenre.

24. Reginald Thomas, "The Rhythm of Rhyme: A Look at Rap Music as an Art Form from a Jazz Perspective," in *African American Jazz and Rap: Social and Philosophical Examinations of Black Expressive Behavior*, ed. James L. Conyers (London: McFarland & Company, 2001), 165–66. For examples of underground rap scenes, see Marcyliena Morgan, *The Real Hiphop* (Durham: Duke University, 2009); and Anthony Kwame Harrison, *Hip Hop Underground: The Integrity and Ethics of Racial Identification* (Philadelphia: Temple University Press, 2009). Cinematic examples of such battles can be found in the Eminem quasi-biopic *8 Mile*, dir. Curtis Hansen, 110 min. (Imagine Entertainment, USA, 2002; DVD, 2003).

25. The term *new jazz swing* can be found in Maultsby, "Africanisms in African American Music," 327. Jazz rap or alternative rap had also been deemed (and dismissed as) "college boy" rap, no doubt influenced by the highbrow topics of groups like Digable Planets and jazz's associations with college-educated, middle-class audiences. Many groups, such as A Tribe Called Quest, did become popular on college campuses before expanding to a wider audience. College radio stations also had successful underground hip-hop communities that would organized events on campus. See Chang, *Can't Stop Won't Stop*, 422; Shawn Taylor, *People's Instinctive Travels and the Paths of Rhythm* (New York: Continuum, 2007), 66; Krims, *Rap Music*, 65.

26. One example of a producer influenced by his parents' jazz tastes is DJ Premier; see Ty Williams, "Rap Session—Hip-Bop: The Rap/Jazz Connection," *Source*, Sept. 1992, 21; see also Toop, *Rap Attack 2*, 189; and B. Coleman, *Check the Technique*, 164–65, 235.

27. Chang, *Can't Stop Won't Stop*, 258.

28. Grandmaster D.ST was featured on the 1983 Herbie Hancock single "Rock It," one of the earliest high-profile collaborations between jazz and hip-hop artists (Fernando, *New Beats*, 140).

29. Butterfly, "Examination of What" (track 14), on Digable Planets, *Reachin' (a new refutation of time and space)*, 1:45.

30. Bourdieu makes the distinction between social capital and cultural capital in "The Forms of Capital," in *Handbook of Theory and Research for the Sociology of Education*, ed. John G. Richardson (London: Greenwood Press, 1986), 243–48.

31. Taylor, *People's Instinctive Travels*, 9–10.

32. Krims, *Rap Music*, 65–70. Bohemianism is certainly a feature of the language and style of the 1950s "hipsters," who also looked to jazz as part of a early cold war sensibility of hipness; see Phil Ford, "Hip Sensibility in an Age of Mass Counter-culture," *Jazz Perspectives* 2, no. 2 (2008): 121–63. As Ford reminds us, "Elitism is essential to hipness," not only in contemporary jazz, but also in Cold War hip sensibilities more generally (142).

33. A harmon mute is a specific type of mute for brass instruments that is made of metal and creates a quieter, tinny sound. The mute has a ring of cork around the outside so that air through the instrument can only escape through the mute. It has a sharp, metallic sound that was often used to change the timbre of the trumpet or trombone in jazz big band music. It can be played with or without a metal "stem" inserted in the mute, drastically changing its sound. Its sound is associated with Miles Davis, more than anyone, who used the mute (without stem) frequently during his long career.

34. This approach to jazz codes is particularly indebted to the semiotic methodologies of John Fiske and Philip Tagg.

35. Steve Redhead and John Street, "Have I the Right? Legitimacy, Authenticity and Community in Folk's Politics," *Popular Music* 8, no. 2 (1989): 180. Redhead and Street interpret Sting's collaboration with jazz musicians for his first solo album *The Dream of the Blue Turtles* (1985) as a gesture of political legitimacy.

36. Rai Zabor and Vic Garbarini, "Wynton vs. Herbie: The Purist and the Crossbreeder Duke it Out," in Walser, *Keeping Time*, 342.

37. Philip Tagg, *Introductory Notes to the Semiotics of Music*, version 3 (1999), 26–27, http://www.tagg.org/xpdfs/semiotug.pdf.

38. Matthew W. Butterfield, "The Power of Anacrusis: Engendered Feeling in Groove-Based Musics," *Music Theory Online* 12, no. 4 (2006), http://mto.society musictheory.org/issues/mto.06.12.4/mto.06.12.4.butterfield.html.

39. *Categorical perception* is a term that Eric Clarke uses to describe the way we perceive music in certain durational categories (such as quarter note, eighth note, half note, etc.). See Eric Clarke, "Rhythm and Timing in Music," in *The Psychology of Music*, ed. Diana Deutch, 2nd ed. (Burlington: Burlington Academic Press, 1999), 490.

40. Butterfield, "Power of Anacrusis," 4.

41. Simon Frith, "The Music Industry," in *The Cambridge Companion to Pop and Rock*, ed. Simon Frith, John Street, Will Straw (Cambridge: Cambridge University Press, 2001), 35.

42. A Tribe Called Quest was formed in Queens in 1988. The members of the group were producer/DJ Ali Shaheed Muhammad, MC/producer Q-Tip (Jonathan Davis), and MCs Phife (Malik Taylor) and Jarobi (only on the first album). Their debut album *People's Instinctive Travels and the Paths of Rhythm* (1990) also featured a number of jazz samples. For analyses of unity between beat and flow in A Tribe Called Quest's "Scenario," "Can I Kick It," and "Push It Along," see Kyle Adams, "Aspects of the Music/Text Relationship in Rap," *Music Theory Online* 14, no. 2 (2008), http://www.mtosmt.org/issues/mto.08.14.2/toc.14.2.html.

43. New jack swing is a style from the late 1980s/early 1990s that fused hip-hop and R&B into a hybrid pop style. Notable producers include Teddy Riley, Jimmy Jam, and Terry Lewis. The song "Show Business" discusses the difficulties of working in the rap music industry, structuring the common artist/group vs. music industry paradigm.

44. The use of the word *proper* in this instance is a reference to the catchphrase used by MC Hammer in a 1991 Pepsi commercial, which introduced him as "MC Hammer: rap star and Pepsi drinker."

45. This phrase is sampled from "Love Your Life" by the Average White Band from *Soul Searching* (1976) (also sampled by Fatboy Slim for "Love Life"). The song also samples "Hydra" by Grover Washington Jr. from *Feels So Good* (1975) and the bass line from Minnie Riperton's "Baby This Love I Have" and Steve Miller Band's "Fly like an Eagle."

46. This bass riff is from "A Chant for Bu" by Art Blakey and the Jazz Messengers. The original is in 3/4 time, and producer Q-Tip was able to copy-and-paste the first two quavers of the bar to create a beat in common time: "I took the original bass line, which was in 3/5 time, and I put a beat onto the last measure to make it 4/4. I made the drums underneath smack, so it had that big sound. And I put a reverse [Roland TR-] 808 [drum machine] behind it, right before the beat actually kicks in. I loved that Last Poets sample on there, too" (quoted in B. Coleman, *Check the Technique*, 443)s.

47. Of course, this distancing from pop was a phenomenon before the 1980s: bebop musicians distanced themselves from "commercial" swing music of the 1930s and 1940s, and rock and punk musicians have often defined themselves against pop in lyrics and interviews. Even earlier, Louis Armstrong received criticism for surviving the Great Depression by having a singing career on Broadway.

48. The idea of being "uncommercial" or not "selling out" is a characteristic of authenticity found in a number of music genres and exists as far back as Romantic notions of transcendence and timelessness in nineteenth-century music. Bourdieu has written about the idea of economic disintrestedness as a bourgeois production illusion; see Bourdieu, "Forms of Capital," 242.

49. Ford, "Hip Sensibility," 123.

50. Formed in 1989, Digable Planets included members Butterfly (Ishmael Butler, from Brooklyn), Doodlebug (Craig Irving, from Philadelphia), and Ladybug (Mary Ann Viera, from Maryland).

51. "Rebirth of Slick (Cool like Dat)" was released in Nov. 1992 in anticipation of the Feb. 1993 album release of *Reachin' (A New Refutation of Time and Space)*. "Rebirth of Slick" received heavy radio airplay by January, the accompanying music video was prevalent on both MTV and BET, and it had sold four hundred thousand copies by early February. This single is by far the most well known from the group; it reached number 1 on the Billboard Hot Rap chart and number 15 on the Billboard Hot 100 Singles chart, and the album reached number 15 on the Billboard Top 200. "Rebirth of Slick (Cool like Dat)" also received a Grammy in 1994 for Rap Performance by a Duo or Group.

52. The "cocoon club" is perhaps a reference to the famous Cotton Club of Harlem, as well as continuing the insect metaphors in the group's lyrics and stage names.

53. The most extensive study of "liveness" is Philip Auslander, *Liveness: Performance in a Mediatized Culture* (London: Routledge, 1999).

54. "Last of the Spiddyocks," a track with numerous jazz musician references that features a harmon-muted trumpet in the beat, ends with audience applause, which is another signifier of liveness.

55. The bass line also features as *leitmotiv* in "Appointment at the Fat Clinic" (track 11) and "Escapism (Gettin' Free)" (track 10), not as central to the basic beat as in "Rebirth of Slick," but as a small moment within the other two songs. This bass line, now associated with Digable Planets' moment of success, has been sampled by later rap artists (such as E-40 for "Yay Area" on *My Ghetto Report Card* in 2006).

56. The bass line and horn figures derive from Art Blakey and the Jazz Messengers' "Stretchin'" from the album *Reflections in Blue* (1978).

57. See Adams, "Aspects of the Music/Text Relationship in Rap."

58. I do not mean to imply here that finding unity should be the goal in music analysis of any kind. Smaller units of meaning can be worthy of investigation in the close reading of music recordings. See J. A. Williams, "Beats and Flows."

59. Diana Crane, *The Production of Culture: Media and the Urban Arts* (London: Sage, 1992), 10.

60. Chuck Eddy, "Review of *People's Instinctive Travels and the Paths of Rhythm*," *Rolling Stone* 576, Apr. 19, 1990, 15.

61. John Bush, "A Tribe Called Quest," allmusic.com, http://allmusic.com/cg/amg.dll?p=amg&sql=11:dcfixq95ld6e (accessed June 1, 2007).

62. Peter Shapiro, *The Rough Guide to Hip-Hop*, 2nd ed. (London: Rough Guides Ltd., 2005), 363, 365.

63. B. Coleman, *Check the Technique*, 435.

64. Big B, "Record Report—Arrested Development," *Source*, May 1992, 32, 56. See also "Jazz Rap," in *The All Music Guide to Hip Hop*, by Vladimir Bogdanov, Chris Woodstra, John Bush, et al. (San Francisco: Backbeat Books, 2003), ix.

65. "Given its more intellectual bent, it's not surprising that jazz-rap never really caught on as a street favorite, but then it wasn't meant to": "Jazz Rap," in Bogdanov et al., *All Music Guide to Hip Hop*, ix.

66. "Among the leading proponents of this more reflective style (including De La Soul and the Jungle Brothers), A Tribe Called Quest was arguably the most accomplished": J. D. Considine and Mac Randall, "A Tribe Called Quest," in *The New Rolling Stone Album Guide*, Rollingstone.com, 2004, http://www.rollingstone.com/artists/atribecalledquest/biography (accessed June 1, 2007).

67. Editors, "Pop Life," *Source*, Jan. 1994, 26.

68. Kevin Powell, "Review of *Reachin' (A Refutation of Time and Space)*," *Rolling Stone* 650, Feb. 18, 1993, 61. Powell is most likely referencing the MC Lyte song "I Cram to Understand You," as intertextual references were often as important to hip-hop journalism as they were to music.

69. Christopher Farley, "Hip-Hop Goes Bebop," *Time*, July 12, 1993, http://www.time.com/time/magazine/article/0,9171,978844,00.html.

70. Both Digable Planets ("Rebirth of Slick [Cool like Dat]") and Dr. Dre ("Nuthin' but a 'G' Thang") had a single and a music video permeating media space at the same time. See *Billboard*, Feb. 6, 1993. Both singles were nominated for the Best Rap Performance by a Duo or Group Grammy Award, with Digable Planets winning the award.

71. See Chang, *Can't Stop Won't Stop*, 420; and Eithne Quinn, *Nuthin' but a "G" Thang: The Culture and Commerce of Gangsta Rap* (New York: Columbia University Press, 2005), 161.

72. Kevin Powell, "Review of *Midnight Marauders* and *Buhloone Mindstate*," *Vibe*, Nov. 1993, 103.

73. David Malley, "Digable Planets," *Rolling Stone Album Guide*, Rollingstone.com, 2004, http://www.rollingstone.com/artists/digableplanets/biography (accessed June 1, 2007).

74. Many other hip-hop groups, such as Organized Konfusion, Stetsasonic, Main Source, Black Moon, Freestyle Fellowship, the Roots, Quasimoto, and Souls of Mischief, have incorporated jazz codes that have contributed to their alternative rap categorizations. Although the media gave much less attention to jazz rap after the mid-1990s, the link between jazz and hip-hop continues into the twenty-first century with artists such as US trumpeter/rapper Russell Gunn, US pianist Robert Glasper, and UK saxophonist/rapper Soweto Kinch.

75. These musical tropes were still used in the 1980s, one example being the use of saxophone in the action series *MacGyver* for a sexually charged fantasy sequence between MacGyver and a woman.

76. For example, three years after Gang Starr's successful "Jazz Thing" (where rapper Guru stated, "The '90s will be the decade of a jazz thing"), Guru made a hip-hop album entitled *Jazzmatazz Vol. 1* (1993) in collaboration with various jazz musicians including Branford Marsalis, Donald Byrd, and Courtney Pine and later produced three subsequent volumes of the series (*Vol. 2* in 1995, *Vol. 3* in 2004, and *Vol. 4* in 2007). At this time, jazz musicians such as Herbie Hancock, Branford Marsalis, Quincy Jones, Wallace Roney, and Greg Osby were making hip-hop-influenced albums. Additionally, Blue Note Records allowed the group US3 (led by British producers Geoff Wilkinson and Mel Simpson) to sample extensively from its catalog free of charge, producing *Hand on the Torch* (1993), which became the top-selling album on Blue Note Records at the time and the first to reach platinum sales in the United States. Their single "Cantaloop (Flip Fantasia)" received widespread radio play and added to the jazz and hip-hop fusion trends at the time. For information on the use of electronics, turntables, and sampling technology in more recent jazz, see chap. 6, "Future Jazz," in Nicholson, *Is Jazz Dead?*, 129–62.

77. Robert Fink, "Elvis Everywhere," *American Music* 16, no. 2 (1998): 146.

78. The use of classical idioms and instruments to elevate jazz and African American culture has a long history, best described in John Howland, *Ellington Uptown: Duke Ellington, James P. Johnson, and the Birth of Concert Jazz* (Ann Arbor: University of Michigan Press, 2009). In light of these traditions, it is interesting to note that, on a general level, jazz has a similar function for hip-hop as classical forms had for concert jazz. The current case may emphasize the African American cultural linkage, whereas the former emphasized the hybridity between European (white) styles and African American ones.

79. Gary Tomlinson, "Authentic Meaning in Music," in *Authenticity and Early Music*, ed. Nicholas Kenyon (Oxford: Oxford University Press, 1988), 123.

80. Matt Diehl has described East Coast rap as "interior," for contemplative Walkman listening on the subway as opposed to the West Coast automobile-

centric listening of "pop rap": Matt Diehl "Pop Rap," in *The Vibe History of Hip Hop*, ed. Alan Light (New York: Three Rivers Press, 1999), 129.

81. For an example of sampling to create atmosphere in Brand Nubian, see Miyakawa, *Five Percenter Rap*, 111–14.

82. For attention to this third dimension from a geographical perspective, see Edward Soja, *Thirdspace: Journeys to Los Angeles and Other Real-and-Imagined Places* (Oxford: Blackwell, 1996).

83. Stuart Hall, "Culture, Media, and the Ideological Effect," in *Mass Communication and Society*, ed. James Curran, Michael Gurevitch and Janet Woolacott (London: Open University Press, 1977).

84. This is aligned with Ford's writing on 1950s hip sensibilities: "The ethic of exclusion, of trials and secret knowledge—in short, an ethic of elitism" ("Hip Sensibility," 140).

Chapter 3

1. Quoted in Lucinda Lewis, *Roadside America: The Automobile and the American Dream* (New York: Harry N. Abrams, 2000), 19.

2. Quoted in Robert Levine, "The Death of High Fidelity," *Rolling Stone*, Dec. 27, 2007, http://www.rollingstone.com/news/story/17777619/the_death_of_high_fidelity/print.

3. Jonathan Gold, "Day of Dre," *Rolling Stone* 666, Sept. 30, 1993, 41, http://www.rollingstone.com/artists/drdre/articles/story/5937496/cover_story_day_of_the_dre.

4. For a more thorough presentation of this phenomena, see Krims, *Music and Urban Geography*. Regarding the design intensity of spaces, see Scott Lash and John Urry, *Economies of Sign and Space* (London: Sage Publications, 1994), 15.

5. Rose, *Black Noise*, 75. She also notes similarities with Caribbean musics such as Jamaica's talk over and dub.

6. Gilroy writes, "It raises the provocative possibility that their distinctive history of propertylessness and material deprivation has inclined them towards a disproportionate investment in particular forms of property that are publicly visible and the status that corresponds to them": Paul Gilroy, "Driving while Black," in *Car Cultures*, ed. Daniel Miller (Oxford: Berg, 2001), 84.

7. Gilroy, "Driving while Black," 97.

8. Gilroy, "Driving while Black," 85.

9. Gilroy, "Driving while Black," 84.

10. Demers, "Sampling the 1970s," 84. Henry Louis Gates Jr. locates the chariot trope in African American art forms, as well as its variation manifested in references to trains(*Signifying Monkey*, 8).

11. Roni Sarig, *Third Coast: OutKast, Timbaland and How Hip-Hop Became A Southern Thing* (Cambridge: Da Capo Press, 2007), 12–19.

12. L'Trimm "Cars with the Boom," *Grab It!* (1988). See also Sarig, *Third Coast*, 30.

13. For more information, see the IASCA website: www.iasca.com. For more on "boom cars," see Brandon Labelle, *Acoustic Ecologies: Sound Culture and Everyday Life* (London: Continuum, 2010), 151–61. See also Frank W. Hoffmann and William G. Bailey, "Boom Cars," in *Sports and Recreation Fads* (Philadelphia: Haworth Press, 1991), 71–72.

14. See the National Alliance Against Loud Car Stereo Assault, www.lowertheboom.org. Anti boom car legislation is not the first case of communities' seeking legal action for noise pollution associated with car culture, as some citizens as early as 1935 were fighting for laws against the noise pollution stemming from the then-new phenomenon known as drive-in theaters. See Kerry Seagrave, *Drive-In Theaters: A History from Their Inception in 1933* (London: McFarland and Company, 1992), 26.

15. Joe Pettitt, *How to Design and Install High-Performance Car Stereo* (North Branch: Car Tech, 2003), 59.

16. Christopher Anet, "An Insight into Subwoofers," *Resolution Magazine* 2, no. 7 (Oct. 2003), 60–62.

17. Andrew Yoder, *Auto Audio* (New York: McGraw Hill, 2000), 96. Subwoofers normally need to produce 80dB SPL to be heard or felt (Pettitt, *How to Design*, 60).

18. Yoder, *Auto Audio*, 96.

19. The division of frequencies to certain speakers is provided by a "crossover" that allows some frequencies to pass through and some to be blocked for a given speaker. These frequency levels are called "crossover points" and can be adjusted in custom systems. For example, a subwoofer crossover could have a crossover point of 90 Hz, and the signal would be blocked at any frequency above 90 Hz. See Doug Newcomb, *Car Audio for Dummies* (New York: Wiley Publishing, 2008), 207. These "crossover points" for any given speaker are variable and adjustable, largely dependent on the practicalities of the technology and the tastes of listeners and manufacturers.

20. Polk Audio, "Tips, Tweaks and Common Sense About Car Audio" (Baltimore: Polk Audio), http://www.polkaudio.com/downloads/12vhndbk.pdf (accessed July 23, 2008).

21. Yoder, *Auto Audio*, 168.

22. Peter Marsh and Peter Collett, *Driving Passion: The Psychology of the Car* (London: Jonathan Cape, 1986), 36. Before the automobile, coach builders would customize carriages for the rich, as a tailor would do for clothes (*carrossiers*). It was not uncommon for celebrities in the early automotive era to hire custom designers for their automobiles. Harley Earl and General Motors president Alfred Sloan simply brought the already existing customization appearance to the wider public in the late 1920s. Hollywood-born Earl, before leading the first Art and Color division of a major automobile manufacturer, was a custom car designer for celebrities such as Fatty Arbuckle and Cecil B. DeMille. See Marsh and Collett, *Driving Passion*, 31; David Gartman, *Auto Opium: A Social History of American Automobile Design* (London: Routledge, 1994), 211.

23. Gartman, *Auto Opium*, 68–75. The term *Sloanism* is used in Karal Ann Marling, "America's Love Affair with the Automobile in the Television Age," in *Autopia: Cars and Culture*, ed. Peter Wollen and Joe Kerr (London: Reakton Books, 2002), 355. Sloan hired Earl in the mid-1920s to compete with Ford's Model T. GM's La Salle, from the Cadillac division in 1927, was the first mass-produced car planned from bumper to bumper by one man (Earl). Earl was also the first to put trademarked tail fins on a 1949 Cadillac, inspired by the P-38 Lightning pursuit plane. See Gartman, *Auto Opium*, 75, 148.

24. John Urry, "The 'System' of Automobility," in *Automobilities*, ed. Mike Featherstone, Nigel Thrift, and John Urry (London: Sage, 2005), 26.

25. Michael Bull, "Automobility and the Power of Sound," in Featherstone, Thrift, and Urry, *Automobilities*, 248.

26. David McCartney, "Automobile Radios," in *The Encyclopedia of Radio*, ed. Christopher H. Sterling (New York: Taylor and Francis, 2004), 138.

27. McCartney, "Automobile Radios," 139.

28. Pond, *Head Hunters*, 132.

29. Suzanne E. Smith, *Dancing in the Street: Motown and the Cultural Politics of Detroit* (Cambridge: Harvard University Press, 1999), 123.

30. David Morse, *Motown and the Arrival of Black Music*, quoted in Smith, *Dancing in the Street*, 123.

31. Warren Belasco, "Motivatin' with Chuck Berry and Fredrick Jackson Turner," in *The Automobile and American Culture*, ed. David C. Lewis and Laurence Goldstein (Ann Arbor: University of Michigan Press, 1980), 264.

32. Levine writes, "Rock and pop producers have always used compression to balance the sounds of different instruments and to make music sound more excit-

ing, and radio stations apply compression for technical reasons. In the days of vinyl records, there was a physical limit to how high the bass levels could go before the needle skipped a groove. . . . Intensely compressed albums like Oasis' 1995 *(What's the Story) Morning Glory?* set a new bar for loudness; the songs were well-suited for bars, cars and other noisy environments" ("Death of High Fidelity").

33. For examples of how the phonograph influenced music composition, see Katz, *Capturing Sound.*

34. For example, producer Elliot Schneider says that he uses a DI for the bass guitar because "the amp signal just doesn't have enough definition; it just contributes a lot of low end": quoted in Howard Massey, *Behind the Glass: Top Record Producers Tell Us How They Craft the Hits* (San Francisco: Backbeat Books, 2000), 60. Of course, other producers may want heavier low end, such as many hip-hop music producers.

35. As one car audio technician writes, "To put it bluntly, car interiors are about the worst listening environments imaginable. Your location in the car is set. Listener seating is to the side of acoustic space in relation to the speakers" (Pettitt, *How to Design,* 20).

36. Brendan Baber, "The Incredible Shrinking Sound System," *Bnet.com,* Sept. 1997, http://findarticles.com/p/articles.

37. A cinematic example of this can be found in the film *Once* (2006): after the band records their demo, the engineer takes them out for a drive to hear the mix.

38. Patrick Olguin, email correspondence with the author, June 3, 2008. Olguin has worked with a number of commercially successful groups and artists, such as Papa Roach, Black Eyed Peas, rapper E-40, and Cake.

39. Patrick Olguin, email correspondence with the author, Sept. 19, 2008.

40. Hank Shocklee of the production team the Bomb Squad recounted to me the existence of a custom car audio system in New York's Sony Studios: Hank Shocklee, interview with the author, Mar. 8, 2009.

41. Krims, *Music and Urban Geography,* 161. Krims writes that some popular music genres "help to provide a soundscape for design-intensive urban interiors, and they do so, arguably, just as classical recordings do, by targeting a soundscape to the design or desired ethos of the private playback space" (*Music and Urban Geography,* 157).

42. Krims, *Music and Urban Geography,* 160.

43. Gold, "Day of Dre," 40.

44. This link between Dr. Dre's music and that of the 1970s is a formidable one, particularly in the borrowing of elements from 1970s funk and of imagery and characters from 1970s blaxploitation film. See Demers, "Sampling the 1970s."

45. The riff and other snippets from the single are used in a number of international rap singles, as the G-funk era was often the first experience that non-US countries had of rap music. As Dre and Snoop reached mainstream success in the United States, they were able to secure international distribution on a larger scale. One example is the Spanish rap group Arma Blanca, on their track "El Musicólogo," which samples from a number of American hits, and DJ Tomek's "G Thang 2008," from Berlin. Ben Folds's cover version of Dr. Dre's "Bitches Ain't Shit" (from *The Chronic*) uses a high-pitched synthesizer in the middle eight similar to one that Dre might use. The Folds cover is characteristically representative of his own piano/ singer-songwriter style, but the inclusion of the synthesizer adds another layer of musical signification not normally found on his recordings.

46. It is important, here, to draw the distinction between publishing fees and master recording (or mechanical) fees. When Dr. Dre rerecords songs, he only has to pay the publishing fees and not the mechanical fees in addition to the publishing, as would be the case if he digitally sampled the sounds. Kembrew McLeod writes, "When clearing a sample taken from a record, two types of fees must be paid: publishing fees and master recording (or mechanical) fees. The publishing fee, which is paid to the company or individual owning a particular song, often consists of a flexible and somewhat arbitrary formula that calculates a statutory royalty rate set by Congress" (*Owning Culture*, 91). See also Schloss, *Making Beats*, 175.

47. "Control is Dre's thing. Every Dre track begins the same way, with Dre behind a drum machine in a room full of trusted musicians. (They carry beepers. When he wants to work, they work.) They'll program a beat, then ask the musicians to play along; when Dre hears something he likes, he isolates the player and tells him how to refine the sound. 'My greatest talent,' Dre says, 'is knowing exactly what I want to hear.'" See Josh Tyrangiel, "In the Doctor's House," *Time*, Sept. 15, 2001, http://www.time.com/time/magazine/article/0,9171,1000775,00.html.

48. Kurtis Blow says, "The 808 is great because you can *detune* it and get this low-frequency hum. It's a car speaker destroyer. That's what we try and do as rap producers—break car speakers and house speakers and boom boxes. And the 808 does it. It's African music!" (quoted in Rose, *Black Noise*, 75).

49. Most accounts portray Dr. Dre as a "studio work-horse." One journalist notes, "Dre works in spurts. This week he's had three studio sessions of 19 hours or more. Last week he did a marathon 56-hour session. If he didn't go to the parking lot for the occasional car-stereo listening test, he'd have no idea whether it was night or day" (Tyrangiel, "In the Doctor's House"). Referring to Dr. Dre, Snoop Dogg has said, "I went and did a song with the nigga, the nigga made me do each word, word

for word, until I got it right. See what people don't understand is, when you dealing with Dr. Dre, you dealing with a perfectionist. It's like if you dealing with God. So you have to be perfection when you do a record with him, because his sound is right, his direction is right. Everybody ain't prepared for that!" See Nima, "Interview with Snoop Dogg," Dubcnn.com, http://www.dubcnn.com/interviews/snoopdogg06/ part1/ (accessed Oct. 22, 2008).

50. Kylee Swenson, "Captain Contagious," *Remix Magazine*, June 1, 2006, http://www.remixmag.com/artists/remix_captain_contagious/index.html.

51. Gold, "Day of Dre," 40.

52. Kay Dickinson, *Off Key: When Film and Music Won't Work Together* (Oxford: Oxford University Press, 2008), 124. See also Theo Cateforis, chap. 6, "Roll Over Guitar Heroes, Synthesizers Are Here . . . ," in *Are We Not New Wave? Modern Pop at the Turn of the 1980s* (Ann Arbor: University of Michigan Press, 2011), 151–81.

53. Goodwin, "Sample and Hold," 263. Goodwin also points out how while the keyboard musician had once been criticized for being cold and alienated, that criticism was transferred in the late 1980s to "musicians" who sit at the computer and choose to compose by way of digital sampler, rather than by playing an instrument.

54. Goodwin, "Sample and Hold," 265.

55. Massey, *Behind the Glass*, 25.

56. Massey, *Behind the Glass*, 159.

57. Cheo Hodari Coker, "N.W.A.," in Light, *Vibe History of Hip Hop*, 261.

58. Jon Pareles, "Still Tough, Still Authentic. Still Relevant?" *New York Times*, Nov. 14, 1999, http://query.nytimes.com/gst/fullpage.html?res=9F03E6DF103A F937A25752C1A96F958260.

59. Gold, "Day of Dre," 41.

60. Brendan I. Koerner, "The Game Is Up: Why Dr. Dre's Protégés Always Top the Charts," *Slate* 1, no. 10, Mar. 10, 2005, http://www.slate.com/id/2114375.

61. Robert Marriott, "Gangsta, Gangsta: The Sad, Violent Parable of Death Row Records," in Light, *Vibe History of Hip Hop*, 321.

62. Many of Dr. Dre's lyrics also express the centrality of the automobile to his perceived lifestyle. In "Nuthin' but a 'G' Thang," he states, "You never been on a ride like this before," and the chorus of "Gin and Juice" begins, "Rollin' down the street, smokin' indo." Nate Dogg raps, "We're gonna rock it till the wheels fall off," at the end of "The Next Episode," a song from Dr. Dre's second solo album, *Chronic 2001* (1999).

63. Eithne Quinn labels the G-funk era as "post-soul," referencing Nelson George's book *Post-Soul Nation* (2004). See Quinn, *Nuthin but a "g" Thang*, 143.

64. For a compelling argument for this, see Kelefa Sanneh, "'Rapping about Rapping': The Rise and Fall of a Hip-Hop Tradition," in *This Is Pop*, ed. Eric Weisbard (Cambridge: Harvard University Press, 2004), 230.

65. Michael Eric Dyson, "Black Youth, Pop Culture, and the Politics of Nostalgia," in *The Michael Eric Dyson Reader* (New York: Basic Civitas Books, 2004), 421.

66. Diehl, "Pop Rap," 129.

67. Brian Cross, *It's Not about a Salary: Rap, Race and Resistance in Los Angeles* (London: Verso, 1993), 197 (emphasis added). A similar sentiment was shared by producer Marley Marl when he said that he made the album *Steering Pleasure* "for people who wanna have som'n cool playin' in their rides. You won't get the same effect if you play the tracks through a regular system; you need a hype car system. The beats are programmed to make the speakers howl, you know what I'm saying" (quoted in Keyes, "At the Crossroads," 239).

68. Josh Tyrangiel has written about Death Row Records president Suge Knight's ability to understand the importance of MTV airplay in promoting his artists: Tyrangiel, "Hip-Hop Video," in Light, *Vibe History of Hip Hop*, 141.

69. Snoop Dogg has been quoted as saying that "one of the first things I did with my profits was to buy myself a car, a '77 cutlass supreme four-door I got off one of the homeboys from Compton for three hundred dollars. It didn't drive for shit, and every time you hit the brakes you could hear it squealing like a bitch in heat, but I loved the lines of that car and the way I looked sitting behind the wheel" (quoted in Gilroy, "Driving while Black," 81).

70. Born Calvin Broadus Jr., rapper Snoop Doggy Dogg changed his MC name to "Snoop Dogg" in 1998 when he left Death Row Records for No Limit Records. I use the two names interchangeably throughout the book.

71. Gold, "Day of Dre," 41.

72. "Stack cheese" is urban slang for making money.

73. Urry, "'System' of Automobility," 30.

74. Labelle, *Acoustic Ecologies*, 145–51.

75. Krims, *Music and Urban Geography*, 161.

76. Though the subwoofer was the product of a number of developments by a number of inventors, Los Angeles was crucial to its development and distribution. In the late 1960s, Ken Kreisel teamed up with Jonas Miller (of Jonas Miller Sound in Beverly Hills) and created M&K Sound in 1974, the second floor of the shop devoted to subwoofers. Kreisel's advancements with subwoofers in the early 1970s originated from a desire to reproduce successfully the low frequencies that he heard from the bass of pipe organs in Los Angeles. He went to Harvard, MIT, and Bell Labs to collaborate on acoustical research that influenced his products. See Wes

Phillips, "Audio Odyssey: Ken Kreisel of M&K," *Stereophile*, Mar. 1997, http://www.stereophile.com/interviews/136/.

77. Marsh and Collett, *Driving Passion*, 85.

78. Ashleigh Brilliant, *The Great Car Craze: How Southern California Collided with the Automobile in the 1920s* (Santa Barbara: Woodbridge Press, 1989), 121–22.

79. Brilliant, *Great Car Craze*, 27.

80. Quoted in Urry, "'System' of Automobility," 31.

81. Motown Corporation also made a version of *American Graffiti* targeted to an African American audience called *Cooley High* (1975).

82. Peter Wollen, "Introduction," in Wollen and Kerr, *Autopia*, 13–14.

83. Ralph Sutton, quoted in Massey, *Behind the Glass*, 293.

84. "*The Chronic* became to gangsta rap what Bob Marley's *Legend* was to reggae—the record that started a mainstream fan on the true path. Dr. Dre perfected the Gangsta Pop formula with Snoop Doggy Dogg's *Doggystyle*—pop songs with the hardcore aura intact, rendered broadcast-ready by radio edits that, somehow, didn't castrate the groove." See Cheo Hodari Coker, *Unbelievable: The Life, Death, and Afterlife of the Notorious B.I.G.* (New York: Three Rivers Press, 2003), 143.

85. Quoted in Frances Basham and Bob Ughetti, *Car Culture* (London: Plexus 1984), 40.

86. Katherine Hayles, *How We Became Posthuman: Virtual Bodies in Cybernetics, Literature, and Informatics* (Chicago: University of Chicago Press, 1999). This echoes the statement from Auner that "in no aspect of our lives has the penetration of the human by machines been more complete than in music. . . . We no longer even recognize complex devices such as a piano as technological artefacts." See Joseph Auner, "'Sing It for Me': Posthuman Ventriloquism in Recent Popular Music," *Journal of the Royal Musicological Association* 128, no. 1 (2003): 99.

87. Auner discusses Radiohead's "Fitter, Happier" and Moby's "Porcelain" as examples of posthuman voices ("'Sing It for Me'"). For an example of the use of the vocoder as an example of empowering femininity in Cher's "Believe," see Kay Dickinson, "'Believe'? Vocoders, Digitised Female Identity and Camp," *Popular Music* 20, no. 3 (2001): 333–47. Unlike these examples, Snoop Dogg's voice is far from that of a cyborg-esque posthuman ventriloquism. In contrast, the humanness of his voice is supported and framed by the synthesized sounds, male vocal effects, group singing, and the female voice of the coda.

88. This line from "Atomic Dog" is also quoted (without effects) in "F—wit Dre Day" on *The Chronic*, a song similar in harmonic structure and instrumentation to "Who Am I?"

89. It is noteworthy that "Who Am I?" was Snoop Doggy Dogg's official debut;

emphasizing his realness and humanness would be especially important to ensure future success. Dr. Dre has introduced a number of protégés since who also had debut singles produced by him, including Eminem, 50 Cent, and The Game (see chap. 5).

90. "Simple verse-chorus" form is a popular song form where the harmonic material of the verse matches the harmonic material of the chorus, as opposed to "contrasting verse-chorus" form, where the two sections have different harmonic progressions. See John Covach, "Form in Rock Music: A Primer," in *Engaging Music: Essays in Music Analysis*, ed. Deborah Stein (Oxford: Oxford University Press, 2005).

91. Dyer, *Pastiche*, 80.

92. Of course, sample-based hip-hop can suggest realness as well, explicated in Krims's discussion of the Bomb Squad's production on Ice Cube's "The Nigga You Love to Hate" (*Rap Music*, 93–102). "Who Am I?" may reflect shifting sonic representations of "realness" within the reality rap music subgenre, partly influenced by Dre's shift away from sample-based production.

93. In terms of theorizing sound frequency, though he focuses mostly on case studies of sound generally rather than on music (though he has chapters on dub and Muzak), a good start is the work of Steve Goodman: *Sonic Warfare: Sound, Affect, and the Ecology of Fear* (Cambridge: MIT Press, 2010).

94. Evidence of this in hip-hop production may be found in the phenomenon of "detuned" layers; if certain layers of sound do not correspond to exact notes in the well-tempered chromatic scale, then this supports the idea that producers think of sound in terms of frequency, rather than in terms of Western pitches. For example, Dr. Dre's "F—wit Dre Day" is in a key somewhere between c minor and c# minor. For more on detuned layers, see Krims, *Rap Music*. Not all rap songs are detuned, however; for example, "Who Am I? (What's My Name)" is closer to a traditional key than not.

95. Michael Bull, "Soundscapes of the Car," in *The Auditory Culture Reader*, ed. Michael Bull and Les Back (Oxford: Berg, 2003), 371.

96. Jonathan Bell, *Carchitecture: When the Car and the City Collide* (London: Birkhäuser, 2001), 11.

97. Marsh and Collett, *Driving Passion*, 4.

98. Bull writes that "sound engulfs the spatial, thus making the relation between subject and object problematic" ("Soundscapes of the Car," 361). Both Urry and Bull have recognized that drivers experience inhabiting the car rather than inhabiting the road or street on which one drives.

99. Mimi Sheller, "Automotive Emotions: Feeling the Car," in Featherstone, Thrift, and Urry, *Automobilities*, 222.

100. Urry, "'System' of Automobility," 25.

Chapter 4

1. Quoted in Plinio Prioreschi, *A History of Human Responses to Death* (Lampeter: Edwin Mellen Press, 1990), 97.

2. Eminem, "Sing for the Moment," *The Eminem Show* (2002).

3. David Giles, *Illusions of Immortality: A Psychology of Fame and Celebrity* (London: Macmillian Press, 2000), 135. For the classic text on stardom in the context of film, see Richard Dyer, *Stars* (London: British Film Institute, 1998).

4. See Anthony DeCurtis, "Kurt Cobain: 1967–1994," *Rolling Stone* 683, June 2, 1994, 30. David Fricke, in "Heart-Shaped Noise: The Music and the Legacy," (also in *Rolling Stone* 683, June 2, 1994), writes in reference to Nirvana's first hit "Smells like Teen Spirit": "it takes one song to define an epoch—or at least to mark the starting line" (66). See also Sharon R. Mazzarella and Norman Pecora, "Kurt Cobain, Generation X, and the Press; College Students Respond," *Popular Music and Society* 19, no. 2 (1995): 3–22; Sharon R. Mazzarella "'The Voice of a Generation'? Media Coverage of the Suicide of Kurt Cobain," *Popular Music and Society* 19, no. 2 (1995): 49–68; Steve Jones, "Covering Cobain: Narrative Patterns in Journalism and Rock Criticism," *Popular Music and Society* 19, no. 2 (1995): 103–18.

5. See Douglas J. Davies, *Death, Ritual, and Belief* (London: Cassell, 1997), 177. One significant death as cultural event was that of Princess Diana in 1997. Her funeral was shown around the world and included Elton John's performance of "Candle in the Wind," which went on to become one of the best-selling singles of all time. C. W. Watson goes as far as to consider Diana symbolically as the royal sacrificial victim who died for the British nation's sins. He writes, "just as the blood of martyrs is the seed of the church, so the death of secular social martyrs can be regarded as the seed for the regeneration of the nation": C. W. Watson, "'Born a Lady, Became a Princess, Died a Saint': The Reaction to the Death of Diana, Princess of Wales," *Anthropology Today* 13, no. 6 (1997): 7.

6. The concept of symbolic immortality, as theorized by Robert Jay Lifton, is discussed at length in the third chapter of the book *Living and Dying*, which Lifton coauthored with Eric Olson (London: Wildwood House, 1974). See also Lifton, *The Future of Immortality and Other Essays for a Nuclear Age* (New York: Basic

Books, 1987); and Lifton, *The Broken Connection: On Death and the Continuity of Life* (Washington, DC: American Psychiatric Press, 1999). Giles's study of fame notes the "long literary tradition of presenting fame as immortality, from Virgil ("I too may . . . fly in victory on the lips of men") through to the lyrics of Irene Cara's song: "Fame! I want to live forever" (*Illusions of Immortality*, 49).

7. Tupac Shakur was gunned down at an intersection in Las Vegas following his attendance of the Mike Tyson–Bruce Seldon fight on Sept. 7, 1996. The Notorious B.I.G. (Christopher Wallace) was shot in similar fashion on Mar. 9, 1997, in Los Angeles. Tupac was twenty-five years old when he was murdered, and Wallace was twenty-four. As of this writing, no one has been arrested for either murder.

8. There are a number of theories surrounding both murders that have spawned numerous books and documentary films. See Randall Sullivan, *Labyrinth: Corruption and Vice in the L.A.P.D.* (Edinburgh: Canongate Books, 2002); and Nick Broomfield's documentary *Biggie and Tupac*, 108 min. (Film Four, UK, 2002; DVD, 2004). See also Cathy Scott, *The Killing of Tupac Shakur* (London: Plexus Publishing, 1997).

9. Kulkarni, *Hip Hop Bring the Noise*, 100.

10. Andrew Gumbel, "Tupac: The Life. The Legend. The Legacy," *Independent*, Sept. 13, 2006, 24.

11. Alan Clayson, *Death Discs: Ashes to Smashes: An Account of Fatality in the Popular Song* (London: Gollancz, 1992), 88.

12. Janne Mäkelä, *John Lennon Imagined: Cultural History of a Rock Star* (London: Peter Lang Publishing, 2004), 261. In regard to Hendrix and less "official" posthumous releases, Steven Roby writes, "Since his death, more than five hundred recorded titles have appeared that are devoted to him entirely or in part": Steven Roby, *Black Gold: The Lost Archives of Jimi Hendrix* (New York: Billboard Books, 2002), 2. I would like to thank Jan Butler for bringing the last book to my attention.

13. Deena Weinstein, "Art versus Commerce: Deconstructing a (Useful) Romantic Illusion," in *Stars Don't Stand Still in the Sky: Music and Myth*, ed. Karen Kelly and Evelyn McDonnell (London: Routledge, 1999), 66–67. On the romantic death of artists, Lee Marshall writes, "It has to be a particular kind of death—a 'heroic' death—and it has to be at an early age. Both of these emerge from Romantic ideology. The Romantics valorized youth as a time of both political and aesthetic radicalism ('Bliss was it in that dawn to be alive,' wrote Wordsworth, 'but to be young was very Heaven'). Youth was a time before the disenchantment of science and rationalism overtook one's self, when the world could be seen through new eyes.

It was a time for breaking the rules created by previous generations, and it was a time for excess, to indulge in all the bounteous tastes the world has to offer— drugs, drink, sex, freedom": Lee Marshall, *Bob Dylan: The Never Ending Star* (Cambridge: Polity Press, 2007), 143–44.

14. Recording Industry Association of America, "Diamond Awards," http://www.riaa.com/gp/bestsellers/diamond.asp (accessed Dec. 20, 2006). Directly after the death of Notorious B.I.G., many record stores moved his debut *Ready to Die* to the front of their stores and ordered additional copies of *Life after Death*. One store manager told Cheo Hodari Coker: "Whenever an artist dies, we pack the shelves" (Coker, *Unbelievable*, 250).

15. Recording Industry Association of America, "Top Artists," http://www.riaa.com/gp/bestsellers/topartists.asp (accessed Dec. 20, 2006).

16. Michael Datcher and Kwame Alexander, eds., *Tough Love: The Life and Death of Tupac Shakur* (Alexandria: Alexander Publishing Group, 1997), 46.

17. Rob Sheffield, "R U Still Down (Remember Me?)," *Rolling Stone* 778, Jan. 22, 1998, 53.

18. Coker, *Unbelievable*, 293.

19. See http://www.makaveli-branded.com/ (accessed Dec. 20, 2006): "keeping the legacy alive through fashion." For a list of clothing lines and hip-hop artists, see the appendix in Emmett G. Price III, *Hip Hop Culture* (Santa Barbara: ABC-CLIO, 2006), 214.

20. *Vibe Magazine*, Dec. 2006, 89.

21. Coker, *Unbelievable*, 263.

22. Coker, *Unbelievable*, 264–65.

23. Roger Beebe, "Mourning Becomes . . . ? Kurt Cobain, Tupac Shakur, and the 'Waning of Affect,'" in *Rock over the Edge: Transformations in Popular Music Culture,* ed. Roger Beebe, Denise Fulbrook, and Ben Saunders (Durham: Duke University Press, 2002), 328. Beebe also cites the Lox's "We'll Always Love Big Poppa" and Puff Daddy's "I'll Be Missing You" as songs that encourage mourning.

24. Marshall, *Bob Dylan*, 129. In the context of Kurt Cobain, Camille Paglia takes this one step further when she writes, "Cobain's a martyr to the god of rock in some way. Buying his merchandise is like buying the relics of the saints": quoted in Steve Jones, "Better Off Dead," in *Afterlife as Afterimage: Understanding Posthumous Fame,* ed. Steve Jones and Joli Jensen (New York: Peter Lang, 2005), 8.

25. As Armond White writes, "for anyone interested in the art of rap, the ball clearly remained in Biggie's corner": Armond White, *Rebel for the Hell of It* (New York: Thunder's Mouth Press, 2002), 186. Both White's and Dyson's books on Tu-

pac make this distinction, as does some of the journalism regarding the East Coast–West Coast feud.

26. Neil Strauss, "Hip-Hop Requiem," in *Tupac: A Thug Life*, ed. Sam Brown (London: Plexus, 2005), 185 (originally published in the *New York Times*).

27. Greg Dimitriadis, *Performing Identity/Performing Culture: Hip-Hop as Text, Pedagogy, and Lived Practice* (Oxford: Peter Lang, 2001), 107.

28. Kevin Powell, who interviewed him for *Vibe Magazine* countless times, said, "He talked about dying, always" (quoted in Scott, *Killing of Tupac Shakur*, 91).

29. S. Brown, *Tupac*, 121.

30. "Last Testament," in *Tupac Shakur*, ed. Alan Light (London: Plexus, 1997), 125. The idea that Tupac was a martyr has also been supplemented by the idea of the promise of a resurrection, or at least an alluding to a Messianic return, in various rap lyrics. As one of the members of the Outlawz asks in "One Day st a Time," from the *Tupac: Resurrection* soundtrack, "So if he died and came back, would he try and save rap?" Rapper 50 Cent proclaims in the first line of the chorus to "The Realest Killaz": "'Till Makaveli returns, it's all eyes on me," a reference to Tupac's 1996 album *All Eyez on Me*, as well as a reference to Tupac as a messiah figure.

31. This is far from the only instance of crucifixion imagery or rhetoric in rap and other popular musics. An early example includes John Lennon's line from the "Ballad of John and Yoko": "the way things are going, they're going to crucify me." Rappers have used crucifixion terminology and imagery to make a point regarding disrespect from the media or other artists, such as in N.W.A.'s "Quiet on the Set" from *Straight Outta Compton* (1988), Public Enemy's "Welcome to the Terrordome," Eminem's "Sing for the Moment," Twista's "Dirty Game," and Tupac's own "Blasphemy." One of the original rap covers to use the "crucifixion pose" was the 1993 "Dre Dog" album *The New Jim Jones*. Nas's music video for "Hate Me Now" includes him with a crown of thorns, carrying a cross while being stoned by the public, and later images in the video include him rapping while up on the cross. Kanye West appeared on the cover of *Rolling Stone* wearing a crown of thorns. See Joe Carter, "Pop Semiotics: The Passion of the Rappers," *Evangelical Outpost*, Jan. 31, 2006, http://www.evangelicaloutpost.com/archives/001806.html.

32. Michael Eric Dyson, *Holler if You Hear Me* (New York: Basic Civitas Books, 2002), 264–65.

33. This number will often vary in journalistic accounts, depending on what they constitute as an "official release," which for most includes *The Don Killuminati: The 7 Day Theory* (1996), *R U Still Down (Remember Me?)* (1997), *Greatest Hits* (1998), *Still I Rise* (1999), *Until the End of Time* (2001), *Better Dayz* (2002), *Tupac: Resur-*

rection Soundtrack (2003), *Loyal to the Game* (2004), and *Pac's Life* (2006). All except the first included Tupac's mother, Afeni Shakur, as executive producer.

34. Dyson, *Holler if You Hear Me*, 10–11. Johnny J, one of his producers when he was with Death Row Records, said, "You know I'd get there about an hour or two earlier, whatever. And I'd just have the track ready. He walks in and hears the beat: 'give me a pen and pad, a pencil . . . come on give me a pencil. I know exactly what I want to do. Let's go for it' . . . In one day we'd do about 4 or 5 cuts a day, depending on the flow": Johnny J, interview, on *Thug Angel: The Life of an Outlaw*, dir. Peter Spirer, 92 min. (QD3 Entertainment, USA, 2002; DVD, 2002), 36:00.

35. Dyson, *Holler if You Hear Me*, 75.

36. Frank Alexander, *Got Your Back: Life as Tupac Shakur's Bodyguard in the Hardcore World of Gangsta Rap* (New York: St. Martin's Press, 1998), 63.

37. Coker, *Unbelievable*, 170.

38. Allison Samuels, "Who Stole Tupac's Soul?" *Rolling Stone* 789, June 25, 1998, 17. Often mythologized is the Faustian pact Tupac made with Suge Knight: a handwritten three-album contract signed Tupac to Death Row Records in exchange for the 1.4 million dollars bail he needed to be released from jail. Accounts say that with no other option, he signed his life away to be caught up in a record label and lifestyle that eventually led to his murder.

39. A story found in many sources relates that when Tupac was ten years old, Reverend Hubert Daughtry asked him what he wanted to be when he grew up, and he responded, "I'm gonna be a revolutionary." See asha bandele, "Meditations in the Hour of Mourning," in Datcher and Alexander, *Tough Love*, 29. A similar version of the anecdote is in White, *Rebel*, 1.

40. Accounts include White, *Rebel*, 16–17; and an interview Tupac gave while he was in prison, found on the DVD *Tupac Vs.*, dir. Ken Peters, 64 min. (Concrete Treehouse Productions, USA, 2004; DVD, 2007), 11:55.

41. Daniel Chua has written that Mozart was characterized as the first "poor artist" (Romantically speaking); his poverty is a "necessary myth" for biographies as a foil to the freedom of his music. Chua notes that Mozart died just before the nineteenth-century shift from music as material commodity to music as intellectual idea, with Mozart "used as the exchange rate." See Daniel K. L. Chua, "Myth: Mozart, Money, Music," in *Mozart Studies*, ed. Simon P. Keefe (Cambridge: Cambridge University Press, 2006), 198.

42. Dyson, *Holler if You Hear Me*, 48. An interview with Greg Jacobs ("Shock G" of Digital Underground) compares different rappers' styles and specifically links Tupac's delivery and style in his raps with a black revolutionary heritage: "Humpty

Hump and Slick Rick rhyme from the nasal palette. Nas rhymes from the back of his throat. Biggie is a swinger. He swings like a horn player over jazz. . . . Pac, on the other hand, Tupac pulled from Martin Luther King, Malcolm X . . . it's like pouring those words out because you mean it. And that's why, you know [does impression of Tupac]: 'I never had a father figure, but I was raised by the thugs and the drug dealers, that's why I love niggas.' That singing that Pac was doing in his stuff." See the interview with Greg Jacobs in *The Art of 16 Bars: Get Ya' Bars Up*, dir. Peter Spirer, 80 min. (QD3 Entertainment, 2005; DVD), 40:48.

43. Jordan Harper, "All Oddz on Me," in S. Brown, *Tupac*, 178.

44. George Kamberelis and Greg Dimitriadis, "Collectively Remembering Tupac: The Narrative Mediation of Current Events, Cultural Histories, and Social Identities," in S. Jones and Jensen, *Afterlife as Afterimage*, 166.

45. Anthony B. Pinn, ed., *Noise and Spirit: The Religious and Spiritual Sensibilities of Rap Music* (New York: New York University Press, 2003).

46. John Teter and Alex Gee, *Jesus and the Hip-Hop Prophets: Spiritual Insights from Lauryn Hill and 2Pac* (Downers Grove: InterVarsity Press, 2003).

47. Theresa L. Reed, *The Holy Profane: Religion in Black Popular Music* (Lexington: University of Kentucky Press, 2002), 159

48. Susan Sontag, "The Artist as Exemplary Sufferer," in *Against Interpretation* (New York: Farrar Straus Giroux, 1966), 42. Though Sontag primarily considers writers in her essay, it would certainly be appropriate to add various musicians to her thoughtful critique.

49. Other examples of Tupac in academia include the Greg Dimitradis book *Performing Identity/Performing Culture*, which includes a chapter Dimitriadis cowrote with George Kamberelis, entitled "The Symbolic Mediation of Identity in Black Popular Culture: The Discursive Life, Death, and Rebirth of Tupac Shakur." The final chapter of Eithne Quinn's *Nuthin but a "G" Thang* is entitled "Tupac Shakur and the Legacies of Gangsta." One article goes so far as to make a tenuous attempt to compare the Lacanian "Real" with the idea of Tupac's manifestation of the "real" as "the dominant cultural logic in hip-hop": see Thomas Kane, "Bringing the Real: Lacan and Tupac," *Prospects: An Annual of American Cultural Studies* 27 (2002): 642.

50. Billy Jam, "Strictly for my Clazzmatez: Tupac Joins Academia's Literary Canon," in Light, *Tupac Shakur*, 147.

51. Nathan Abrams also shows that contemporary rap artists, specifically hardcore rap artists such as Chuck D, Paris, KRS-One, Grandmaster Flash, and Eric B and Rakim, contain characteristics similar to Gramsci's concept: Nathan D. Abrams, "Antonio's B-Boys: Rap, Rappers, and Gramsci's Intellectuals," *Popular Music and Society* 19, no. 4 (1995): 1–19.

52. Tupac Shakur, *The Rose That Grew from Concrete* (New York: MTV, 1999), 25.

53. *Tupac: Hip-Hop Genius*, dir. Charlotte Lewin, 64 min. (Chrome Dreams Video, USA, 2005; DVD, 2005).

54. Angela Ardis, *Inside a Thug's Heart* (New York: Kensington Publishing Corp., 2004).

55. Shakur, *Rose That Grew from Concrete*, xiii.

56. Thomas Swiss, "Jewel Case: Pop Stars, Poets, and the Press," in *Pop Music and the Press*, ed. Steve Jones (Philadelphia: Temple University Press, 2002), 179. The singer-songwriter Jewel published a book of her poetry entitled *A Night without Armor* (1998). Jewel had been constructed as a poet in the press, and the book was successful, selling 432,000 copies that year. A spoken-word CD version was also available. Swiss writes how Jewel's endeavor fit the tradition of Bob Dylan, Jim Morrison, and Patti Smith of pop musicians/poets. Like Tupac's poetry books and Kurt Cobain's journal collection, the cover of Jewel's book is handwritten, suggesting a deep form of authenticity. The Notorious B.I.G. has also been labeled as a poet and has been compared to various poets: "People tend to forget that one of America's premiere poets, Biggie Smalls, and another, Walt Whitman, were both from Brooklyn": Paul D. Miller, "The City in Public versus Private," in Chang, *Total Chaos*, 151.

57. Or perhaps the idea that chamber music gives an audience a sense of eavesdropping on the innermost thoughts and feelings of the composer is what becomes desirable. Chamber music has connotations of an upper-class cultural art form, and poetry may still have links with an aristocratic connoisseurship. For more on the covert values associated with descriptions of music as "chamber-music-like," see Janet M. Levy, "Covert and Casual Values in Recent Writings about Music," *Journal of Musicology* 5, no. 1 (1987).

58. Tupac's mother, Afeni, organized the construction of the statue, a product of the Tupac Amaru Shakur foundation, which she founded after his death.

59. S. Jones, "Better off Dead," 5.

60. Kamberelis and Dimitriadis, "Collectively Remembering Tupac," 145. They outline four main functions of narratives: mediating between ordinary and exceptional ideas and events, affirming or validating moral or ethical imperatives, regulating affect, and constructing and maintaining coherent social and cultural identities.

61. Nicholas Cook, "The Domestic *Gesamtkunstwerk*, or Record Sleeves and Reception," in *Composition-Performance-Reception*, ed. Wyndham Thomas (Aldershot: Ashgate, 1998), 115.

62. Eshun, *More Brilliant than the Sun*,

63. Sontag, "Artist as Exemplary Sufferer," 42.

64. Sontag, "Artist as Exemplary Sufferer," 42.

65. "Star Profiles II," in Frith, Straw, and Street, *Cambridge Companion to Pop and Rock*, 204.

66. Peggy J. Bowers and Stephanie Houston Grey, "Karen: The Hagiographic Impulse in the Public Memory of a Pop Star," in S. Jones and Jensen, *Afterlife as Afterimage*, 107.

67. Samuels, "Who Stole Tupac's Soul?" 17.

68. One example of postmortem sampling of the image of Elvis was a "duet" performance of Celine Dion and a hologram-like image of Elvis Presley singing "If I Can Dream" for the *American Idol* 2007 "Idol Gives Back" charity show. Another example is the ZZ Top music video to "Viva Las Vegas" from their 1992 *Greatest Hits Album*, using Elvis's image from the eponymous film.

69. Gary Burns, "Refab Four: Beatles for Sale in the Age of Music Video," in *The Beatles, Popular Music and Society*, ed. Ian Inglis (London: Macmillan Press, 2000), 176–77. See also Janne Mäkelä, "Who Owns Him?: The Debate on John Lennon," in S. Jones and Jensen, *Afterlife as Afterimage*, 177–78.

70. Fred Goodman, "Duets with the Dead: Homage or Exploitation?" *New York Times*. Jan. 16, 2000, www.nytimes.com.

71. See "Pat Metheny Declares War on Kenny G," Vh1.com, June 14, 2000, http://www.vh1.com/artists/news/1436591/20000614/g_kenny.jhtml. See also Tony Whyton, chap. 3, "Not a Wonderful World: Louis Armstrong Meets Kenny G," in *Jazz Icons* (Cambridge: Cambridge University Press, 2010); 57–81. Whyton's book discusses the importance of the role of the "African-American hero" figure in jazz (e.g., Armstrong, Ellington, Coltrane), and I believe many of these ideas can also apply to the hip-hop generation and its heroes.

72. Roland Barthes, "The Grain of the Voice," in *Image Music Text*, ed. and trans. Stephen Heath (Hammersmith: Fontana Press, 1977), 188.

73. Michel Chion, *The Voice in Cinema*, trans. and ed. Claudia Gorbman (New York: Columbia University Press, 1999), 1. Chion and other film theorists writing about Lacanian psychoanalysis cite Lacan's Seminar XI: *The Four Fundamental Concepts of Psychoanalysis*. The seminar was given in 1964 and was the first of his seminars to be published (in 1973). Chion also points out that in Freudian psychoanalysis, "everything happens in and through the voice" (1). Another example includes Mary Ann Doane, "The Voice in Cinema: The Articulation of Body and Space," in *Film Sound: Theory and Practice*, ed. Elisabeth Weis and John Belton (New York: Columbia University Press, 1985), 170.

74. In 1878, one *Scientific American* article stated: "Speech has become, as it were, immortal": quoted in Jonathan Sterne, "Dead Rock Stars 1990," in S. Jones and Jen-

sen, *Afterlife as Afterimage*, 254–55. Sterne cites a number of early writings on the phonograph that deal with the death discourse regarding early recorded sound and the immortality of the recorded voice.

75. Jason Toynbee, *Making Popular Music* (Oxford: Oxford University Press, 2000), 45.

76. Marshall, *Bob Dylan*, 43.

77. Mikhail Bakhtin, "Discourse in the Novel," in *The Dialogic Imagination*, ed. Michel Holquist (Austin: University of Austin Press, 1982), 342, also quoted in Reynolds, *Motives for Allusion*, 84.

Bakhtin makes the distinction between "authoritative discourse" in the novel and "internally persuasive discourse," "which is more akin to retelling a text in one's own words, with one's own accents, gestures, modifications," Bakhtin, 424.

78. This also means, of course, that the recorded voice can be manipulated digitally as well, and the next chapter presents some examples of Eminem's manipulation of 2 Pac's voice.

79. The term *acousmêtre* is most extensively theorized in Chion, *Voice in Cinema*, 36.

80. This "unplugged" aesthetic was perhaps most apparent in youth culture as part of a series of concerts called *MTV: Unplugged*, which featured a number of groups popular at the time that essentially played covers of their songs with relatively acoustic instrumentation. See Philip Auslander, "Liveness," in *The Popular Music Studies Reader*, ed. Andy Bennett, Barry Shank, and Jason Toynbee (London: Routledge, 2006), 89.

81. Nas says in one interview, "As soon as I heard it [the rap], I was with it. It was something I wanted to do with just a guitar playing, not really drums—something you could hear the words [on]." See Shaheem Reid, "On Tupac Video Set, Nas Says Rapper Better than Shakespeare," *MTV News*, Dec. 3, 2004, http://www.mtv.com/news/articles/1458966/20021203/nas.jhtml.

82. "At least since the early 1960s, acoustic playing has stood for authenticity, sincerity, and rootsiness; hence, the dismay that greeted Bob Dylan's use of an electric guitar at the 1965 Newport Folk Festival. Live performance, too, has long been understood as the realm of the authentic, the true test of musicianship undisguised by studio trickery" (Auslander, "Liveness," 89).

83. Sontag, "Artist as Exemplary Sufferer," 42.

84. *Thug Angel*, 34:29.

85. Ta-Nehisi Coates, "Tupac: The Reality Show," in Hermes and Michel, *Spin*, 145.

86. dream hampton, "Hell-Raiser," in *"And it Don't Stop": The Best American*

Hip-Hop Journalism of the Last 25 Years, ed. Raquel Cepeda (New York: Faber and Faber, Inc., 2004), 132. Her observations reflect the Jan. 31, 1994, Blue Palms Recording Studio session in Burbank.

87. The irony of the Nas alliance with Tupac is that Tupac showed his disdain for Nas on some of his records. The opening pseudo-news report from *The Don Killuminati* album opens describing Nas as the "alleged ringleader" of a conspiracy to "assassinate the character of not only Mr. Shakur, but Death Row Records as well." And on the track "Against All Odds" from the same album, Tupac criticizes Dr. Dre, Mobb Deep, Puffy, and Nas, saying of Nas, "This little nigga named Nas thinks he live like me / Talkin' 'bout he left the hospital, took five like me / You living fantasies, nigga I reject your deposit." Suge Knight considered Nas's "collaboration" to be "real disrespectful to Pac." He continues, "Don't go [do a song] knowing a certain individual didn't care for you": Shaheem Reid, "Suge Knight Calls Tupac/Nas Track 'Disrespectful,'" *MTV News*, Apr. 21, 2003, http://www.mtv.com/news/articles/1471376/20030418/knight_marion_suge_.jhtml.

88. Todd Boyd, *The New H.N.I.C. (Head Nigga in Charge): The Death of Civil Rights and the Reign of Hip Hop* (New York: New York University Press, 2003), 90.

89. Faith Evans also sang on the Puff Daddy memorial song "I'll Be Missing You." Though they had been estranged at the time of his death, the marriage bond provides an authentic sense of tribute and conveys the sense that Faith has a right to honor her husband (a family sentiment similar to Natalie Cole's "Unforgettable"). Jay-Z (as opposed to Nas and Tupac), however, had an actual connection and friendship with the Notorious B.I.G., who appeared on Jay-Z's debut album *Reasonable Doubt* (1996).

90. Coker writes that "*Ready to Die* sold 500,000 copies in its first week alone. Suddenly the video for 'Juicy' was all over MTV, the radio was playing his song three times an hour, and it seemed like everywhere he went, people knew who the Notorious B.I.G. was" (*Unbelievable*, 114).

91. "Juicy" sampled the beat from the 1983 single "Juicy Fruit" by the group Mtume. By sampling a song from the early 1980s, Biggie uses nostalgia, musically, to accompany the rags-to-riches story of his growing up ("I used to read Word Up magazine . . . Every Saturday, Rap Attack, Mr. Magic, Marley Marl"). He gives thanks to those who supported him in the past and describes both the contrast between his past and present living conditions and also the state of rap music ("Remember Rappin Duke? 'Duh-ha duh-ha.' You never thought hip-hop would take it this far"). Overall, the lyrics and the musical accompaniment are "positive," the sample in a major key. The UK hip-hop magazine *Hip-Hop Connection*, in its tribute

to Notorious B.I.G. a decade after his murder, refers to "Juicy" as as "uplifting a rap song as you'll ever hear, and one without an ounce of schmaltz to it." See Angus Batey, Andrew Emery, Phillip Mlynar, Rob Pursey, "Notorious B.I.G.: A Tribute," *Hip-Hop Connections* 209, Mar. 2007, 73.

92. Comparing Biggie to Tupac, Coker writers, "Biggie's legacy is different. Wallace's lasting imprint on hip hop is more musical than iconographic. He is a master of flow, of lyrical rhythm and technique—the Jordan to Rakim's Magic. While his catalogue of unreleased records isn't as large as Tupac's, the quality of many of the surviving freestyles is unsurpassed" (*Unbelievable*, 8). Anthony DeCurtis writes, "The Notorious B.I.G., for his part, was eminently of this world. He had perhaps the greatest emotional range and straight-up literary skill of any rapper before or after him. His rhymes could be riotously funny on a purely verbal level ('... escargot / My car go ...'), and he could seamlessly move from fury to vulnerability to sensuality to a poignancy within a few lines. His ceaseless profanity—as in so many hip hop lyrics—lends his raps a conversational tone, the language of the streets": Anthony DeCurtis, "Word," in Light, *Vibe History of Hip Hop*, 97.

93. Accounts of this can be found in Coker, *Unbelievable*, 96, 102.

94. Examples include Lil' Kim, "Suck My Dick"; Method Man and Mary J. Blige, "I'll Be There for You/You're All I Need"; Smitty, "Diamonds on My Neck" (which uses the hook from "Dangerous MCs"); Bossman, "Untouchable"; Big Pun, "Super Lyrical" (which uses excerpts from "One More Chance"); and Michael Jackson, "Unbreakable." Faith Evans uses the "Juicy"/Mtume beat for her 2001 song "Faithfully."

95. Jerry L. Barrow, "Under the Influence," *Source* 207, Feb. 2007, 78.

96. Ellen Rosand, "Lament," in Macy, *Grove Music Online*, http://www.grovemusic.com (accessed Nov. 23, 2006).

97. Susan McClary, on *Thug Angel*, DVD Extras.

98. Susan McClary, on *Thug Angel*, DVD Extras.

99. Susan McClary and Robert Walser discuss this concept in their article "Start Making Sense!": "Thus to try to make the case that a particular configuration sounds mournful (something that may be obvious to virtually all listeners, especially those not perverted by musical training) is to have to invent a philosophical argument for meaning in music and to try to reconstruct forgotten codes out of centuries of music": Susan McClary and Robert Walser, "Start Making Sense!: Musicology Wrestles with Rock," in Frith and Goodwin, *On Record*, 283.

100. Quoted in Rosand, "Lament."

101. Effects such as echo, reverb, double-tracking, and compression can be used to varying degrees to create such a "big" sound.

102. Richard Middleton, "'O Brother Let's Go Down Home': Loss, Nostalgia and the Blues," *Popular Music* 26, no. 1 (2007): 56.

103. The concept of detuned layers is one feature of what Krims calls the "hip-hop sublime." See Krims, *Rap Music*, 73.

104. Coker, *Unbelievable*, 330–31.

105. The Mack, "A Dream," *This Is a Kanye West Production*, http://www.the mack.org/KanyeList.html (accessed December 20, 2006). The term *jawn* is a Philadelphia urban slang term that is often used in place of any noun, but usually a "thing."

106. Missy Elliot, "Back in the Day," *Under Construction* (2002).

Chapter 5

1. As seen in recent histories of hip-hop, "generations" tend to last five to six years, with dominant artists, geographical locations, and styles as defining features. Because of the short time span of generations in popular music subgenres compared to generations of human life, one might be inclined to call these "microgenerations" within popular music. A similar example of historicization in rock music is demonstrated by the BBC documentary *The Seven Ages of Rock*, which divides the past fifty years of rock music into seven distinct eras.

2. These time periods, of course, differ between writers and fans, but I will use one example from William Jelani Cobb to show that there is a historical consciousness that recognizes multiple "periods" of the genre's history: "Art respects no borders and time frames, but for our own concerns, hip hop can be divided into four overlapping eras: the Old School, 1974–1983, the Golden Age, 1984–1992, the Modern Era, 1992–1997, and the Industrial Era, 1998–2005" (*To the Break of Dawn*, 41). See also Chang, *Can't Stop Won't Stop*.

3. Krims, *Rap Music*, 70–80.

4. For more on mixtapes, see Bakari Kitwana, *Why White Kids Love Hip-Hop: Wankstas, Wiggers, Wannabes, and the New Reality of Race in America* (New York: Basic Civitas Books, 2005), 92.

5. Robert P. Morgan, "Tradition, Anxiety, and the Musical Scene," in Kenyon, *Authenticity and Early Music*, 65.

6. Quoted in Morgan, "Tradition, Anxiety," 63–64. Stravinsky also writes, "A real tradition is not the relic of a past that is irretrievably gone; it is a living force that animates and informs the present.... This sense of tradition which is a natural need must not be confused with the desire which the composer feels to affirm the kin-

ship he finds across the centuries with some master of the past" (quoted in Morgan, "Tradition, Anxiety," 63).

7. Historically conscious hip-hop artists and groups have also made links with pre-hip-hop musical forms in a variety of ways, such as with the music of James Brown, jazz (see chap. 2), and funk styles. See also Joanna Demers, "Sampling as Lineage in Hip-Hop" (PhD thesis, Princeton University, 2002); and Demers, "Sampling the 1970s."

8. Eminem, "Patiently Waiting," 50 Cent, *Get Rich or Die Tryin'* (2003).

9. This line could also be a reference to the single "The Realest Killaz," which features 50 Cent, on the *Tupac: Resurrection* soundtrack. The idea of a double-voiced utterance, a concept theorized by Bakhtin, has been utilized by writers such as Henry Louis Gates Jr. who believe that that the double-voiced utterance is a primary quality of black discourse. For the application of the double-voiced utterance to James Brown's "Superbad," see Brackett, *Interpreting Popular Music*, 123.

10. Lynne D. Johnson, "Hip-Hop's Holy Trinity," in *Da Capo Best Music Writing 2004*, ed. Mickey Hart (Cambridge: Da Capo Press, 2004), 139.

11. Since Ayler's comment was made after Coltrane died, this may be a case of Ayler attempting to place himself within a particular canon without having the luxury of a response from Coltrane.

12. L. D. Johnson, "Hip-Hop's Holy Trinity," 139, 143.

13. For more on the multiple functions at work in society regarding posthumous fame, see Joli Jensen, "Posthumous Patsy Clines: Constructions of Identity in Hillbilly Heaven," in S. Jones and Jensen, *Afterlife as Afterimage*, 123.

14. Antoine Hennion states, for example, "The invention of a tradition and the social production of the past has been traced for several repertories, ranging from Beethoven (DeNora 1995) to country music (Peterson 1997)": Antoine Hennion, "Music and Mediation," in *The Cultural Study of Music*, ed. Martin Clayton, Trevor Herbert, and Richard Middleton (London: Routledge, 2006), 84.

15. Eric W. Rothenbuhler, "Robert Johnson's Records," in S. Jones and Jensen, *Afterlife as Afterimage*, 221.

16. Pete Frame, *The Rock Family Trees: The Development and History of Rock Performers* (London: Omnibus Press, 1983).

17. Richard Taruskin writes that Furtwängler's and Schoenberg's approaches "rely on a sense of continuity—and hence direct transmission—of tradition that many in the twentieth century believe to be lost": Richard Taruskin, "The Pastness of the Present and the Presence of the Past," in Kenyon, *Authenticity and Early Music*, ed 158. Robert Morgan echoes this observation: "Always implicit in Schoenberg's

remarks is the belief that music history is linear in nature—that one compositional development leads logically and inexorably to the next, producing the progressive growth of an ever more varied, complex, and differentiated musical language" ("Tradition, Anxiety," 62). For a critique of this as manifested in jazz historiography, see Scott DeVeaux, "Constructing the Jazz Tradition: Jazz Historiography," *Black American Literature Forum* 25, no. 3 (1991): 525–60. For examples outside of music see Eric Hobsbawm and Terence Ranger, eds., *The Invention of Tradition* (Cambridge: Cambridge University Press, 1992).

18. Examples include Josquin des Prez/Jean Molinet, "Nymphes de bois" (1497) and Guillaume Cretin, "Déploration dur le trépas de J. Ockeghem" (1497). See Paula Higgins, "Lamenting 'Our Master and Good Father': Intertexuality and Creative Patrilineage in Tributes by and for Johannes Ockeghem," in *Cum maioribus lachrymis et fletu immenso: Der Tod in Musik und Kultur des Spätmittelalters*, ed. Birgit Lodes and Stefan Gasch (Tutzing: Hans Schneider, 2007), 277–314. See also Paula Higgins, "Musical 'Parents' and Their 'Progeny': The Discourse of Creative Patriarchy in Early Modern Europe," in *Music in Renaissance Cities and Courts: Essays in Honor of Lewis Lockwood*, ed. Jessie Ann Owens and Anthony M. Cumming (Warren, MI: Harmonie Park Press, 1997), 170–82.

19. Tia DeNora, *Beethoven and the Construction of Genius: Musical Politics in Vienna, 1792–1803* (Berkeley: University of California Press, 1995), 16 (my emphasis).

20. DeNora, *Beethoven and the Construction of Genius*, 84.

21. Yet there is no evidence in Mozart's letters that he ever actually heard Ludwig van Beethoven play. See DeNora, *Beethoven and the Construction of Genius*, 114.

22. Kris Ex, "2Pac," in *Classic Material: The Hip-Hop Album Guide*, ed. Oliver Wang (Toronto: ECW Press, 2003), 156.

23. Bozza, *Whatever You Say I Am*, 167.

24. Bozza, *Whatever You Say I Am*, 65.

25. Jason Tanz confirms this sentiment: "Eminem could also boast a seal of approval from his mentor and producer, Dr. Dre, the former member of N.W.A. whose solo album, *The Chronic*, became one of the most beloved gangsta-rap albums ever. Unlike some other white rappers, Eminem's top priority seemed to be winning over the respect of the hip-hop community rather than climbing the pop charts": Jason Tanz, *Other People's Property: A Shadow History of Hip-Hop in White America* (New York: Bloomsbury USA, 2007), 161.

26. Todd Boyd, *The New H.N.I.C. (Head Nigga in Charge): The Death of Civil Rights and the Reign of Hip Hop* (New York: New York University Press, 2003). 136.

27. Both references allude to Tupac's "Thug Life" philosophy and are the words famously tattooed on his abdomen.

28. See Charles Aaron, "Eminem," in Hermes, *Spin*, 252. See also Bozza, *Whatever You Say I Am*, 37–38.

29. Bozza, *Whatever You Say I Am*, 35.

30. Notorious B.I.G., "Suicidal Thoughts," and Eminem "Encore/Curtains Down." The Eminem single notably features Dr. Dre, 50 Cent, and himself.

31. Shaheem Reid, "Eminem: Reconstructing Tupac," *MTV News*, http://www.mtv.com/bands/t/tupac/news_feature_102703/index.jhtml (accessed Feb. 23, 2007).

32. L. Marshall, *Bob Dylan*, 261.

33. Like his mentor Dr. Dre, Eminem has a number of collaborators who feature in production credits, e.g., the Detroit Bass Brothers (Mark Bass and Jeff Bass) and keyboardist and producer Luis Resto. When I refer to Eminem as producer, I am acknowledging that Eminem's sonic signature is a product of these collaborations and not simply of Eminem as auteur. Using language such as "Eminem's production" or "Eminem's sonic signature" is simply shorthand for "the result of a number of agents involved in a production credited to Eminem."

34. A brief list of Eminem-produced tracks for other artists would include Jay-Z's "Renegade" and "Moment of Clarity" and Nas's "The Cross," as well as tracks for the Game ("We Ain't") and 50 Cent ("Patiently Waiting"), to name a few. His star persona as an MC, however, receives much more media focus and promotion than his production work.

35. Steve Knopper, "Eminem Brings Tupac to Life," *Rolling Stone* 963, Dec. 9, 2004, 36.

36. The song includes an opening verse by Tupac, followed by a verse by Eminem. Tupac's lyrics open with the lines: "Sometimes it's hard, to wake up in the morning. Mind full of demons I don't wanna hear them anymore," reinforcing a persona of the suffering artist that constitutes part of his postmortem mythology, a trait that Eminem has used to a much greater extent for his own persona(e).

37. Mark Gillespie, "'Another Darkchild Classic': Phonographic Forgery and Producer Rodney Jerkins' Sonic Signature" (MMus diss., Université Laval, Quebec, 2006). Gillespie differentiates between "sound signatures" (nonvocal sonic material) and "name-signatures" (allonymic—the producer is named by someone other than the producer—and autonymic—the producer names him- or herself). His taxonomy of sound signatures includes (A) discrete (immediately recognizable sounds, e.g., Timbaland's "flute" sound); (B) abstract (e.g., particular rhythmic patterns); (C) performative ("feel," use of quantization); (D) structural (organization, how the track is put together); (E) orchestral (specific combinations of patches); (F) sound-effects; and (G) phonographic staging (31).

38. Krims, *Music and Urban Geography*, 161.

39. Quoted in Jake Brown, *Dr. Dre in the Studio: From Compton, Death Row, Snoop Dogg, Eminem, 50 Cent, The Game and Mad Money The Life, Times and Aftermath of the Notorious Record Producer Dr. Dre* (New York: Colossus Books, 2006), 82.

40. A more well-known association between Elton John and Eminem is their famous performance of "Stan" at the Grammy Awards in 2001.

41. The decision to label verses A, B, and C is based on differences in the harmonic progressions.

42. Rarely detailed in academic writing on sampling are differences in "sequencing," the act of putting samples in some sort of sequential order. Mark Gillespie makes the distinction between "syntagmatic sequencing" and "morphemic sequencing," where the latter samples short sounds (such as a snare hit), and the former utilizes longer musical phrases and passage ("'Another Darkchild Classic,'" 75, 98). He also differentiates between sample-based producers (e.g., the Bomb Squad) and sequence-based producers (e.g., Puff Daddy). For example, the Bomb Squad's early 1990s output demonstrates morphemic sequencing, whereas Puff Daddy and Eminem often use longer loops in their productions. This is similar to Richard Middleton's distinction between musematic repetition (repetition of shorter "riffs") and discursive repetition (repetition of longer phrases, such as in AABA song form), albeit more specific to digital sampling and borrowing: Middleton, *Studying Popular Music*.

43. Driving eighth notes could be said to be a more direct variation on what Mark Spicer calls the "safety pin riff," alluding to punk style in the music of the Police: Mark Spicer, "'Regatta de Blanc': Analyzing Style in the Music of the Police," in *Sounding Out Pop, Analytical Essays in Popular Music*, ed. Mark Spicer and John Covach (Ann Arbor: University of Michigan Press, 2010), 136.

44. Allan Moore, *Rock: The Primary Text* (Buckingham: Open University Press, 1993), 182. Glenn Pillsbury notes such a pattern in the context of thrash metal, the low E riff in Metallica's "Whiplash," which he describes as a "rhythmically insistent single note riff," as part of an "energy cycle": Glenn T. Pillsbury, *Damage Incorporated: Metallica and the Production of Musical Identity* (London: Routledge, 2006), 6.

45. "The Watcher," Dr. Dre, *Chronic 2001* (1999); "It Has Been Said," *Duets: The Final Chapter* (2005); "Thug 4 Life," *Loyal to the Game* (2004); "Crazy in Love," *Encore* (2004); "Ghetto Gospel," *Loyal to the Game* (2004); "Runnin (Dyin' to Live)," *Tupac: Resurrection* (2003); "Patiently Waiting," *Get Rich or Die Trying* (2003); "Mockingbird," *Encore* (2004); "One Day at a Time," *Tupac: Resurrection* (2003).

46. Like Jay-Z's "A Dream" from the previous chapter, the descending chords in Aeolian mode suggest a lament that never reaches its relative point of stability of the dominant (according to McClary, on *Thug Angel*, DVD Extras). If we wish to treat these two examples as derivative of rock harmonies, and consider rock's harmonic language separate in logic from Western classical music as Allan Moore does, then the VII acts as a dominant of sorts: "Clearly, the VII-I cadence does not have the finality of the traditional V-I, although it is articulated as a full close in all the examples I have presented. In terms of poetics, it seems to me to qualify the certainty of V-I with 'nevertheless.'" See Allan Moore, "The So-Called 'Flattened Seventh' in Rock," *Popular Music* 14, no. 2 (1995): 193.

47. Premiere, "Loyal to the Game," *Sixshot.com, Electronic Hip-Hop Magazine*, www.sixshot.com/articles/4719 (accessed Jan. 6, 2009).

48. Dave, "Loyal to the Game," *Rap News Network*, Dec. 17, 2004, www.rapnews direct.com/0–202–259812–0.html?tag=artistnav.

49. Usman Sajjad, "Review—*Loyal to the* Game," *Situation*, www.thesituation. co.uk/reviews/05/tupac.html (accessed Jan. 6, 2009). Some reviews were more generous, applauding that he was "helping keep 2Pac fresh in 2004," but most internet reviews I have found were less than complementary. See Steve "Flash" Juon, "RapReview of the Week—*Loyal to the Game*," *RapReviews.com*, December 14, 2004, http://www.rapreviews.com/archive/2004_12F_loyalto.html (accessed Jan. 6, 2009).

50. Recording Industry Association of America, http://www.riaa.com/gp/data base/search_results.asp (accessed Dec. 20, 2006).

51. This, of course, simplifies the argument slightly, since there are plenty of critics of the practice of "digital sampling" in general. The important point is that hip-hop fans and writers who might defend the practice generally would be opposed to the manipulation of the voice of an iconic persona within the genre.

52. The music video for "I Ain't Mad at Cha" is not technically a posthumous tribute since it was created before Shakur died. He did, however, die soon after shooting, and the music video was released posthumously and was largely received as a tribute.

53. D. J. Davies, *Death, Ritual, and Belief,* 2.

54. This argument is based on Beebe, "Mourning Becomes . . . ?" (see chap. 4). Beebe argues that Cobain did not die symbolically because the media continued to treat him as if nothing had changed, showing the Nirvana *MTV Unplugged* footage as if it were a new music video. Tupac, he contrasts, was the subject of a number of memorial projects, music videos such as "Changes" that encouraged mourning.

Beebe's article was published prior to the release of *Loyal to the Game*, and I would argue that this "updated" 2Pac example complicates his dichotomy significantly.

55. "To add insult to injury, the song Hennessey contains a constant playing accordion, which sounds like something you would find the Clampetts dancing a jig to in The Beverly Hillbillies. This 'red-neck' style of music is something no 2Pac fan should have to listen to with 2Pac's name stamped on it" (Dave, "Loyal to the Game").

56. Higgins, "Lamenting 'Our Master and Good Father,'" 278.

57. Touré, "The Life of a Hunted Man," *Rolling Stone* 919, Apr. 3, 2003, 48.

58. L. D. Johnson, "Hip-Hop's Holy Trinity," 141.

59. In the mould of Tupac and Biggie, and Jay Z and Nas, 50 Cent and Eminem (and G-Unit) had a public feud, or "beef," with Ja Rule and his record label, Murder Inc. G-Unit produced one single as a "diss record" of Ja Rule in the form of a trope of 2Pac's "Hail Mary" (originally released under the pseudonym Makaveli) on a DJ Kay Slay mixtape. The single features Eminem, 50 Cent, and Busta Rhymes. Eminem sings the opening vocal line associated with Tupac in the original version: "Come get me / If you muthafuckas want Shady / If Pac was still here now / he would never ride with Ja /na na na na na na na na na" (an allosonic quotation of the vocal line, with different lyrics). Eminem, in his rap, accuses Ja Rule of "stealin Pac's shit like he just wrote it." Many of the lyrics in this song, and many other diss songs about Ja Rule, claim that the rapper is imitating Tupac.

60. "The Massacre," *Rolling Stone*, March 10, 2005.

61. S. Craig Watkins, *Hip-Hop Matters: Politics, Pop Culture, and the Struggle for the Soul of a Movement* (Boston: Beacon Press, 2005), 2.

62. L. Marshall, *Bob Dylan*, 5.

63. 50 Cent, "Tupac Shakur," *Rolling Stone* 972, Apr. 21, 2005

64. 50 Cent, "Tupac Shakur."

65. 50 Cent, in *Tupac: Resurrection*, dir. Lauren Lazin, 112 min. (Paramount, USA, 2003; DVD, 2004), DVD Extras.

66. Coker, *Unbelievable*, 330.

67. His debut commercial album, *Get Rich or Die Tryin'* (2003), was released in the United States on Feb. 6, 2003; the *Bad Boys II Soundtrack* was released on July 15, 2003; and the *Tupac Resurrection* soundtrack was released on Nov. 14, 2003 (the film having been released three days earlier).

68. Eminem, "Patiently Waiting," 50 Cent, *Get Rich or Die Tryin'* (2003).

69. Eminem's rap begins with a hospital-machine-like beeping to present the

description of 50 Cent's surviving his gunshots ("As you layin' on the table, they operatin' to save you / It's like an angel came to you sent from the heavens above").

70. Quoted in Nicholas Cook, *Music, Imagination, and Culture* (Oxford: Oxford University Press, 1990), 26.

71. Directly before this moment, Eminem raps, "You know what's coming you muthafuckas don't even know, do you?" The most obvious reading of this declaration is Eminem trumpeting the arrival of 50 Cent on the mainstream rap scene in general, but it could also be heard as a double-voiced utterance, introducing "what's coming" as the crux and climax of the song, including the references to Biggie and Tupac, as well as Eminem's signature rhythm.

72. Brackett, *Interpreting Popular Music*, 128.

73. Zygmunt Bauman, *Mortality, Immortality, and Other Life Strategies* (Stanford: Stanford University Press, 1992), 57.

74. Floyd, *Power of Black Music*, 231.

Conclusion

1. I borrow the term *open source culture* from Jonathan Lethem, who uses it in the context of blues and jazz ("Ecstasy of Influence," 27).

2. Paul D. Miller, "Algorithms: Erasures and the Art of Memory," in Cox and Warner, *Audio Culture*, 352.

3. Paul D. Miller, "In through the Out Door: Sampling and the Creative Act," in Miller, *Sound Unbound*, 14.

4. L. Marshall, *Bob Dylan*, 240. The quote is from an email sent to Paul Williams, published in Williams's book *Bob Dylan: Performing Artist 1986–1990 and Beyond*. Marshall further theorizes on the role of the internet and other technology in experiencing music and considers how Dylan's deliberate use of quotation puts him in relation with various traditions, echoing a similar process in certain realms of hip-hop.

5. Miller, "In through the Out Door," 6.

6. Floyd, *Power of Black Music*, 10.

7. Quoted in Gates, *Signifying Monkey*, 118.

8. Gates, *Signifying Monkey*, 113–18.

9. Anderson, *Imagined Communities*, 10.

BIBLIOGRAPHY

50 Cent. "Tupac Shakur." *Rolling Stone* 972, April 21, 2005. Available at: http://www .rollingstone.com/music/lists/100-greatest-artists-of-all-time-19691231/tu-pac-shakur-19691231.

Aaron, Charles. "Eminem." In Hermes and Michel, *Spin*, 250–55.

Abrams, Nathan D. "Antonio's B-Boys: Rap, Rappers, and Gramsci's Intellectuals." *Popular Music and Society* 19, no. 4 (1995): 1–19.

Adams, Kyle. "Aspects of the Music/Text Relationship in Rap." *Music Theory Online* 14, no. 2 (2008). http://www.mtosmt.org/issues/mto.08.14.2/toc.14.2.html.

Adams, Kyle. "On the Metrical Techniques of Flow in Rap Music." *Music Theory Online* 15, no. 5 (2009). http://www.mtosmt.org/issues/mto.09.15.5/mto.09.15.5. adams.html#FN1.

Ahern, Charlie. *Wild Style: The Sampler*. New York: Powerhouse Books, 2007.

Ake, David. *Jazz Cultures*. Berkeley: University of California Press, 2002.

Alexander, Frank. *Got Your Back: Protecting Tupac in the Hardcore World of Gangster Rap*. New York: St. Martin's Griffin, 2000.

Allen, Graham. *Intertextuality*. New York: Routledge, 2000.

Allen, Harry. "Dreams of a Final Theory." In Chang, *Total Chaos*, 7–9.

Alvarez, Gabriel. "Gangsta Rap in the '90s." In Light, *Vibe History of Hip Hop*, 285–95.

Anderson, Benedict. *Imagined Communities: Reflections on the Origin and Spread of Nationalism*. 2nd ed. London: Verso, 1991.

Anet, Christopher. "An Insight into Subwoofers." *Resolution Magazine* 2, no. 7 (October 2003): 60–62.

Ardis, Angela. *Inside a Thug's Heart*. New York: Dafina Books, 2004.

Ariés, Philippe. *Western Attitudes towards Death: From the Middle Ages to the Present*. Baltimore: Johns Hopkins University Press, 1975.

Auner, Joseph. "'Sing It for Me': Posthuman Ventriloquism in Recent Popular Music." *Journal of the Royal Musicological Association* 128, no. 1 (2003): 98–122.

Auslander, Philip. "Liveness." In Bennett, Shank, and Toynbee, *Popular Music Studies Reader*, 85–91.

Auslander, Philip. *Liveness: Performance in a Mediatized Culture*. London: Routledge, 1999.

Austerlitz, Paul. *Jazz Consciousness: Music, Race, and Humanity*. Middletown: Wesleyan University Press, 2005.

Baber, Brendan. "The Incredible Shrinking Sound System." *Bnet.com*, September 1997. http://findarticles.com/p/articles.

Bakhtin, Mikhail. "Discourse in the Novel." In *The Dialogic Imagination*, ed. Michel Holquist, 259–422. Austin: University of Texas Press, 1982.

Ballantine, Christopher. "Charles Ives and the Meaning of Quotation in Music." *Musical Quarterly* 65 (1979): 167–84.

bandele, asha. "Meditations in the Hour of Mourning," in Datcher and Alexander, *Tough Love*, 25–30. Alexandra, VA: Black Words, Inc., 1996.

Barrow, Jerry L. "Under the Influence." *Source* 207, February 2007, 78.

Barry, David. *Street Dreams: American Car Culture from the Fifties to the Eighties*. London: Macdonald Orbis, 1988.

Barthes, Roland. *Image Music Text*. Hammersmith: Fontana Press, 1977.

Bartlett, Andrew. "Airshafts, Loudspeakers, and the Hip Hop Sample: Contexts and African American Musical Aesthetics." *African American Review* 28 (1994): 639–52.

Basham, Frances, and Bob Ughetti. *Car Culture*. London: Plexus, 1984.

Bastfield, Darrin Keith. *Back in the Day: My Life and Times with Tupac Shakur*. New York: One World/Ballantine, 2002.

Batey, Angus, Andrew Emery, Phillip Mlynar, and Rob Pursey, "Notorious B.I.G.: A Tribute." *Hip-Hop Connection* 209, March 2007: 73.

Bauman, Zygmunt. *Mortality, Immortality and Other Life Strategies*. Oxford: Polity Press, 1992.

Becker, Ernest. *The Denial of Death*. New York: Free Press, 1997.

Becker, Howard. *Art Worlds*. Berkeley: University of California Press, 1982.

Beebe, Roger. "Mourning Becomes ... ? Kurt Cobain, Tupac Shakur, and the 'Waning of Affect.'" In *Rock over the Edge: Transformations in Popular Music Culture*, ed. Roger Beebe, Denise Fulbrook, and Ben Saunders, 311–34. Durham: Duke University Press, 2002.

Belasco, Warren. "Motivatin' with Chuck Berry and Fredrick Jackson Turner." In *The Automobile and American Culture*, ed. David C. Lewis and Laurence Goldstein, 262–79. Ann Arbor: University of Michigan Press, 1980.

Bell, Jonathan. *Carchitecture: When the Car and the City Collide*. London: Birkhäuser, 2001.

Bennett, Andy, Barry Shank, and Jason Toynbee, eds. *The Popular Music Studies Reader*. London: Routledge, 2006.

Berger, Michael L. *The Automobile in American History and Culture: A Reference Guide*. London: Greenwood Press, 2001.

Bicknell, Jeanette. "The Problem of Reference in Musical Quotation." *Journal of Aesthetics and Art Criticism* 59, no. 2 (2001): 185–91.

Big B. "Record Report—Arrested Development." *Source*, May 1992, 32, 56.

Birnbaum, Larry. "Jazz for the Hip-Hop Nation." *Downbeat*, February 1993, 33–36.

Bogdanov, Vladamir, Chris Woodstra, John Bush, et. al. *The All Music Guide to Hip Hop*. San Francisco: Backbeat Books, 2003.

Bonner, Dyl. "Ready-Made Music." *Music and Musicians* 23, no. 12 (1975): 28–30.

Bourdieu, Pierre. "The Forms of Capital." In *Handbook of Theory and Research for the Sociology of Education*, ed. John G. Richardson, 241–58. London: Greenwood Press, 1986.

Bourdieu, Pierre. "The Market of Symbolic Goods." *Poetics* 14 (1985): 13–44.

Bourne, Michael. "Bill Cosby Loves Jazz!: A Conversation with Bill Cosby." *Downbeat*, July 1988, 22–23.

Bowers, Peggy J., and Stephanie Houston Grey. "Karen: The Hagiographic Impulse Anorexia in the Public Memory of a Pop Star." In S. Jones and Jensen, *Afterlife as Afterimage*, 97–120.

Boyd, Todd. *Am I Black Enough for You: Popular Culture from the Hood and Beyond*. Bloomington: Indiana University Press, 1997.

Boyd, Todd. *The New H.N.I.C. (Head Nigga in Charge): The Death of Civil Rights and the Reign of Hip Hop*. New York: New York University Press, 2003.

Bozza, Anthony. *Whatever You Say I Am: The Life and Times of Eminem*. New York: Three Rivers Press, 2003.

Brackett, David. *Interpreting Popular Music*. Berkeley: University of California Press, 2000.

Brackett, Nathan, and Christian Hoard. *The New Rolling Stone Album Guide*. 4th ed. New York: Fireside, 2004.

Breihan, Tom. "Jurassic 5: Feedback." *Pitchfork Media*, July 28, 2006. http://www.pitchforkmedia.com/article/record_review/37529-feedback.

Brewster, Bill, and Frank Broughton. *Last Night a DJ Saved My Life: The History of the Disc Jockey*. London: Headline, 2006.

Brown, Jake. *Dr. Dre in the Studio: From Compton, Death Row, Snoop Dogg, Eminem, 50 Cent, The Game and Mad Money The Life, Times and Aftermath of the Notorious Record Producer Dr. Dre*. New York: Colossus Books, 2006.

Brown, Sam, ed. *Tupac: A Thug Life*. London: Plexus, 2005.

Brilliant, Ashleigh. *The Great Car Craze: How Southern California Collided with the Automobile in the 1920s*. Santa Barbara: Woodbridge Press, 1989.

Bull, Michael. "Automobility and the Power of Sound." In Featherstone, Thrift, and Urry, *Automobilities*, 243–59.

Bull, Michael. *Sound Moves: iPod Culture and Urban Experience*. London: Routledge, 2007.

Bull, Michael. "Soundscapes of the Car." In *The Auditory Culture Reader*, ed. Michael Bull and Les Back, 357–80. Oxford: Berg, 2004.

Burkholder, Peter. *All Made of Tunes: Charles Ives and the Uses of Musical Borrowing*. New Haven: Yale University Press, 1995.

Burkholder, Peter. "Borrowing," In Macy, *Grove Music Online*. http://www.oxford musiconline.com/subscriber/article/grove/music/52918?q=Borrowing&searc h=quick&pos=1&_start=1#firsthit. Accessed September 16, 2007.

Burns, Gary. "Refab Four: Beatles for Sale in the Age of Music Video." In *The Beatles, Popular Music and Society*, ed. Ian Inglis, 176–88. London: Macmillan Press, 2000.

Bush, John. "A Tribe Called Quest." allmusic.com. http://allmusic.com/cg/amg .dll?p=amg&sql=11:dcfixq95ld6e. Accessed June 1, 2007.

Bush, John. "*People's Instinctive Travels and the Paths of Rhythm*." allmusic.com. http://www.allmusic.com/cg/amg.dll?p=amg&sql=10:kzfexqlgldte. Accessed July 3, 2007.

Butterfield, Matthew W. "The Power of Anacrusis: Engendered Feeling in Groove-Based Musics." *Music Theory Online* 12, no. 4 (2006). http://mto.societymusic theory.org/issues/mto.06.12.4/mto.06.12.4.butterfield.html.

Bynoe, Yvonne. *Encyclopedia of Rap and Hip Hop Culture*. London: Greenwood Press, 2006.

Campbell, Joseph. *The Hero with a Thousand Faces*. London: Fontana Press, 1993.

Carroll, Charles Michael. "Musical Borrowing." *College Music Symposium* 18 (1978): 11–18.

Carter, Joe. "Pop Semiotics: The Passion of the Rappers." *Evangelical Outpost*, January 31, 2006. http://www.evangelicaloutpost.com/archives/001806.html.

Cateforis, Theo. *Are We Not New Wave? Modern Pop at the Turn of the 1980s*. Ann Arbor: University of Michigan Press, 2011.

"CEA Predicts Sales of In-vehicle Electronics Will Grow to $12.8 Billion." *Carsound.com*, February 28, 2008. http://www.carsound.com/artman2/publish/ news/CEA_PREDICTS_SALES_OF_IN-VEHICLE_ELECTRONICS_ WILL_GROW_TO_12_8_BILLION.shtml.

Chang, Jeff. *Can't Stop Won't Stop: A History of the Hip-Hop Generation.* London: Ebury Press, 2005.

Chang, Jeff, ed. *Total Chaos: The Art and Aesthetics of Hip-Hop.* New York: Basic Books, 2006.

Chion, Michel. *The Voice in Cinema.* Trans. and ed. Claudia Gorbman. New York: Columbia University Press, 1999.

Choron, Jacques. *Death and Western Thought.* New York: Macmillan, 1963.

Chua, Daniel K. L. "Myth: Mozart, Money, Music." In *Mozart Studies,* ed. Simon P. Keefe, 193–213. Cambridge: Cambridge University Press, 2006.

Clarke, Eric F. "The Impact of Recording on Listening." *Twentieth-century Music* 4, no. 1 (2007): 47–70.

Clarke, Eric F. "Rhythm and Timing in Music." In *The Psychology of Music,* ed. Diana Deutsch, 2nd ed., 473–97. Burlington, MA: Burlington Academic Press, 1999.

Clayson, Alan. *Death Discs: Ashes to Smashes: An Account of Fatality in the Popular Song.* London: Gollancz, 1992.

Coates, Ta-Nehisi. "Tupac: The Reality Show." In Hermes and Michel, *Spin,* 144–47.

Cobb, William Jelani. *To the Break of Dawn: A Freestyle on the Hip Hop Aesthetic.* New York: New York University Press, 2007.

Coker, Cheo Hodari. "N.W.A." In Light, *Vibe History of Hip Hop,* 251–63.

Coker, Cheo Hodari. *Unbelievable: The Life, Death, and Afterlife of the Notorious B.I.G.* New York: Three Rivers Press, 2003.

Coleman, Brian. *Check the Technique: Liner Notes for Hip-Hop Junkies.* New York: Villard Books, 2007.

Coleman, Mark. *Playback: From the Victrola to MP3, 100 Years Of Music, Machines, and Money.* Cambridge: Da Capo Press, 2003.

Coleman, Mark. Review of *It Was Written,* by Nas. *Rolling Stone,* September 19, 1996. http://www.rollingstone.com/artists/nas/albums/album/301203/review/6068277/it_was_written.

Considine, J. D., and Mac Randall. "A Tribe Called Quest." In *The New Rolling Stone Album Guide.* Rollingstone.com. 2004. http://www.rollingstone.com/artists/atribecalledquest/biography. Accessed June 01, 2007.

Conyers, James L., Jr., ed. *African American Jazz and Rap: Social and Philosophical Examinations of Black Expressive Behaviour.* London: McFarland and Company, 2001.

Cook, Nicholas. *Analysing Musical Multimedia.* Oxford: Oxford University Press, 1998.

Cook, Nicholas. "The Domestic *Gesamtkunstwerk*, or Record Sleeves and Reception." In *Composition-Performance-Reception*, ed. Wyndham Thomas, 105–15. Aldershot: Ashgate, 1998.

Cook, Nicholas. *Music, Imagination, Culture*. Oxford: Oxford University Press, 1990.

Cook, Richard. *Blue Note Records: The Biography*. London: Secker and Warburg, 2001.

Cooke, Mervyn. *Jazz*. London: Thames and Hudson, 1998.

Cooke, Mervyn. "Jazz among the Classics, and the Case of Duke Ellington." In *The Cambridge Companion to Jazz*, ed. Mervyn Cooke and David Horn, 153–76. Cambridge: Cambridge University Press, 2002.

Cooke, Mervyn, and David Horn, eds. *The Cambridge Companion to Jazz*. Cambridge: Cambridge University Press, 2002.

Covach, John. "Form in Rock Music: A Primer." In *Engaging Music: Essays in Music Analysis*, ed. Deborah Stein, 65–76. Oxford: Oxford University Press, 2005.

Cox, Christoph, and Daniel Warner, eds. *Audio Culture*. London: Continuum, 2004.

Crane, Diana. "High Culture versus Popular Culture Revisited: A Reconceptualization of Recorded Cultures." In *Cultivating Differences: Symbolic Boundaries and the Making of Inequality*, ed. Michèle Lamont and Marcel Fournier, 58–74. Chicago: University of Chicago Press, 1992.

Crane, Diana. *The Production of Culture: Media and the Urban Arts*. London: Sage Publications, 1992.

Cross, Brian. *It's Not about a Salary: Rap, Race and Resistance in Los Angeles*. London: Verso, 1993.

Crouch, Stanley. "Wynton Marsalis Interview: 1987." *Downbeat*, November 1987, 17–19, 57.

Cunningham, Mark. *Good Vibrations: A History of Record Production*. 2nd ed. London: Sanctuary, 1998.

Cutler, Chris. "Plunderphonia." In Cox and Warner, *Audio Culture*, 138–56.

Dahlhaus, Carl. *Foundations of Music History*. Trans. J. B. Robinson. Cambridge: Cambridge University Press, 1983.

Dant, Tim. "The Driver-Car." In Featherstone, Thrift, and Urry, *Automobilities*, 61–79.

Datcher, Michael, and Kwame Alexander, eds. *Tough Love: The Life and Death of Tupac Shakur*. Alexandria: Alexander Publishing Group, 1997.

Dave. "Loyal to the Game." *Rap News Network*, December 17, 2004. www.rapnewsdirect.com/0–202–259812–00.html?tag=artistnav.

Davies, Douglas J. *Death, Ritual, and Belief*. London: Cassell, 1997.

Davies, Hugh. "A History of Sampling." *Organised Sound* 1, no. 1 (1996): 3–11.

Davies, Jon, ed. *Ritual and Remembrance: Responses to Death in Human Societies.* Sheffield: Sheffield Academic Press, 1994.

Davis, Francis. *In The Moment: Jazz in the 1980s.* New York: Da Capo Press, 1996.

Dawsey, Kierna Mayo. "Days like This." *Source,* December 1993, 76–78.

DeCurtis, Anthony. "Kurt Cobain: 1967–1994," *Rolling Stone* 683, June 2, 1994, 30.

DeCurtis, Anthony. "Word." In Light, *Vibe History of Hip Hop,* 91–93.

DeGenova, Nick. "Gangster Rap and Nihilism in Black America: Some Questions of Life and Death." *Social Text* 43 (1995): 89–132.

Demers, Joanna. "Sampling as Lineage in Hip-Hop." PhD diss. Princeton University, 2002.

Demers, Joanna. "Sampling the 1970s in Hip-Hop." *Popular Music* 22, no. 1 (2003): 41–56.

Demers, Joanna. *Steal This Music: How Intellectual Property Law Affects Musical Creativity.* Athens: University of Georgia Press, 2006.

DeNora, Tia. *Beethoven and the Construction of Genius: Musical Politics in Vienna, 1792–1803.* Berkeley: University of California Press, 1995.

DeNora, Tia. *Music in Everyday Life.* Cambridge: Cambridge University Press, 2000.

D'Errico, Michael. "Behind the Beat: Technical and Practical Aspects of Instrumental Hip-Hop Composition." MA thesis. Tufts University, 2011.

Dettelbach, Cynthia Golomb. *In the Driver's Seat: The Automobile in American Literature and Popular Culture.* London: Greenwood Press, 1976.

DeVeaux, Scott. "Constructing the Jazz Tradition: Jazz Historiography." *Black American Literature Forum* 25, no. 3 (1991): 525–60.

Dickinson, Kay. "'Believe'? Vocoders, Digitised Female Identity and Camp." *Popular Music* 20, no. 3 (2001): 333–47.

Dickinson, Kay. *Off Key: When Film and Music Won't Work Together.* Oxford: Oxford University Press, 2008.

Diehl, Matt. "Pop Rap." In Light, *Vibe History of Hip Hop,* 121–33.

Dimitriadis, Greg. *Performing Identity/Performing Culture: Hip-Hop as Text, Pedagogy, and Lived Practice.* Oxford: Peter Lang, 2001.

DJ Premier. *Red Bull Music Academy.* http://www.redbullmusicacademy.com/TUTORS.9.0.html?act_session=368. Accessed February 16, 2008.

Doane, Mary Ann. "The Voice in Cinema: The Articulation of Body and Space." In *Film Sound: Theory and Practice,* ed. Elisabeth Weis and John Belton, 162–76. New York: Columbia University Press, 1985.

Dougan, John. "Objects of Desire: Canon Formation and Blues Record Collecting." *Journal of Popular Music Studies* 18, no. 1 (2006): 40–65.

Dubrow, Heather. *Genre*. London: Taylor & Francis, 1982.

Dyer, Richard. *Pastiche*. London: Routledge, 2007.

Dyer, Richard. *Stars*. London: British Film Institute, 1998.

Dyson, Michael Eric. "Black Youth, Pop Culture, and the Politics of Nostalgia." In *The Michael Eric Dyson Reader*, 418–40. New York: Basic Civitas Books, 2004.

Dyson, Michael Eric. *Holler if You Hear Me: Searching for Tupac Shakur*. New York: Basic Civitas Books, 2002.

Dyson, Michael Eric. *Know What I Mean? Reflections on Hip Hop*. New York: Basic Civitas Books, 2007.

Eddy, Chuck. "Review of *People's Instinctive Travels and the Paths of Rhythm*." *Rolling Stone* 576, April 19, 1990, 15.

Editors. "Pop Life." *Source*, January 1994, 26.

Erlewine, Stephen Thomas. "2Pac." allmusic.com. http://www.allmusic.com/cg/ amg.dll. Accessed February 19, 2007.

Eshun, Kodwo. *More Brilliant than the Sun: Adventures in Sonic Fiction*. London: Quartet Books, 1999.

Evans, Ron. *The Creative Myth and the Cosmic Hero: Text and Context in Ernest Becker's the Denial of Death*. Oxford: Peter Lang, 1992.

Farley, Christopher John. "Hip-Hop Goes Bebop." *Time*, July 12, 1993. http://www .time.com/time/magazine/article/0,9171,978844,00.html.

Farley, Christopher John. "Hip-Hop Nation." *Time*, February 8, 1999. http://www .time.com/time/magazine/article/0,9171,990164,00.html.

Featherstone, Mike, Nigel Thrift, and John Urry, eds. *Automobilities*. London: Sage, 2005.

Ferency-Viars, Robert. "Introduction to Car Stereo." *Crutchfield*. http://www.crutch field.com/learn/learningcenter/car/car_stereo/intro.html. Accessed October 30, 2008.

Fernando, S. H. "Hip-Hop Alternatives—Greg Osby *3-D Lifestyles*." *Source*, July 1993: 73.

Fernando, S. H. *The New Beats*. New York: Anchor Books, 1994.

Fink, Robert. "Analyzing Rhythmic Teleology in African American Popular Music." *Journal of the American Musicological Society* 64, no. 1 (2011): 179–237.

Fink, Robert. "Elvis Everywhere: Musicology and Popular Music Studies at the Twilight of the Canon." *American Music* 16, no. 2 (1998): 135–79.

Fish, Stanley. *Is There a Text in the Class? The Authority of Interpretive Communities.* Cambridge: Harvard University Press, 1980.

Fiske, John. *Television Culture.* London: Methuen, 1987.

Fiske, John, and John Hartley. *Reading Television.* 2nd ed. London: Routledge, 2003.

Floyd, Samuel A., Jr. *The Power of Black Music: Interpreting Its History from Africa to the United States.* New York and Oxford: Oxford University Press, 1995.

Ford, Philip. "Hip Sensibility in an Age of Mass Counterculture." *Jazz Perspectives* 2, no. 2 (2009): 121–63.

Ford, Philip. "Somewhere/Nowhere: Hipness as an Aesthetic." *Musical Quarterly* 86, no. 1 (2002): 49–81.

Forman, Murray. *The 'Hood Comes First: Race, Space and Place in Rap and Hip-Hop.* Middletown: Wesleyan University Press, 2002.

Forman, Murray, and Mark Anthony Neal, eds. *That's the Joint! The Hip-Hop Studies Reader.* London: Routledge, 2004.

Foucault, Michel. "Nietzsche, Genealogy and History." In *Language, Counter-memory, Practice,* ed. and trans. Donald F. Bouchard, 139–64. Ithaca: Cornell University Press, 1977.

Frame, Pete. *The Rock Family Trees: The Development and History of Rock Performers.* London: Omnibus Press, 1983.

Fricke, David. "Heart-Shaped Noise: The Music and the Legacy." *Rolling Stone* 683, June 2, 1994, 63–67.

Fricke, Jim, and Charlie Ahearn, eds. *Yes Yes Y'all: The Experience Music Project Oral History of Hip-Hop's First Decade.* Oxford: Perseus Books Group, 2002.

Frith, Simon. "Art, Ideology and Pop Practice." In *Marxism and the Interpretation of Culture,* ed. Cary Nelson and Lawrence Grossberg, 461–76. London: Macmillan Education, 1988.

Frith, Simon. "The Popular Music Industry." In *The Cambridge Companion to Pop and Rock,* ed. Simon Frith, John Street, and Will Straw, 26–52. Cambridge: University of Cambridge Press, 2001.

Frith, Simon, and Andrew Goodwin, eds. *On Record: Rock, Pop, and the Written Word.* London: Routledge, 1990.

Frith, Simon, and Lee Marshall, eds. *Music and Copyright.* 2nd ed. London: Routledge, 2004.

Frith, Simon, Will Straw, and John Street, eds. *The Cambridge Companion to Pop and Rock.* Cambridge: University of Cambridge Press, 2001.

Fuller, Linda K. *The Cosby Show: Audiences, Impact, and Implications.* London: Greenwood Press, 1992.

Futterman, Steve. "Review of *Tune in Tomorrow: The Original Soundtrack* by Wynton Marsalis." *Rolling Stone* 599, March 7, 1991, 84–85.

Gabbard, Krin. *Jammin at the Margins: Jazz and the American Cinema*. Chicago: University of Chicago Press, 1996.

Gabbard, Krin, ed. *Jazz among the Discourses*. Durham: Duke University Press, 1995.

Gabbard, Krin, ed. *Representing Jazz*. Durham: Duke University Press, 1995.

Gans, Herbert. *Popular Culture and High Culture: An Analysis and Evaluation of Taste*. 2nd ed. New York: Basic Books, 1999.

Garcia, Luis Manuel. "On and On: Repetition as Process and Pleasure in Electronic Dance Music." *Music Theory Online* 11, no. 4 (2005). http://www.music-theory.org/mto/.

Gartman, David. *Auto Opium: A Social History of American Automobile Design*. London: Routledge, 1994.

Gates, Henry Louis, Jr. *The Signifying Monkey: A Theory of African-American Literary Criticism*. New York and Oxford: Oxford University Press, 1989.

Gennari, John. "Jazz Criticism: Its Development and Ideologies." *Black American Literature Forum* 25, no. 3 (1991): 449–523.

George, Nelson. *Hip-Hop America*. Harmondsworth: Penguin Books, 1998.

George, Nelson. "Introduction." In *Yes Yes Y'all: The Experience Music Project Oral History of Hip-Hop's First Decade*, ed. Jim Fricke and Charlie Ahearn, vii–x. Oxford: Perseus Books Group, 2002.

George, Nelson. "Sample This." In *That's the Joint! The Hip-Hop Studies Reader*, ed. Murray Forman and Mark Anthony Neal, 437–41. London: Routledge, 2004.

Geraghty, Christine. *Now a Major Motion Picture: Film Adaptations of Literature and Drama*. Plymouth, UK: Rowman and Littlefield, 2008.

Giddins, Gary. *Rhythm-a-ning: Jazz Tradition and Innovation in the '80s*. New York: Oxford University Press, 1985.

Giles, David. *Illusions of Immortality: A Psychology of Fame and Celebrity*. London: Macmillian Press, 2000.

Gillespie, Mark. "'Another Darkchild Classic': Phonographic Forgery and Producer Rodney Jerkins' Sonic Signature." MMus dissertation. Université Laval, Quebec, 2006.

Gilmore, Mikal. *Night Beat: A Shadow History of Rock and Roll*. New York: Picador, 1999.

Gilroy, Paul. *The Black Atlantic: Modernity and Double-Consciousness*. London: Verso, 1993.

Gilroy, Paul. "Driving while Black." In *Car Cultures*, ed. Daniel Miller, 81–104. Oxford: Berg, 2001.

Gold, Jonathan. "Day of Dre." *Rolling Stone* 666, September 30, 1993. http://www .rollingstone.com/artists/drdre/articles/story/5937496/cover_story_day_of_ the_dre.

Goodman, Steve. *Sonic Warfare: Sound, Affect, and the Ecology of Fear*. Cambridge: MIT Press, 2010.

Goodwin, Andrew. "Sample and Hold: Pop Music in the Digital Age of Reproduction." In Frith and Goodwin, *On Record*, 258–74.

Gorbman, Claudia. *Unheard Melodies: Narrative Film Music*. Bloomington: University of Indiana Press, 1987.

Gorer, Geoffrey. "The Pornography of Death." In *Death, Grief and Mourning in Contemporary Britain*, 169–75. London: Cresset Press, 1965.

Gorman, Christine. "Shake Rattle and Roar: Thunder in the Distance?" *Time*, March 6, 1989. http://www.time.com/time/magazine/article/0,9171,957183,00 .html?iid=chix-sphere.

Grant, Catherine. "Recognising Billy Budd in *Beau Travail*: Epistemology and Hermeneutics of Auteurist 'Free' Adaptation." *Screen* 43, no. 1 (2002): 57–73.

Gray, Herman. *Watching Race: Television and the Struggle for Blackness*. Minneapolis: University of Minnesota Press, 1995.

Greenblatt, Leah. "Still Life: Even in Death, Tupac Remains a Best Seller." *Entertainment Weekly* 844–45, October 14, 2005.

Gridley, Mark, Robert Maxham, and Robert Hoff. "Three Approaches to Defining Jazz." *Musical Quarterly* 73, no. 4 (1989): 513–31.

Guevara, Nancy. "Women Writin' Rappin' Breakin'." In *Droppin' Science*, ed. William Eric Perkins, 49–62. Philadelphia: Temple University Press, 1996.

Gumbel, Andrew. "Tupac: The Life. The Legend. The Legacy." *Independent*, September 13, 2006, 24.

Hagins, Ogbonna. "A Great Day in Hip-Hop: The Rap Elite Recreates A Great Day in Harlem." *Philadelphia Citypaper.net*, October 15–22, 1998. http://www .citypaper.net/articles/101598/music.hiphop.shtml.

Hall, Stuart. "Culture, Media, and the Ideological Effect." In *Mass Communication and Society*, ed. James Curran, Michael Gurevitch, and Janet Woolacott, 315–48. London: Open University Press, 1977.

hampton, dream. "Hell-Raiser." In *"And It Don't Stop": The Best American Hip-Hop Journalism of the Last 25 Years*, ed. Raquel Cepeda, 131–46. New York: Faber and Faber, 2004.

hampton, dream. "Record Report—*Midnight Marauders*." *Source*, December 1993, 88.

Harlos, Christopher. "Jazz Autobiography: Theory, Practice Politics." In *Representing Jazz*, ed. Krin Gabbard, 131–66. Durham: Duke University Press, 1995.

Harper, Jordan. "All Oddz on Me." In S. Brown, *Tupac*, 178–79.

Harrison, Anthony Kwame. *Hip Hop Underground: The Integrity and Ethics of Racial Identification*. Philadelphia: Temple University Press, 2009.

Hayles, N. Katherine. *How We Became Posthuman: Virtual Bodies in Cybernetics, Literature, and Informatics*. Chicago: University of Chicago Press, 1999.

Head, Thomas. *Hagiography and the Cult of Saints: The Diocese of Orleans 800–1200*. Cambridge: Cambridge University Press, 1990.

Heard, Randolph. "Guru's *Jazzmatazz*." *Rap Pages*, July 1993: 15.

Hebdige, Dick. *Subculture: The Meaning of Style*. London: Routledge, 1979.

Helland, Dave. "Wynton: Prophet in Standard Time." *Downbeat*, September 1990, 16–19.

Hennion, Antoine. "Music and Mediation." In *The Cultural Study of Music*, ed. Martin Clayton, Trevor Herbert, and Richard Middleton, 80–91. London: Routledge, 2006.

Hermes, Will, and Sia Michel, eds. *Spin: 20 Years of Alternative Music*. New York: Three Rivers Press, 2005.

Hess, Mickey. *Is Hip Hop Dead? The Past, Present, and Future of America's Most Wanted Music*. London: Praeger, 2007.

Higgins, Paula. "The Apotheosis of Josquin des Prez and Other Mythologies of Musical Genius." *Journal of the American Musicological Society* 57, no. 3 (2005): 443–510.

Higgins, Paula. "Lamenting 'Our Master and Good Father': Intertexuality and Creative Patrilineage in Tributes by and for Johannes Ockeghem." In *Cum maioribus lachrymis et fletu immenso: Der Tod in Musik und Kultur des Spätmittelalters*, ed. Birgit Lodes and Stefan Gasch, 277–314. Tutzing: Hans Schneider, 2007.

Higgins, Paula. "Musical 'Parents' and Their 'Progeny': The Discourse of Creative Patriarchy in Early Modern Europe." In *Music in Renaissance Cities and Courts: Essays in Honor of Lewis Lockwood*, ed. Jessie Ann Owens and Anthony M. Cummings, 169–86. Warren, MI: Harmonie Park Press, 1997.

Hobsbawm, Eric, and Terence Ranger, eds. *The Invention of Tradition*. Cambridge: Cambridge University Press, 1992.

Hoffmann, Frank W., and William G. Bailey. "Boom Cars." In *Sports and Recreation Fads*, 71–72. Philadelphia: Haworth Press, 1991.

Horn, David. "The Identity of Jazz." In *The Cambridge Companion to Jazz*, ed.

Mervyn Cooke and David Horn, 9–32. Cambridge: Cambridge University Press, 2002.

Hosokowa, Shukei. "The Walkman Effect." In *Popular Music 4*, 165–80. Cambridge: Cambridge University Press, 1984.

Howard, David N. *Sonic Alchemy: Visionary Music Producers and their Maverick Recordings*. Milwaukee: Hal Leonard, 2004.

Howland, John. *Ellington Uptown: Duke Ellington, James P. Johnson, and the Birth of Concert Jazz*. Ann Arbor: University of Michigan Press, 2009.

Huey, Steve. "The Notorious B.I.G." allmusic.com. http://www.allmusic.com/cg/amg.dll?p=amg&sql=11:309hs34ba3xg. Accessed February 19, 2007.

Jam, Billy. "Strictly for my Clazzmatez: Tupac Joins Academia's Literary Canon." In *Tupac Shakur*, ed. Alan Light, 147. London: Plexus, 1998.

Jensen, Joli. *Is Art Good For Us? Beliefs about High Culture in American Life*. New York: Rowman and Littlefield, 2002.

Jensen, Joli. "Posthumous Patsy Clines: Constructions of Identity in Hillbilly Heaven." In S. Jones and Jensen, *Afterlife as Afterimage*, 121–41.

Johnson, E. Patrick. *Appropriating Blackness: Performance and the Politics of Authenticity*. Durham: Duke University Press, 2003.

Johnson, Lynne D. "Hip-Hop's Holy Trinity." In *Da Capo Best Music Writing 2004*, ed. Mickey Hart, 138–44. Cambridge: Da Capo Press, 2004.

Johnson, Martin. "Digable Planets: The Trio Pays Homage to Early Jazz Greats." *Rolling Stone* 652, March 18, 1993, 23.

Jones, LeRoi. "The Changing Same (R&B and New Black Music)." In *Black Music*, 180–211. London: MacGibbon and Kee, 1969.

Jones, Steve. "Better Off Dead." In S. Jones and Jensen, *Afterlife as Afterimage*, 3–16.

Jones, Steve. "Covering Cobain: Narrative Patterns in Journalism and Rock Criticism." *Popular Music and Society* 19, no. 2 (1995): 103–18.

Jones, Steve, ed. *Pop Music and the Press*. Philadelphia: Temple University Press, 2002.

Jones, Steve, and Joli Jensen, eds. *Afterlife as Afterimage: Understanding Posthumous Fame*. New York: Peter Lang, 2005.

Joseph, Jamal, ed. *Tupac Shakur: Legacy*. London: Simon & Schuster, 2006.

Juon, Steve "Flash." "RapReview of the Week—*Loyal to the Game*." *RapReviews.com*. http://www.rapreviews.com/archive/2004_12F_loyalto.html. Accessed Jan 6, 2009.

Kallberg, Jeffrey. "The Rhetoric of Genre: Chopin's Nocturne in G Minor." *Nineteenth-Century Music* 11 (1987–88): 238–61.

Kamberelis, George, and Greg Dimitriadis. "Collectively Remembering Tupac: The

Narrative Mediation of Current Events, Cultural Histories, and Social Identities." In S. Jones and Jensen, *Afterlife as Afterimage*, 143–70.

Kane, Thomas. "Bringing the Real: Lacan and Tupac." *Prospects: An Annual of American Cultural Studies* 27 (2002): 641–63.

Katz, Mark. *Capturing Sound: How Technology Has Changed Music.* Berkeley: University of California Press, 2004.

Keller, Daphne. "The Musician as Thief: Digital Culture and Copyright Law." In Miller, *Sound Unbound*, 135–50.

Kenny, Glenn. "A Tribe Called Quest—*Midnight Marauders*." *Rolling Stone* 670, November 25, 1993, 116.

Kenyon, Nicholas, ed. *Authenticity and Early Music.* Oxford: Oxford University Press, 1988.

Kernfeld, Barry, ed. *The New Grove Dictionary of Jazz.* New York: Macmillan & Co., 1988.

Keyes, Cheryl. "At the Crossroads: Rap Music and Its African Nexus." *Ethnomusicology* 40, no. 2 (1996): 239–40.

Kistner, Gavin. "Hip-Hip Sampling and Twentieth Century African-American Music: An Analysis of Nas' 'Get Down' (2003)." MMus dissertation. Université Laval, Quebec, 2006.

Kitwana, Bakari. *The Hip Hop Generation: Young Blacks and the Crisis in African American Culture.* New York: Basic Civitas Books, 2003.

Kitwana, Bakari. *Why White Kids Love Hip-Hop: Wangstas, Wiggers, Wannabes, and the New Reality of Race in America.* New York: Basic Civitas Books, 2005.

Kivy, Peter. *The Possessor and the Possessed: Handel, Mozart, Beethoven and the Idea of Musical Genius.* New Haven: Yale University Press, 2001.

Klasco, Mike. "A Short History of Compact Deep Bass Subwoofers." *Car Audio and Electronics.* http://www.caraudiomag.com/specialfeatures/0109cae_history_compact_deep_bass_subwoofer/index.html. Accessed June 28, 2008.

Knapp, Raymond. "Review of *Motives for Allusion: Context and Content in Nineteenth-Century Music* by Christopher Reynolds and *Quotation and Cultural Meaning in Twentieth-Century Music* by David Metzer." *Journal of the American Musicological Society* 58, no. 3 (2005): 736–48.

Knopper, Steve. "Eminem Brings Tupac to Life." *Rolling Stone* 963, December 9, 2004, 36.

Koerner, Brendan I. "The Game Is Up: Why Dr. Dre's Protégés Always Top the Charts." *Slate* 1, no. 10, March 10, 2005. http://www.slate.com/id/2114375.

Krieger, Leonard. *Ranke: The Meaning of History.* London and Chicago: University of Chicago Press, 1977.

Krims, Adam. "The Hip-Hop Sublime as a Form of Commodification." In *Music and Marx*, ed. Regula Burckhardt Qureshi, 63–78. London: Routledge, 2002.

Krims, Adam. "Marxism, Urban Geography and Classical Recording: An Alternative to Cultural Studies." *Music Analysis* 20, no. 3 (2001): 347–63.

Krims, Adam. "Marxist Music Analysis without Adorno: Popular Music and Urban Feography." In *Analysing Popular Music*, ed. Allan Moore, 131–57. Cambridge: Cambridge University Press, 2003.

Krims, Adam. *Music and Urban Geography*. London: Routledge, 2007.

Krims, Adam. *Rap Music and the Poetics of Identity*. Cambridge: Cambridge University Press, 2000.

Kugelberg, Johan. *Born in the Bronx: A Visual Record of the Early Days of Hip Hop*. New York: Rizzoli International Publications, 2007.

Kulkarni, Neil. *Hip Hop Bring the Noise: The Stories behind the Biggest Songs*. London: Carlton Books, 2004.

Labelle, Brandon. *Acoustic Ecologies: Sound Culture and Everyday Life*. London: Continuum, 2010.

Lacan, Jacques. *The Four Fundamental Concepts of Psychoanalysis (The Seminar of Jacques Lacan, Book XI)*. Ed. Jacques-Alain Miller. Trans. Alan Sheridan. New York: W. W. Norton & Co., 1998.

Lacasse, Serge. "Intertextuality and Hypertextuality in Recorded Popular Music." In *The Musical Work: Reality or Invention?* ed. Michael Talbot, 35–58. Liverpool: Liverpool University Press, 2000.

Lacy, Karen. *Blue-Chip Black*. Berkeley: University of California Press, 2007.

Laing, Dave. "A Voice without a Face: Popular Music and the Phonography in the 1890s." *Popular Music* 10, no. 1 (1991): 1–9.

Lash, Scott, and John Urry. *Economies of Sign and Space*. London: Sage Publications, 1994.

Leland, John. *Hip: A History*. New York: Harper Perennial, 2005.

Leland, John, and Steinski. "The Big Steal." *Face Magazine*, March 1988. http://www.globaldarkness.com/articles/big_steal.htm.

Lessig, Lawrence. *Free Culture: The Nature and Future of Creativity*. Harmondsworth: Penguin, 2005.

Lethem, Jonathan. "The Ecstacy of Influence: A Plagiarism Mosaic." In Miller, *Sound Unbound*, 25–52.

Levine, Lawrence. *Highbrow/Lowbrow: The Emergence of Cultural Hierarchy in America*. Cambridge: Harvard University Press, 1988.

Levine, Robert. "The Death of High Fidelity." *Rolling Stone* 1042143, December 27,

2007.   http://www.rollingstone.com/news/story/17777619/the_death_of_
high_fidelity/print .

Levy, Janet M. "Covert and Casual Values in Recent Writings about Music." *Journal of Musicology* 5, no. 1 (1987): 3–27.

Lewis, Lucinda. *Roadside America: The Automobile and the American Dream.* New York: Harry N. Abrams, 2000.

Lifton, Robert J. *The Broken Connection: On Death and the Continuity of Life.* Washington, DC: American Psychiatric Press, 1999.

Lifton, Robert J. *The Future of Immortality and Other Essays for a Nuclear Age.* New York: Basic Books, 1987.

Lifton, Robert J., and Eric Olson. *Living and Dying.* London: Wildwood House, 1974.

Light, Alan. "Beastie Boys: White Dudes in the House." In Hermes and Michel, *Spin*, 81.

Light, Alan. "De La Soul." *Rolling Stone* 602, April 18, 1991, 57.

Light, Alan, ed. *Tupac Shakur.* London: Plexus, 1997.

Light, Alan, ed. *The Vibe History of Hip Hop.* New York: Three Rivers Press, 1999.

Litman, Jessica. *Digital Copyright.* Amherst, NY: Promethus Books, 2001.

Lopes, Paul. *The Rise of a Jazz Art World.* Cambridge: Cambridge University Press, 2002.

The Mack. "A Dream." *This Is a Kanye West Production.* http://www.themack.org/KanyeList.html. Accessed December 20, 2006.

Macy, Laura, ed. *Grove Music Online.* http://www.grovemusic.com.

Mäkelä, Janne. *John Lennon Imagined: Cultural History of a Rock Star.* Oxford: Peter Lang, 2004.

Mäkelä, Janne. "Who Owns Him? The Debate on John Lennon." In S. Jones and Jensen, *Afterlife as Afterimage*, 171–90.

Malley, David. "Digable Planets." *Rolling Stone Album Guide.* Rollingstone.com. 2004. http://www.rollingstone.com/artists/digableplanets/biography. Accessed June 1, 2007.

Mandel, Howard. "Wynton Marsalis: The Interview." *Downbeat*, July 1984, 17–18.

Mansbach, Adam. "On Lit Hop." In Chang, *Total Chaos*, 92–101.

Marling, Karal Ann. "America's Love Affair with the Automobile in the Television Age." In *Autopia: Cars and Culture*, ed. Peter Wollen and Joe Kerr, 354–62. London: Reakton Books, 2002.

Marriott, Robert. "Gangsta, Gangsta: The Sad, Violent Parable of Death Row Records." In Light, *Vibe History of Hip Hop*, 319–25.

Marsh, Peter, and Peter Collett. *Driving Passion: The Psychology of the Car.* London: Jonathan Cape, 1986.

Marshall, Lee. *Bob Dylan: The Never Ending Star.* Cambridge: Polity Press, 2007.

Marshall, Wayne. "Giving Up Hip-Hop's Firstborn: A Quest for the Real after the Death of Sampling." *Callaloo* 29, no. 3 (2006): 868–92.

"The Massacre." *Rolling Stone,* March 10, 2005: 107–8.

Massey, Howard. *Behind the Glass: Top Record Producers Tell Us How They Craft the Hits.* San Francisco: Backbeat Books, 2000.

Matos, Michelangelo. "All Roads Lead to 'Apache.'" In *Listen Again: A Momentary History of Pop Music,* ed. Eric Weisbard, 200–209. Durham: Duke University Press, 2007.

Maultsby, Portia K. "Africanisms in African American Music." In *Africanisms in American Culture,* ed. Joseph Holloway. 2nd ed., 437–41. Bloomington: Indiana University Press, 2005.

Maxwell, William. "Sampling Authenticity: Rap Music, Postmodernism, and the Ideology of Black Crime." *Studies in Popular Culture* 14, no. 1 (1991): 1–15.

Mazzarella, Sharon R. "'The Voice of a Generation'? Media Coverage of the Suicide of Kurt Cobain." *Popular Music and Society* 19, no. 2 (1995): 49–68.

Mazzarella, Sharon R., and Norman Pecora. "Kurt Cobain, Generation X, and the Press: College Students Respond." *Popular Music and Society* 19, no. 2 (1995): 3–22.

McAdams, Janine. "Planets Probe Rap Frontier: 'Digable' Debut Jazzes up Genre." *Billboard,* February 6, 1993, 1, 81.

McCarthy, Kerry. "'Brought to Speake English with the Rest': Byrd's Motet Contrafacta." *Musical Times* 148, no. 3 (2007): 51–60.

McCartney, David. "Automobile Radios." In *The Encyclopedia of Radio,* ed. Christopher H. Sterling, 138–39. New York: Taylor & Francis, 2004.

McClary, Susan, and Robert Walser. "Start Making Sense! Musicology Wrestles with Rock." In Frith and Goodwin, *On Record,* 237–49.

McDonald, Chris. "'Rock, Roll and Remember?': Addressing the Legacy of Jazz in Popular Music Studies." *Popular Music History* 1, no. 2 (2006): 126–42.

McDonough, John. "Jazz Sells." *Downbeat,* October 1991, 34.

McLeod, Kembrew. *Owning Culture: Authorship, Ownership and Intellectual Property Law.* New York: Peter Lang, 2001.

McQuillar, Tayannah Lee. *When Rap Music Had a Conscience: The Artists, Organizations, and Historic Events That Inspired and Influenced the "Golden Age" of Hip-Hop from 1989 to 1996.* New York: Thunder's Mouth Press, 2007.

Meconi, Honey, ed. *Early Musical Borrowing*. London: Routledge, 2001.

Metzer, David. *Quotation and Cultural Meaning in Twentieth Century Music*. Cambridge: Cambridge University Press, 2003.

Meyer-Baer, Kathi. *Music of the Spheres and the Dance of Death: Studies in Musical Iconology*. Princeton: Princeton University Press, 1970.

Middleton, Richard. "'O Brother Let's Go Down Home': Loss, Nostalgia and the Blues." *Popular Music* 26, no. 1 (2007): 47–64.

Middleton, Richard. *Studying Popular Music*. Milton Keynes: Open University Press, 1990.

Miller, Paul D. "Algorithms: Erasures and the Art of Memory." In Cox and Warner, *Audio Culture*, 348–54.

Miller, Paul D. "The City in Public versus Private," In Chang, *Total Chaos*, 149–57.

Miller, Paul D. "In through the Out Door." In Miller, *Sound Unbound*, 14, 5–19.

Miller, Paul D., ed. *Sound Unbound: Sampling Digital Music and Culture*. London: MIT Press, 2008.

Miyakawa, Felicia M. *Five Percenter Rap: God Hop's Music, Message, and Black Muslim Mission*. Bloomington: Indiana University Press, 2005.

Monson, Ingrid. "Doubleness and Jazz Improvisation: Irony, Parody, and Ethnomusicology." *Black Music Research Journal* 22, no. 2 (1994): 283–313.

Moore, Allan. *Rock: The Primary Text*. Buckingham: Open University Press, 1993.

Moore, Allan. "The So-Called 'Flattened Seventh' in Rock." *Popular Music* 14, no. 2 (1995): 185–202.

Morgan, Marcyliena. *The Real Hiphop: Battling for Knowledge, Power, and Respect in the LA Underground*. Durham: Duke University Press, 2009.

Morgan, Robert P. "Tradition, Anxiety, and the Musical Scene." In Kenyon, *Authenticity and Early Music*, 57–82.

Nattiez, Jean-Jacques. *Music and Discourse: Toward a Semiology of Music*. Trans. Carolyn Abbate. Princeton: Princeton University Press, 1990.

Negus, Keith. "The Work of Cultural Intermediaries and the Enduring Distance between Production and Consumption." *Cultural Studies* 16, no. 4 (2002): 501–15.

Newcomb, Doug. *Car Audio for Dummies*. New York: Wiley Publishing, 2008.

Nicholson, Stuart. *Is Jazz Dead? (Or Has It Moved to a New Address)*. London: Routledge, 2005.

Nicholson, Stuart. *Jazz: The 1980s Resurgence*. New York: Da Capo Press, 1995.

Nima. "Interview with Snoop Dogg." Dubcnn.com. http://www.dubcnn.com/interviews/snoopdogg06/part1/. Accessed October 22, 2008.

Nisenson, Eric. *Blue: The Murder of Jazz*. New York: Da Capo Press, 2000.

Partin, Nat. "Review of *Ultimate Breaks and Beats: The Ultimate Collection,*" *Pitchfork,* February 16, 2007. http://www.pitchforkmedia.com/article/record_review/41174-ultimate-breaks-beats-the-complete-collection.

Patillo, Mary. *Black Picket Fences.* Chicago: University of Chicago Press, 1997.

"Pat Metheny Declares War on Kenny G." Vh1.com, June 14, 2000. http://www.vh1.com/artists/news/1436591/20000614/g_kenny.jhtml.

Perkins, William Eric, ed. *Droppin' Science: Critical Essays on Rap Music and Hip Hop Culture.* Philadelphia: Temple University Press, 1996.

Perry, Imani. *Prophets of the Hood: Politics and Poetics in Hip Hop.* Durham: Duke University Press, 2004.

Pettitt, Joe. *How to Design and Install High-Performance Car Stereo.* North Branch: Car Tech, 2003.

Phillips, Wes. "Audio Odyssey: Ken Kreisel of M&K." *Stereophile,* March 1997. http://www.stereophile.com/interviews/136/.

Pillsbury, Glenn. *Damage Incorporated: Metallica and the Production of Musical Identity.* London: Routledge, 2006.

Pinn, Anthony B., ed. *Noise and Spirit: The Religious and Spiritual Sensibilities of Rap Music.* New York: New York University Press, 2003.

Polk Audio. "Tips, Tweaks and Common Sense about Car Audio." Baltimore: Polk Audio. http://www.polkaudio.com/downloads/12vhndbk.pdf. Accessed July 28, 2008.

Pond, Steven. *Head Hunters: The Making of Jazz's First Platinum Album.* Ann Arbor: University of Michigan Press, 2005.

Porcello, Thomas. "The Ethics of Digital Audio Sampling: Engineers Discourse." *Popular Music* 10, no. 1 (1991): 69–84.

Potter, Russell A. *Spectacular Vernaculars: Hip-Hop and the Politics of Postmodernism.* New York: State University of New York Press, 1995.

Powell, Kevin. "Review of *Midnight Marauders* by A Tribe Called Quest and *Bulhoone Mindstate* by De La Soul." *Vibe,* November 1993, 103–4.

Powell, Kevin. "Review of *Reachin' (A Refutation of Time and Space)." Rolling Stone* 650, February 18, 1993, 61.

Prashad, Vijay. *Everybody Was Kung Fu Fighting: Afro-Asian Connections and the Myth of Cultural Purity.* Boston: Beacon Press, 2002.

Premiere, "Loyal to the Game." *Sixshot.com: Electronic Hip-Hop Magazine.* www.sixshot.com/articles/4719. Accessed January 6, 2009.

Price, Emmett G., III. *Hip Hop Culture.* Santa Barbara: ABC-CLIO, 2006.

Prioreschi, Plinio. *A History of Human Responses to Death: Mythologies, Rituals and Ethics.* New York: Edwin Mellen Press, 1990.

Quinn, Eithne. *Nuthin' but a "G" Thang: The Culture and Commerce of Gangsta Rap.* New York: Columbia University Press, 2005.

Rabaté, Jean-Michel, ed. *The Cambridge Companion to Lacan.* Cambridge: Cambridge University Press, 2003.

Redhead, Steve, and John Street. "Have I the Right? Legitimacy, Authenticity and Community in Folk's Politics." *Popular Music* 8, no. 2 (1989): 177–84.

Reed, Theresa L. *The Holy Profane: Religion in Black Popular Music.* Lexington: University of Kentucky Press, 2002.

Reich, Howard. "Wynton's Decade." *Downbeat*, December 1992, 16–21.

Reid, Shaheem. "Eminem: Reconstructing Tupac." *MTV News.* http://www.mtv.com/bands/t/tupac/news_feature_102703/index.jhtml. Accessed February 23, 2007.

Reid, Shaheem. "On Tupac Video Set, Nas Says Rapper Better than Shakespeare." *MTV News.* December 3, 2004. http://www.mtv.com/news/articles/1458966/20021203/nas.jhtml.

Reid, Shaheem. "Suge Knight Calls Tupac/Nas Track 'Disrespectful.'" *MTV News.* April 21, 2003. http://www.mtv.com/news/articles/1471376/20030418/knight_marion_suge_.jhtml.

Reynolds, Christopher. *Motives for Allusion: Context and Content for Nineteenth-Century Music.* Cambridge: Harvard University Press, 2003.

Rickels, Laurence A. *The Case of California.* Minneapolis: University of Minnesota Press, 2001.

Ro, Ronin. "The Definitive Gang Starr Story: Not Just a Jazz Thing." *Source* (April 1994): 69.

Ro, Ronin. "Hip-Hop Alternatives: Various Artists *Jazzmatazz.*" *Source*, no. 44 (May 1993): 72.

Roby, Steven. *Black Gold: The Lost Archives of Jimi Hendrix.* New York: Billboard Books, 2002.

Rosand, Ellen. "Lament." In Macy, *Grove Music Online.* http://www.grovemusic.com. Accessed November 23, 2006.

Rose, Tricia. *Black Noise: Rap Music and Black Culture in Contemporary America.* Middletown: Wesleyan University Press, 1994.

Rothenbuhler, Eric W. "The Strange Career of Robert Johnson's Records." In S. Jones and Jensen, *Afterlife as Afterimage*, 209–34.

Rumerich, Mark. *Car Stereo Cookbook.* 2nd ed. New York: McGraw Hill, 2005.

Sachs, Wolfgang. *For the Love of the Automobile: Looking Back into the History of our Desires.* Trans. Don Reneau. Berkeley: University of California Press, 1992.

Sales, Grover. *Jazz: America's Classical Music*. New York: Da Capo Press, 1992.

Samson, Jim. "Genre." In *Oxford Music Online*, ed. L. Macy. http://www.oxford musiconline.com/. Accessed August 10, 2009.

Samuels, Allison. "Who Stole Tupac's Soul?" *Rolling Stone* 789, June 25, 1998, 17.

Sandy, Candace, and Dawn Marie Daniels. *How Long Will They Mourn Me?* New York: Random House, 2006.

Sanneh, Kelefa. "'Rapping about Rapping': The Rise and Fall of a Hip-Hop Tradition." In *This Is Pop*, ed. Eric Weisbard, 223–34. Cambridge: Harvard University Press, 2004.

Sajjad, Usman. "Review of *Loyal to the* Game." *Situation*. www.thesituation.co.uk/reviews/05/tupac.html. Accessed January 6, 2009.

Sarig, Roni. *Third Coast: OutKast, Timbaland and How Hip-Hop Became a Southern Thing*. Cambridge: Da Capo Press, 2007.

Schloss, Joseph G. *Foundation: B-Boys, B-Girls, and Hip-Hop Culture in New York*. New York and Oxford: Oxford University Press, 2009.

Schloss, Joseph G. *Making Beats: The Art of Sample Based Hip-Hop*. Middletown: Wesleyan University Press, 2004.

Schumacher, Thomas G. "This Is a Sampling Sport: Digital Sampling, Rap, and the Law of Cultural Production." *Media, Culture, and Society* 17, no. 2 (1995): 253–73.

Schur, Richard L. *Parodies of Ownership: HipHop and Intellectual Property Law*. Ann Arbor: University of Michigan Press, 2009.

Schwarz, David. *Listening Subjects: Music, Psychoanalysis, Culture*. London: Duke University Press, 1997.

Scott, Cathy. *The Killing of Tupac Shakur*. London: Plexus Publishing, 1997.

Seagrave, Kerry. *Drive-In Theaters: A History from Their Inception in 1933*. London: McFarland and Company, 1992.

Shakur, Tupac. *The Rose That Grew from Concrete*. New York: MTV, 1999.

Shapiro, Peter. *The Rough Guide to Hip-Hop*. 2nd ed. London: Rough Guides, 2005.

Sheffield, Rob. "R U Still Down (Remember Me?)." *Rolling Stone* 778, January 22, 1998, 53–54.

Sheller, Mimi. "Automotive Emotions: Felling the Car." In Featherstone, Thrift, and Urry, *Automobilities*, 221–42.

Shumway, David. "Rock 'n' Roll Sound Tracks and the Production of Nostalgia." *Cinema Journal* 38, no. 2 (1999): 36–51.

Shusterman, Richard. "The Fine Art of Rap." In *Pragmatist Aesthetics: Living Beauty, Rethinking Art*, 201–35. Oxford: Rowman and Littlefield, 2000.

Silverman, Kaja. *The Subject of Semiotics*. Oxford: Oxford University Press, 1984.

Sinclair, Tom. "A Tribe Called Quest." *Rolling Stone* 660–61, July 8–22, 1993, 26.

Smith, Danyel. " Gang Starr: Jazzy Situation." *Vibe*, May 1994: 88.

Smith, Suzanne E. *Dancing in the Street: Motown and the Cultural Politics of Detroit*. Cambridge: Harvard University Press, 1999.

Snead, James A. "On Repetition in Black Culture." In *Out There: Marginalization and Contemporary Cultures*, ed. Russell Ferguson et al., 213–30. London: MIT Press, 1990.

Soja, Edward. *Thirdspace: Journeys to Los Angeles and Other Real-and-Imagined Places*. Oxford: Blackwell, 1996. 124–53.

Sontag, Susan. "The Artist as Exemplary Sufferer." In *Against Interpretation and Other Essays*, 39–48. New York: Picador, 2001.

Spicer, Mark. "'Regatta de Blanc': Analyzing Style in the Music of the Police." In *Sounding Out Pop, Analytical Essays in Popular Music*, ed. Mark Spicer and John Covach, 124–53. Ann Arbor: University of Michigan Press, 2010.

Spicer, Mark, and John Covach, eds. *Sounding Out Pop: Analytical Essays in Popular Music*. Ann Arbor: University of Michigan Press, 2010.

Stanbridge, Alan. "Burns, Baby Burns: Jazz History as a Contested Cultural Site." *Source: Challenging Jazz Criticism* 1, no. 4 (2004): 81–99.

Stanbridge, Alan. "Is Jazz Popular Music?" Paper presented at the IASPM US-Canada Conference. April 2007. Boston.

Sterne, Jonathan. "Dead Rock Stars 1900." In S. Jones and Jensen, *Afterlife as Afterimage*, 253–68.

Strauss, Neil. "Hip-Hop Requiem: Mining Tupac Shakur's Legacy." In S. Brown, *Tupac*, 184–86.

Strong, John S. "Relics." In *Death, Afterlife and the Soul*, ed. Lawrence E. Sullivan, 56. New York: Macmillan, 1989.

Stuckey, Sterling. *Slave Culture: Nationalist Theory and the Foundations of Black America*. New York and Oxford: Oxford University Press, 1987.

Sullivan, Randall. *Labyrinth: Corruption and Vice in the L.A.P.D.* Edinburgh: Canongate Books, 2003.

Swenson, Kylee. "Captain Contagious." *Remix Magazine*, June 1, 2006. http://remix mag.com/artists/remix_captain_contagious/index.html.

Swiss, Thomas. "Jewel Case: Pop Stars, Poets, and the Press." In *Pop Music and the Press*, ed. Steve Jones, 171–82. Philadelphia: Temple University Press, 2002.

Szwed, John F. "Props." *Vibe*, September 1993: 140.

Tagg, Philip. *Introductory Notes to the Semiotics of Music*. Version 3. 1999. http://www.tagg.org/xpdfs/semiotug.pdf.

Tagg, Philip. "Subjectivity and Soundscape, Motorbikes and Music." In Bennett, Shank, and Toynbee, *Popular Music Studies Reader*, 44–52.

Tanz, Jason. *Other People's Property: A Shadow History of Hip-Hop in White America*. New York: Bloomsbury USA, 2007.

Taruskin, Richard. "The Pastness of the Present and the Presence of the Past." In Kenyon, *Authenticity and Early Music*, 137–207.

Taylor, Shawn. *People's Instinctive Travels and the Paths of Rhythm*. New York: Continuum, 2007.

Teter, John, and Alex Gee. *Jesus and the Hip-Hop Prophets: Spiritual Insights from Lauryn Hill and 2Pac*. Downers Grove: InterVarsity Press: 2003.

Thomas, Reginald. "The Rhythm of Rhyme." In *African American Jazz and Rap: Social and Philosophical Examinations of Black Expressive Behavior*, ed. James L. Conyers Jr., 163–81. London: McFarland and Company, 2001.

Thornton, Sarah. *Club Cultures: Music, Media and Subcultural Capital*. Middletown: Wesleyan University Press, 1996.

Tomlinson, Gary. "Cultural Dialogics and Jazz: A White Historian Signifies." *Black Music Research Journal* 22 (2002): 71–105.

Tomlinson, Gary. "The Historian, the Performer and Authentic Meaning in Music." In Kenyon, *Authenticity and Early Music*, 115–36.

Toop, David. *Rap Attack 2*. London: Serpent's Tail, 1992.

Touré. "Digging the Planets." *Source*, April 1993, 36.

Touré. "I Live in the Hiphop Nation." In *Never Drank the Kool-Aid*, 333–38. New York: Picador, 2006.

Touré. "The Life of a Hunted Man." *Rolling Stone* 919, April 3, 2003, 44–48.

Toynbee, Jason. *Making Popular Music: Musicians, Creativity and Institutions*. London: Arnold Publishing, 2000.

Tyrangiel, Josh. "Hip-Hop Video." In Light, *Vibe History of Hip Hop*, 137–41.

Tyrangiel, Josh. "In the Doctor's House." *Time*, September 15, 2001. http://www.time.com/time/magazine/article/0,9171,1000775,00.html.

Urry, John. "The 'System' of Automobility." In Featherstone, Thrift, and Urry, *Automobilities*, 25–40.

Vaidhyanathan, Siva. *Copyrights and Copywrongs: The Rise of Intellectual Property and How It Threatens Creativity*. New York: New York University Press, 2003.

Volti, Rudi. *Cars and Culture: The Life Story of a Technology*. London: Technographies, 2004.

von Appen, Ralf, André Doehring, Dietrich Helms, and Thomas Phelps, eds. (2010). *Samples: Online-Publikationen des Arbeitskreis Studium Populärer Musik*. http://aspm.ni.lo-net2.de/samples/.

Walser, Robert, ed. *Keeping Time: Readings in Jazz History*. Oxford: Oxford University Press, 1999.

Wang, Oliver, ed. *Classic Material: The Hip-Hop Album Guide*. Toronto: ECW Press, 2003.

Wang, Oliver. "Trapped in between the Lines: The Aesthetics of Hip-Hop Journalism." In Chang, *Total Chaos*, 165–74.

Watkins, S. Craig. *Hip-Hop Matters: Politics, Popular Culture, and the Struggle for the Soul of a Movement*. Boston: Beacon Press, 2005.

Watson, C. W. "'Born a Lady, Became a Princess, Died a Saint': The Reaction to the Death of Diana, Princess of Wales." *Anthropology Today* 13, no. 6 (1997): 3–7.

Weheliye, Alexander. "'Feenin': Posthuman Voices in Contemporary Black Popular Music." *Social Text* 71 (2002): 21–47.

Weinstein, Denna. "Art versus Commerce: Deconstructing a (Useful) Romantic Illusion." In *Stars Don't Stand Still in the Sky*, ed. Karen Kelly and Evelyn McDonnell, 56–69. London: Routledge, 1999.

Wheeler, Elizabeth A. "'Most of My Heroes Don't Appear on No Stamps': The Dialogics of Rap Music." *Black Music Research Journal* 11, no. 2 (1991): 193–216.

White, Armond. *Rebel for the Hell of It: The Life of Tupac Shakur*. 2nd ed. New York: Thunder's Mouth Press, 2002.

Whyton, Tony. *Jazz Icons*. Cambridge: Cambridge University Press, 2010.

Wilder, Chris. "A Tribe Called Quest: Abstract Attitude." *Source*, no. 26 (1991): 25.

Williams, Justin A. "Beats and Flows: A Response to Kyle Adams." *Music Theory Online* 15, no. 2 (2009). http://mto.societymusictheory.org/issues/mto.09.15.2/mto.09.15.2.williams.html.

Williams, Todd. "Miles Davis: 1926–1991." *Source*, January 1992, 13, 92.

Williams, Ty. "Rap Session—Hip-Bop: The Rap/Jazz Connection." *Source*, September 1992, 21.

Williams, Ty. "Remembering Dizzy." *Source*, April 1993, 22.

Wilson, William Julius. *The Declining Significance of Race*. Chicago: University of Chicago Press, 1978.

Witzer, Michael Karl, and Kurt Bash. *Crusin': Car Culture in America*. Osceola: Motorbooks International, 1997.

Wollen, Peter, and Joe Kerr, eds. *Autopia: Cars and Culture*. London: Reakton Books, 2002.

Yoder, Andrew. *Auto Audio*. 2nd ed. New York: McGraw Hill, 2000.

Zabor, Rai, and Vic Garbarini, "Wynton vs. Herbie: The Purist and Crossbreeder

Duke It Out." In *Keeping Time,* ed. Robert Walser, 339–51. Oxford: Oxford University Press, 1999.

Zamora, Lois Parkinson. *The Usable Past: The Imagination of History in Recent Fiction of the Americas.* Cambridge: Cambridge University Press, 1997.

Selected Discography (all selections are compact disc format)

2Pac. *All Eyez on Me.* Death Row Records, 1996. 524 204-2.

2Pac. *Better Dayz.* Interscope Records, 2002. 0694970702.

2Pac. *Loyal to the Game.* Interscope Records, 2004. B0003861-02.

2Pac. *Tupac Resurrection Soundtrack.* Interscope Records, 2003. 0602498611593.

2Pac. *Until the End of Time.* Interscope Records, 2001. INTR-10345-2.

2Pac/Makaveli. *The Don Killuminati (The 7 Day Theory).* Interscope/Death Row Records, 1996. INT2-90039.

50 Cent. *Get Rich or Die Tryin.* Shady/Aftermath/Interscope, 2003. 069493544-2.

Art Blakey and the Jazz Messengers. *Moanin'.* Blue Note, 1958, 1999. 45-1735.

Art Blakey and the Jazz Messengers. *A Night in Tunisia.* Blue Note, 1960, 1989. CDP 7 840 49 2.

Bambaataa, Afrika. *Looking for the Perfect Beat: 1980–1985.* Rhino/Ada, 2001. B00005ABF6.

Beastie Boys. *To The Five Boroughs.* Capitol, 2004. B00021LRWM.

Boogie Down Productions. *Edutainment.* Jive, 1990. 1358-2-J.

The Branford Marsalis Quartet Featuring Terence Blanchard. *Music from Mo' Better Blues.* CBS, 1990. 467160 2.

Coltrane, John. *Blue Train.* Blue Note, 1957, 1997. CDP 7 460952.

Common Sense. *Resurrection.* Relativity, 1994. 88561-1208-1.

Davis, Miles. *Doo-Bop.* Warner Bros., 1992. 9 26938-2.

De La Soul. *The Grind Date.* Sanctuary Records, 2004. B0002WZT20.

De La Soul. *Three Feet High and Rising.* Tommy Boy, 1989. TBCD 1019.

Digable Planets. *Reachin' (A New Refutation of Time and Space).* Pendulum, 1993. 7243 8 27758 2 9.

Dr. Dre. *The Chronic.* Interscope/Death Row Records, 1992. P2 57128.

Eminem. *The Eminem Show.* Interscope, Records, 2002. 493 327-2.

Eminem. *Encore.* Interscope/Aftermath, 2004. B0003771-72.

The Game. *The Documentary.* Interscope/Aftermath, 2005. B0003947-09.

Gang Starr. *Daily Operation.* Chrysalis, 1992. 3219102.

Gang Starr. *Step in the Arena*. Chrysalis, 1990. F2 21798.

Guru. *Jazzmatazz Volume 1*. Chrysalis/EMI. 1993. 3219982.

Guru. *Jazzmatazz Volume 2: The New Reality*. Chrysalis, 1995. CDP-534290.

Guru. *Jazzmatazz Volume 3 (Streetsoul)*. Virgin Records America, 2000. 7243 8 5018824.

Guru. *Jazzmatazz Volume 4: The Hip Hop Jazz Messenger: "Back to the Future."* Grand Records, 2007. SGR007.

Hancock, Herbie. *Dis Is Da Drum*. Mercury, 1994. 528 185-2.

Hargrove, Roy. *Diamond in the Rough*. Novus, 1990. PD90471.

Ice Cube. *AmeriKKKa's Most Wanted*. Priority Records, 1990. CDL 57120.

The Incredible Bongo Band. *Bongo Rock*. Mr Bongo, 2006. B000G1T072.

Jay-Z. *The Blueprint 2: The Gift and the Curse*. Roc-A-Fella-Records, 2002. 440 063 381-2.

Jones, Quincy. *Back on the Block*. Qwest Records, 1989. 9 26020-2.

Jones, Quincy. *Q's Jook Joint*. Qwest Records, 1995. 9 46109-2.

Jungle Brothers. *Straight Out of the Jungle*. Warlock Records, 1988. WARCD-2704.

Kinch, Soweto. *Conversations with the Unseen*. Dune, 2006. DUNE CD08.

Kinch, Soweto. *A Day in the Life of B19: Tales of the Tower Block*. Dune, 2006. DUNE CD14.

KRS-One. *Hip Hop Lives*. Koch Records, 2007. B00000AOWX.

KRS-One. *Kristyles*. Koch Records, 2003. B00008OLYM.

KRS-One. *KRS-One*. Jive, 1995. B0000052Y.

Kweli, Talib. *The Beautiful Struggle*. Rawkus / Umgd, 2004. B0002XL22U.

L'Trimm. *Grab It!* Atlantic Records, 1988. 7 81925-2.

Miles Davis All Stars. *Walkin'*. Prestige, 1954, 1999. PRCD-7076-2.

Nas. *God's Son*. Sony, 2002. B00007FZIJ.

Nas. *Hip Hop Is Dead*. Def Jam, 2006. B000K7VHXC.

Nas. *Illmatic*. Sony, 1994. B0000029GA.

Nas. *It Was Written*. Columbia, 1996. B000002B1M.

The Notorious B.I.G. *Born Again*. Bad Boy, 1999. 78612-73023-2.

The Notorious B.I.G. *Duets: The Final Chapter*. Bad Boy, 2005. 7567 83885 2.

The Notorious B.I.G. *Ready to Die*. Bad Boy. 78612-73000-2 (1994).

N.W.A. *Straight Outta Compton*. Ruthless Records/Priority Records, 1988. CDL 57102.

O'Neal, Shaquille. *Shaq Diesel*. Jive Records, 1993. B0000050Z.

Osby, Greg. *3-D Lifestyles*. Blue Note, 1993. CDP 0777 798635 2 5.

The Pharcyde. *Bizarre Ride II the Pharcyde*. Delicious Vinyl, 1992. 828 749-2.

Public Enemy. *Fear of a Black Planet*. Def Jam, 1990. 314 523 446-2.

Public Enemy. *It Takes a Nation of Millions to Hold us Back*. Def Jam, 1989. CK 44303.

Public Enemy. *Yo! Bum Rush the Show*. Def Jam, 1987. 527 357-2.

Roberts, Marcus. *Deep in the Shed*. 1990. BMG. 3078-2-N.

Roney, Wallace. *Mystikal*. HighNote, 2005. HCD 7145.

The Roots. *Do You Want More?!!!??!* Geffen Records, 1994. DGCD-24708.

The Roots. *Phrenology*. MCA, 2002. B00007B9DP.

The Roots. *Things Fall Apart*. MCA, 1999. B00000I5JL.

Snoop Doggy Dogg. *Doggystyle*. Interscope/Death Row Records, 1993. 6544-92279-2.

A Tribe Called Quest. *The Low End Theory*. Jive/BMG, 1991. 82876 53549 2.

A Tribe Called Quest. *People's Instinctive Travels and the Paths of Rhythm*. Jive. 1990. 051 272-2 (LC 7925).

Ultimate Beats and Breaks: The Ultimate Collection. Street Beat, 2007. B000LRY9W2.

Filmography

8 Mile. Dir. Curtis Hansen. 110 minutes. Imagine Entertainment, USA, 2002. DVD, 2003.

American Graffiti. Dir. George Lucas. 110 minutes. Universal Pictures, USA, 1973. DVD, 1998.

The Art of 16 Bars: Get Ya' Bars Up. Dir. Peter Spirer. 80 minutes. QD3 Entertainment, USA, 2005. DVD.

Biggie and Tupac. Dir. Nick Broomfield. 108 minutes. FilmFour, UK, 2002. DVD, 2004.

Bird. Dir. Clint Eastwood. 161 minutes. Warner Bros. Pictures, USA, 1988. DVD, 2001.

Boyz n the Hood. Dir. John Singleton. 107 minutes. Columbia Pictures, USA, 1991, DVD, 2001.

Flashdance. Dir. Adrian Lyne. 95 minutes. Paramount Pictures, USA, 1983. DVD, 2007.

The Freshest Kids. Dir. Israel. 94 minutes. QD3 Entertainment, USA, 2001. DVD, 2002.

Hip-Hop: Beyond Beats and Rhymes. Dir. Byron Hurt. 61 minutes. Media Education Foundation, USA, 2006. DVD, 2006.

Juice. Dir. Ernest R. Dickerson. 95 minutes. Paramount Pictures, USA, 1992. DVD, 2001.

Let's Get Lost. Dir. Bruce Weber. 120 minutes. Little Bear Productions, USA/West Germany. 1988. VHS.

Menace II Society. Dir. Albert Hughes and Allen Hughes. 97 minutes. New Line Cinema, USA, 1993. DVD, 1997.

Mo' Better Blues. Dir. Spike Lee. 130 minutes. Universal Pictures, USA, 1990. DVD, 2004.

Once, Dir. John Carney. 85 minutes. Samson Films, Ireland, 2006. DVD, 2007.

Round Midnight. Dir. Bertrand Tavernier. 133 minutes. Warner Bros. Pictures, USA/France, 1986. DVD, 2001.

South Central. Dir. Steve Anderson. 99 minutes. Warner Brothers Pictures, USA, 1992. DVD, 1999.

Thelonious Monk: Straight, No Chaser. Dir. Charlotte Zwerin. 90 minutes. Warner Brothers Pictures, USA, 1988. DVD, 2001.

Thug Angel: The Life of an Outlaw. Dir. Peter Spirer. 92 minutes. QD3 Entertainment, USA, 2002. DVD, 2002.

Thug Immortal: The Tupac Shakur Story. Prod. George Tan. 60 minutes. Sunset Home Visual Entertainment, USA, 2002. DVD, 2002.

Tupac: Hip-Hop Genius. Dir. Charlotte Lewin. 64 minutes. Chrome Dreams Video, USA, 2005. DVD, 2005.

Tupac: Resurrection. Dir. Lauren Lazin. 112 minutes. Paramount, USA, 2003. DVD, 2004.

Tupac Vs. Dir. Ken Peters. 64 minutes. Concrete Treehouse Productions, USA, 2004. DVD, 2007.

The Up in Smoke Tour. Dir. Philip G. Atwell. 150 minutes. Aftermath Entertainment, USA, 2000. DVD, 2000.

Wild Style. Dir. Charlie Ahern. 82 minutes. Wild Style Productions, USA, 1982. DVD, 2007.

INDEX

U.C.B.
LIBRARY